Winning the War on Terror:
Legal and Policy Lessons from the Past

Jeffrey F. Addicott
B.A., J.D., LL.M., S.J.D.

Lawyers & Judges
Publishing Company, Inc.

This publication is designed to provide accurate and authoritative information in regard to the subject matter covered. It is sold with the understanding that the publisher is not engaged in rendering legal, accounting, or other professional service. If legal advice or other expert assistance is required, the services of a competent professional person should be sought.

—From a *Declaration of Principles* jointly adopted by a Committee of the American Bar Association and a Committee of Publishers and Associations.

The publisher, editors and authors must disclaim any liability, in whole or in part, arising from the information in this volume. The reader is urged to verify the reference material prior to any detrimental reliance thereupon. Since this material deals with legal, medical and engineering information, the reader is urged to consult with an appropriate licensed professional prior to taking any action that might involve any interpretation or application of information within the realm of a licensed professional practice.

Copyright ©2003 by Lawyers & Judges Publishing Co., Inc. All rights reserved. All chapters are the product of the Authors and do not reflect the opinions of the Publisher, or of any other person, entity, or company. No part of this book may be reproduced in any form or by any means, including photocopying, without permission from the Publisher.

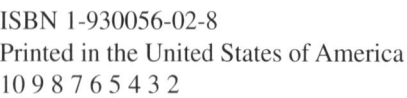

Lawyers & Judges Publishing Company, Inc.

P.O. Box 30040 • Tucson, AZ 85751-0040
(800) 209-7109 • FAX (800) 330-8795
e-mail: sales@lawyersandjudges.com

ISBN 1-930056-02-8
Printed in the United States of America
10 9 8 7 6 5 4 3 2

Dedication

To R. B. Thieme, Jr.—theologian, soldier, educator, patriot

Summary Table of Contents

Dedication iii
Table of Contents vii
Acknowledgments xi
Introduction xiii

Chapter 1: What Is Terrorism? 1
Chapter 2: The War on Terror 17
Chapter 3: Expanding the War on Terror 39
Chapter 4: Civil Liberties and the War on Terror 59
Chapter 5: Necessity and Rationale for the Law of War—
    Lessons from My Lai 95
Chapter 6: A New Paradigm for War
    and Terrorism Avoidance 137
Chapter 7: Leading the Way—
    Pax Americana or the Rule of Law? 177
Chapter 8: The Role of the Military and Army Special Forces
    in Promoting Human Rights 197
Chapter 9: America Must Stay the Course 213

Appendices 221
About the Author 287
Index 289

Table of Contents

Dedication iii

Summary Table of Contents v

Acknowledgments xi

Introduction xiii

Chapter 1: What Is Terrorism? 1
   1.1 Defining Terrorism 2
   1.2 The Goal of Terrorism 4
   1.3 Terrorism and Weapons of Mass Destruction 4
   1.4 State-Sponsored and State-Supported Terrorism 5
   1.5 The Diplomatic Bag 6
   1.6 Sub-State Terrorism 9
   1.7 Individual Terrorism 10
   1.8 Al-Qa'eda-Styled Terrorism 11
   Endnotes 12

Chapter 2: The War on Terror 17
   2.1 September 11, 2001 18
   2.2 An Act of War 20
   2.3 The Rule of Law—Use of Force 22
   2.4 NATO 29
   2.5 Congressional War-Making Power 30
   2.6 The Employment of Lawful Violence 32
   Endnotes 33

Chapter 3: Expanding the War on Terror 39
   3.1 Why They Hate 41
   3.2 Weapons of Mass Murder 43
   3.3 Future Battles and the Rule of Law 44
   3.4 Power versus Words—The Rule of Law 48
   Endnotes 53

Chapter 4: Civil Liberties and the War on Terror 59
   4.1 Past Efforts to Address Terrorism 60
   4.2 Federal Courts and Military Tribunals 62
   4.3 Investigating Terrorist Suspects 70
   4.4 Use of the Military in Domestic Law Enforcement 72
   4.5 Immigration 75
   4.6 New Information-Gathering Technologies 76
   4.7 Assassination 77
   4.8 Increased Security Measures in Public Places 79
   4.9 The Constitution and the War on Terror 79
   Endnotes 80

Chapter 5: Necessity and Rationale for the Law of War—
Lessons from My Lai 95
   5.1 The Law of War 98
   5.2 Voices from the Past—My Lai 101
   5.3 Facts of My Lai 102
   5.4 My Lai Comes to Light 105
   5.5 Impact of My Lai 105
   5.6 Why Did My Lai Happen? 106
   5.7 Leadership 111
   5.8 Lack of a Grand Strategy on the Part of the United States 115
   5.9 Lessons of My Lai 117
   5.10 Lesson One—Rationale for the Law of War 118
   5.11 Lesson Two—Soldiers Must Be Trained in the Law of War ... 121
   5.12 Lesson Three—Preventing Violations of the Law of War
       in the War on Terror 122
   Endnotes 126

Table of Contents

**Chapter 6: A New Paradigm for War
and Terrorism Avoidance** 137
    6.1 The Causes of Aggression and Terrorism 139
    6.2 The New Paradigm for War and Terrorism Avoidance 142
    6.3 Defining Democratic Values and Democracy 144
    6.4 Origins of Human Rights 148
    6.5 The Corpus of Human Rights Law 154
    6.6 United Nations Efforts to Promote Human Rights 155
    6.7 Non-Governmental Organizations Devoted to Human Rights .. 161
    6.8 Regional Organizations to Promote Human Rights 162
    6.9 Traditional Efforts of the United States in
        Promoting Human Rights 164
    Endnotes 172

**Chapter 7: Leading the Way—
Pax Americana or the Rule of Law?** 177
    7.1 Collective Security 177
    7.2 Peace, Freedom and Appeasement—
        Lessons from the Gulf War of 1991 179
    7.3 Stay with the Rule of Law 185
    Endnotes 192

**Chapter 8: The Role of the Military and Army Special Forces
in Promoting Human Right**s 197
    8.1 The United States Global Strategic View 199
    8.2 New Non-Traditional Roles—
        Human Rights as a Force Multiplier 200
    8.3 The Role of Special Forces 205
    Endnotes 211

Chapter 9: America Must Stay the Course 213
    Endnotes 219

Appendices

Appendix A:
Selected Provisions of the Charter of the United Nations 223
Appendix B:
United Nations Security Council Resolution 1368 (2001).............. 241
Appendix C:
Statement by the North Atlantic Council (September 12, 2001) 243
Appendix D:
Authorization for Use of Military Force
(Public Law 107-40, 107th Congress) 245
Appendix E:
War Powers Resolution (Public Law 93-148, 93rd Congress,
H. J. Res. 542, November 7, 1973) 247
Appendix F:
President's Letter to Congress on American Response to Terrorism
(October 9, 2001) 255
Appendix G:
The United States Constitution (Selected Provisions) 257
Appendix H:
Universal Declaration of Human Rights 261
Appendix I:
International Covenant on Civil and Political Rights 269
Appendix J:
Joint Resolution to Authorize the Use of United States
Armed Forces Against Iraq 283

About the Author 287

Index 289

Acknowledgments

Among the colleagues and friends who have supported this book with their insight, time, and thoughtfulness are Professor Robert Summers and Colonel William A. Hudson, Jr. The author wishes to acknowledge the invaluable help of the following research assistants, Christian Hack, Kristy Eddings, and Stephanie Hoppas for expertly dealing with conceptual, bibliographical and organizational problems. The author also wishes acknowledge with appreciation the *University of Florida Journal of International Law*, *Houston Journal of International Law*, *Military Law Review*, and *The Scholar: St. Mary's Law Review on Minority Issues* for permission granted to reprint materials previously published. Finally, special thanks to Dean Bill Piatt, St. Mary's University School of Law, for providing much-needed logistical support to this project.

Introduction

[The War on Terror] is civilization's fight. This is the fight of all who believe in progress and pluralism, tolerance and freedom.[1]
—George W. Bush

Be it the Middle Ages or the Renaissance, the Great War[2] or the Cold War,[3] the trends of human history have always been characterized by epochs or eras. While it is sometimes difficult to find the exact chronological line separating one era from the next, some eras are born in a single dramatic event of such enormity that the very date overshadows the general theme of the times. As December 7, 1941,[4] was to the World War II[5] generation, so too was September 11, 2001,[6] to the new era that many believe has now arrived on the stage of history. Arguably, the post-Cold War[7] period may have indeed given way to a new time in history labeled by most commentators as the "War on Terror."[8]

The challenge that the United States is facing, as is the rest of the civilized world, is to realistically fight and win the War on Terror. In the year since September 11, 2001, many solutions have been suggested to protect this nation from global terrorism. Among them are such things as the institution of new security and intelligence gathering methods, developing streamlined templates for a rapid federal, state and local response in the aftermath of a major terrorist attack and revamping the Immigration and Naturalization Service to better regulate and account for those who enter the United States. These solutions focus on various pressure points of the problem, but will not prove adequate if America hopes to significantly blunt the scourge of global terrorism. The enemy must be clearly understood and then the battle must be brought to the enemy. Who are these terrorists and how can they be defeated?

A fundamental obligation of any state is to protect its citizens from external as well as internal threats to person and property. Nowhere is this obligation more difficult to perform than in the realm of al-Qa'eda-styled terrorism, particularly when one considers the apocalyptic horrors that might be unleashed through the terrorist use of weapons of mass destruction. In the War on Terror, the United States is concerned not only with those renegade states which might commit or sponsor terror attacks using weapons of mass destruction, but also there is deep consternation about how to best deal with international or domestic terrorist groups, and even individuals.

For those who follow the studies and trends, the lethality of terrorism continues to grow, particularly against United States interests. Of course, such studies are rather inconsequential when one considers the aftermath of a terrorist directed nuclear, biological, chemical, or radiological attack in an urban area of the United States. The attacks of September 11, 2001, could very well pale in comparison. Furthermore, to the mass casualties and devastating economic disruption, one must add the troubling impact such an event might have on future civil liberties and freedoms that Americans now enjoy. Considering that al-Qa'eda-styled terrorists have targeted the United States more often than any other country in the world, save Israel, the specter of weapons of mass destruction terrorism demands top priority in our thinking and planning.

Karl von Clausewitz once observed: "Every age has its own kind of war, its own limiting conditions and its own peculiar preconceptions." One characteristic of the War on Terror is undeniable; the United States stands alone as the world's bastion of stability and as the foremost sphere of power and influence. Accordingly, it is absolutely critical that our national strategy for winning the War on Terror successfully accomplish three things. First, the United States must fully identify and appreciate the threat of the new breed of al-Qa'eda-styled global terrorism. Second, United States strategy must undergo a major metamorphosis in order to better bring the battle to the terrorist and to the nations that harbor them. America must go after the radical regimes that stand behind the terrorists. Third, particularly in the context of the new Afghanistan government, America must unabashedly embark on a dedicated democracy building campaign in order to drain the totalitarian swamps in which international terrorism breeds.

This third factor involves the promotion of a new paradigm that is intuitively simplistic and yet absolutely vital to winning the War on Terror. Simply put, since democracies do not engage in terrorism the United States must concentrate resources to do more to promote the normative values of democracy, pluralism, and human rights throughout the community of nations. The United States of America must become the chief advocate of policies which promote global stability and encourage a steadfast adherence to established, well-defined norms of international behavior, i.e., maintaining the rule of law. This democracy building initiative must be the basis for a new and dynamic paradigm whose application points to a more effective way to war and terrorism avoidance, especially in regards to state-sponsors of aggression and terrorism. The al-Qa'eda terrorists and their like cannot successfully operate without host-nation support from a totalitarian regime

At the end of the day, terrorism, like crime, can never be completely eradicated. As the title of this book suggests, however, the new specter of al-Qa'eda terrorism can be better contained. The purpose of this book is to survey the dominant characteristics of the War on Terror and to highlight some of the legal and policy implications that confront the United States with special emphasis on the importance of developing capable military forces on the one hand and promoting democracy as a long-term solution to terrorism avoidance on the other. In this context, even if one is cynical enough to believe that the world politic is ruled primarily by the application or threat of force, it is nevertheless of critical importance from both a national and an international perspective that America rubricate its leadership role by thoughtful concerns for the positive advancement of the rule of law. The world's most precious commodities—the promotion of democratic values and human rights—must not become casualties in the War on Terror. Indeed, these are the very tools that will prove of ultimate value in winning the War on Terror.

Endnotes

1. President George W. Bush address to a joint session of Congress (Sept. 20, 2001).

2. The Great War is commonly known as World War I. It was the first modern world war and said, at the time, to be the "war to end all wars." The Great War lasted from 1914 until 1918 in which the United States, Great Britain, France, Russia, Italy, Japan, and Belgium defeated Germany, Austria-Hungary, Turkey, and Bulgaria.

3. The Cold War lasted from 1945 until December 1991, with the collapse of the Union of Soviet Socialist Republics into a number of independent republics.

4. December 7, 1941 was the date of the infamous attack by Japan on the United States military facilities at Pearl Harbor, Hawaii. This event directly triggered American involvement in World War II. Several American lawmakers equated the shock of the terror attack of Sept. 11, 2001, to the surprise Japanese bombing of Pearl Harbor. See, Miles A. Pomper, "In For the Long Haul," *Congressional Quarterly*, Sept. 15, 2001, at 2118.

5. World War II lasted from 1939-1945 in which the United States, Great Britain, the Soviet Union and other allies, defeated Germany, Japan, and Italy.

6. Erica Goode, "A Day of Terror: The Psychology," *New York Times*, Sept. 12, 2001, at A13 [hereinafter Day of Terror]. On September 11, 2001, a total of 19 members of the terrorist al-Qa'eda network hijacked four domestic U.S. passenger aircraft while in flight (five terrorists in three of the planes and four in the fourth). The terrorists crashed two of the aircraft into the twin towers of the World Trade Center in New York. Another plane was crashed by the terrorists into the Pentagon, Washington, D.C., but the fourth plane was forced down by passengers into a field in Pennsylvania. According to a *New York Times* tally, along with billions of dollars in property loss, approximately 3,067 were killed, not including the 19 terrorists. This figure includes 184 dead at the Pentagon (counting the 59 passengers on the hijacked plane) and 40 dead in Pennsylvania. See "Dead and Missing," *New York Times*, Feb. 10, 2002, at A12.

7. The so-called post-Cold War era began in 1991. It was referred to as the post-Cold War era because no clear new world theme had emerged.

8. See Katharine Q. Seelye and Elisabeth Bumiller, "After the Attacks: The President; Bush Labels Aerial Terrorist Attacks 'Acts of War,'" *New York Times*, Sept. 13, at A16. The phrase "war on terror" was first used by President Bush on September 11, 2001, aboard Air Force One. His first major public address the next day also declared the terrorist attacks as "acts of war." Other synonyms include the "War on Terrorism" and the "War on Global Terrorism."

Chapter 1

What Is Terrorism?

The goal of terror is to kill one and frighten 10,000.

—Chinese proverb

Synopsis
1.1 Defining Terrorism
1.2 The Goal of Terrorism
1.3 Terrorism and Weapons of Mass Destruction
1.4 State-Sponsored and State-Supported Terrorism
1.5 The Diplomatic Bag
1.6 Sub-State Terrorism
1.7 Individual Terrorism
1.8 Al-Qa'eda-Styled Terrorism
Endnotes

Things must be properly defined before they can be intelligently discussed. Although many trace the etymology of the word *terror* to France's "reign of terror" under Robespierre,[1] the employment of terror is a phenomenon that has been around for a very long time in human history.[2] Notwithstanding the fact that terrorism is the antithesis of the rule of law, there exists no global consensus on a precise definition of terrorism[3] either in the international community or in the United States. This is due in part to the tensions of the Cold War era when West and East could agree on precious little, but also continues today under the postmodernist cliché, "one man's terrorist is another man's freedom fighter."[4] For instance, a suicide bomber in Israel who intentionally kills innocent Jewish civilians may be considered a "hero" by certain segments of the Palestinian people and a terrorist by others.[5] Thus, in order to better reflect the inherent terror and illegality of Palestinian suicide bombers, it is far more palatable to reasonable minds to refer to these individuals as "homicide bombers."

1.1 Defining Terrorism

Recognizing the politics associated with reaching an acceptable global definition for terrorism, the United Nations has very often elected to avoid the term terrorism altogether, use it in a general sense only,[6] or to carefully carve out very specific acts in selected international treaties to characterize as "terrorism." Three examples serve to illustrate this delinquency.

First, the International Law Commission's 1954 *Draft Code of Offenses Against the Peace and Security of Mankind* contained the following proposed language at Article 25 to define terrorism: "[T]he undertaking or encouragement by the authorities of a State of terrorist activity in another State, or the toleration by the authorities of a State of organized activities calculated to carry out terrorist acts in another State." Even though the proposed sentence failed to define the term, no agreement could be reached. As of this writing, almost fifty years later, the United Nations General Assembly has still not been able to reach agreement on a final version.[7]

Second, the latest attempt by the United Nations Sub-Commission on Human Rights to come up with a definition of terrorism has met similar troubles. The first draft report of February 2001, listed three essential elements of terrorism. A terrorist act: (1) must be illegal, violating national or international law; (2) must be intended to harm the state for political reasons; and (3) must be capable of generating a state of fear in the general population. However, in order to reach consensus amongst the committee members on its first progress report, the special rapporteur had to delete the entire definition relating to terrorism.[8]

Third, perhaps the greatest missed opportunity for the United Nations to establish a firm international definition of terrorism as it relates to states that sponsor or support terrorists occurred in its failure to employ the word "terrorism" in the context of the key 1957 United Nations General Assembly resolution defining aggression as it relates to when a nation may engage in armed self-defense under Article 51[9] of the United Nations Charter. The United Nations chose to classify the activities of states who send, organize, or support "armed bands, groups, irregulars, or mercenaries, which carry out acts of armed force against a State,"[10] as simply engaging in unlawful aggression in direct violation of the U.N. Charter. It failed to refer to these activities as engaging in terrorism. Terrorism, of course, could have certainly fit into this expression of unlawful aggression, but it was not used.

In the United States, the difficulties in definition are not related to a reluctance to use the term terrorism,[11] but rather rest in the sheer number of different government instrumentalities that have offered independent interpretations of terrorism which, while similar, are not identical.[12] The latest American effort to define terrorism is found at Section 411 of the USA/Patriot Act (Patriot Act), signed into law in November of 2001.[13]

Actually, the Patriot Act provides similar definitions for "terrorist organization," "domestic terrorism," and "international terrorism." A terrorist organization is defined as one that is:

> (1) designated by the Secretary of State as a terrorist organization under the process established under current law; (2) designated by the Secretary of State as a terrorist organization for immigration purposes; or (3) a group of two or more individuals that commits terrorist activities or plans or prepares to commit (including locating targets for) terrorist activities.[14]

Domestic terrorism is defined in the Patriot Act with a slightly different emphasis; domestic terrorism is the "unlawful use, or threatened use, of force or violence by a group or individuals based [in the United States] . . . committed against persons or property to intimidate or coerce a government, the civilian population . . . in furtherance of political or social objectives."[15]

International terrorism is set out in the Patriot Act as follows:

> International terrorism involves violent acts or acts dangerous to human life that violate the criminal laws of the United States or any state, or that would be a criminal violation if committed within the jurisdiction of the United States or any state. These acts appear intended to intimidate or coerce a civilian population, influence the policy of a government by intimidation or coercion, or affect the conduct of a government by assassination or kidnapping. International terrorist acts occur outside the United States or transcend national boundaries in terms of how terrorists accomplish them, the persons they appear intended to coerce or intimidate, or the place in which the perpetrators operate.[16]

1.2 The Goal of Terrorism

Despite the lack of a fixed universal agreement defining terrorism, the essential goal of terrorism is readily identifiable. As the root word implies, the goal of terrorism is to instill fear in a given civilian population by means of violence. In the oft-repeated Chinese proverb, the objective of the terrorist is to kill one and frighten 10,000.[17] While specific acts of terrorism may appear to be mindless and irrational, terrorism is the exact opposite of confused behavior. Terrorism is a goal-directed, calculated, premeditated use of force.

Since the victims of terrorism are invariably innocent civilians, it appears fundamentally logical that a definitional approach should concentrate on the act and not the political, religious, or social causes which motivate the act. Under this regimen, the use of violence on a civilian target with intent to cause fear in a given civilian population is easily classified as a terrorist act.[18] In other words, to the common understanding of the general public, terrorism is immediately associated with violence that is directed at the indiscriminate killing of innocent civilians to create a climate of fear.[19] The ends can never justify the means.

In this light, bombings of public places, the sending of letter bombs or poisons through the mails,[20] hijackings of aircraft, hostage taking, and so on, are all acts of terrorism regardless of the underlying cause said to justify the attack. In a sense, terrorism can simply be described as making "war" on civilians.[21]

1.3 Terrorism and Weapons of Mass Destruction

Apart from the normal *modus vivendi* of terrorism, one must now add weapons of mass destruction as a special definitional subset. In Section 1403 of the National Defense Authorization Act for fiscal year 1997, weapons of mass destruction are defined as "any weapon or device that is intended, or has the capability, to cause death or serious bodily injury to a significant number of people through the release of toxic or poisonous chemicals or their precursors, a disease organism, or radiation or radioactivity."[22] Thus, in its broadest sense, weapons of mass destruction include not only nuclear material, but the full range of biological, chemical, and radioactive agents.

As is true for any terrorist event, there are three general sources from which a weapon of mass destruction terrorist attack can emanate—states, sub-state groups,[23] or individuals.[24] Tragically, in the so-called information age, all three categories have demonstrated a willingness to use weapons of mass murder. States that engage in terrorism and have the potential of using weapons of mass destruction are further divided as either state-sponsors or state-supporters of terrorism.

1.4 State-Sponsored and State-Supported Terrorism

Perhaps the most easily identifiable category of terrorism is the state-sponsored terrorist attack. In recent times, the international community has been shocked to learn that certain renegade states such as Iraq have shown an unabashed willingness to use deadly nerve gas to kill thousands of men, women and children (the Kurds). Indeed, it can be argued that all totalitarian states pose an ever-present threat for the use of weapons of mass destruction at any given time—both against their own people and against other nations. The United States State Department now designates seven countries as sponsors of terrorism against other nations: the gang of seven are Cuba, Iran, Iraq, Libya, North Korea, Sudan, and Syria. In fact, the number is larger. In 1999, John A. Lauder, director of the Central Intelligence Agency's Nonproliferation Center, testified before Congress that a dozen countries, including Iran, Iraq, Libya, North Korea, and Syria, "now either possess or are actively pursuing offensive biological weapons capabilities for use against their perceived enemies, whether internal or external."[25]

In the context of a state use of weapons of mass destruction in a terrorist attack, several commentators seek to distinguish a state-sponsored terrorist act from a state-supported terrorist act. State-sponsored terrorism exists when a state directly but secretly uses its own resources to sponsor acts of terrorism against another country. Since accountability for such acts are denied, the aggressor-state seeks to avoid responsibility. On the other hand, state-supported terrorism refers to the practice of a state providing resources or finances to a terrorist group for training and logistics, as occurred in Afghanistan where the terrorist group headed by Osama bin Laden once took open refuge. In contrast to the state-sponsored scenario, the state-supported terrorist group generally operates in a more independent fashion from the state.

A classic and oft-cited case of a state-sponsored act of terrorism occurred in 1986 when Libyan government agents bombed an American frequented discotheque in then West Berlin, Germany. This secretive act of terror was followed by a second state-sponsored act of terror: the in-flight bombing of Pan Am Flight 800 over Lockerbie, Scotland, in 1989 which killed 278 people.[26]

In the final analysis, it is difficult to make a practical distinction between state-sponsored and state-supported terrorism. The terms really speak only to the degree of culpability. Nevertheless, if the rule of law has any force, states who allow terrorist groups to operate with impunity on their soil should never be able to escape the attendant lawful consequences. While it is subject to legal debate whether a particular terrorist act committed apart from the support or sponsorship of a state would be considered an "act of war" under international law,[27] a terrorist attack with the support or sponsorship of a state could very well be deemed an "act of war."[28]

The early days of concern regarding terrorism and the use of weapons of mass destruction saw most of the emphasis focused primarily on the actions of the totalitarian state. Because many believed that ready access to weapons of mass destruction material was limited, sub-state terrorist groups and individual terrorists were generally given less attention. For these later categories of terrorism, the international community generally concentrated on making specific overt acts international crimes (e.g., airline hijacking or hostage taking). In rgards to renegade states, however, the major issue turned on the proper application of appropriate sanctions against the state that sponsored or supported the terrorist incident.

1.5 The Diplomatic Bag

A particular early concern, which demonstrates the depth of the debate regarding how to deal with a weapon of mass murder terrorist event *vis-à-vis* international legal sanctions, was the use of the diplomatic bag to import and export with impunity assorted prohibited and illegal items into receiving and transit states.[30] The diplomatic bag issue continues to stir disagreement even today. Modern international practice has witnessed the use (or attempted use) of the diplomatic bag to transport illegal foreign currency, illegal drugs, weapons, and even people. While all *malum in se* acts committed under the cover of this diplomatic shield are sorely objectionable, the most insidious and disconcerting activities are those in which the diplomatic bag might be used as a vehicle to commit clearly defined

Chapter 1: What Is Terrorism?

acts of terrorism, especially those related to the employment of a weapon of mass destruction.

Currently, the diplomatic privileges and immunities accorded to the diplomatic bag under treaty and customary international law are set out in Article 27 of the Vienna Convention on Diplomatic Relations.[31] In short, the diplomatic bag is deemed by international law to be inviolable and not subject to detention or search. The central thrust of those who periodically call for a change to the Vienna Convention argue that the protected status given to the diplomatic bag must be significantly revised to account for the legitimate security interests of the receiving state. Again, the major concern is that the diplomatic bag could be used by a foreign actor to commit an act of terrorism with a weapon of mass destruction.

Perhaps the most widely publicized abuse of the diplomatic bag to date, and one which clearly illustrates the controversy over the status of the bag, was committed by the Libyan government of Colonel Qaddafi. In April of 1984, two Libyans gunned down eleven demonstrators and one British constable as they stood outside of the Libyan embassy in London. Despite substantial suspicions that the weapons and other evidence connected with this heinous act of terrorism were put inside of Libyan diplomatic bags, the British authorities allowed the Libyans to carry the diplomatic bags out of the country without searching or scanning them. This incident caused a chorus of protest that the rules of diplomatic immunity were obsolete.

Responding to public fears that diplomatic privileges could be used as a vehicle to commit state-sponsored terrorism related to weapons of mass murder, then-Secretary of Defense Caspar Weinberger publicly indicated in 1986 that the entire doctrine of diplomatic immunity should be greatly limited.[32] Arguing that state-sponsored terrorists were abusing the doctrine, Weinberger called upon "diplomats, with the assistance of the legal profession" to define new limits that would help solve the problem of diplomatic privileges being extended to those states who were connected with terrorists.[33] Weinberger's call to action was not heeded.

No one can argue that all conventional terrorist acts fade in significance when compared to fears that the diplomatic bag might be used illegally to transport weapons of mass destruction. In the wake of the large-scale destruction that would result from even a single weapon of mass destruction event, the demands for security safeguards would seem to far outweigh any status quo that the international rules might seek to maintain. In short, if ordinary weapons can be neatly and easily sent into the receiving state via the diplomatic bag, why not a weapon of mass destruction? One terrorist from a hostile country, for example, could smuggle in a vile of lethal biological material for insertion in a city water supply in the United States. Although this argument is true enough, the privileged status of the diplomatic bag has never been successfully curtailed. This is true for three reasons.

First, most people understand that if the diplomatic bag privilege is limited then the determined terrorist will find yet another way to smuggle materials for mass murder into the United States. In an open society, such as the United States, the state-sponsored terrorist, or any terrorist, can obtain much, if not most, of the needed materials on the domestic open market and, more importantly, do so without leaving a signature.[34]

Second, since nations have an inherent right of self-defense to search out and otherwise protect themselves against viable threats to their national security, the state which sponsored such blatant aggressive behavior takes an inordinate risk by using the diplomatic bag in such a manner. Deterrence would keep the renegade state in check.

Third, like all international agreements, the Vienna Convention can never hope to maintain any form of functional integrity unless it is strictly adhered to. Nations who demand inspection of even the most suspicious diplomatic bags must do so only at the risk of having their own bags subjected to the same process by the sending state.[35] And that practice would quickly undermine the entire process of free diplomatic intercourse. The only real guarantee that other nations, friendly or otherwise, will generally follow international rules rests in this reciprocity analysis—the red thread of international law. We follow the rules because the other guy follows the rules.

As discussed in Chapter 2, the way to deal with a state-sponsored terrorist attack, if linkage is established, is to seek redress under the rule of law—financially, judicially, or militarily.[36] Historically, if a state sponsors a terrorist act, the United States has generally demonstrated that it has the capability and willingness to retaliate under the well-recognized venue of self-defense. Unlike other international disputes between nations, terrorist attacks should never be handled by a third party in the context of dispute resolution. The renegade state must be neutralized in a legitimate manner

Chapter 1: What Is Terrorism?

and forum. Ultimately, the aggrieved state can turn to the classical rules of self-defense, depending on the severity of the terrorist incident. Realistically, if the United States had hard evidence that a state was behind a terrorist attack, it would likely respond under the traditional notions of self-defense and forcible self-help. This, of course, is precisely what occurred in response to the September 11, 2001, attack on the United States. Any nation will certainly do what is necessary to protect itself from illegal acts of violence.

1.6 Sub-State Terrorism

Sub-state terrorist groups can either be domestic or international terrorist organizations and are generally categorized by either religious or political ideologies. In 1995, for example, "25 of 58, or 42 per cent of known, active, international terrorist groups had a predominately religious component or motivation."[37] In addition, from a rule of law perspective sub-state terrorist organizations do not operate with the approval or sponsorship of the host nation.

The first use of a weapon of mass destruction by a sub-state group occurred on March 20, 1995, when members of the Aum Shinrikyo cult in Japan released a lethal nerve agent, sarin, in a Tokyo underground subway. This weapon of mass destruction attack killed twelve people and injured 3,000 others.

While attacks by sub-state groups against United States interests have yet to use weapons of mass destruction (as of this writing), many groups have shown a viciousness and disregard for human life that clearly points to a willingness to use such weapons in the future. For instance, an Islamic radical group with ties to al-Qa'eda and headed by Ramzi Ahmad Yousef, conducted the 1993 bombing of New York City's World Trade Center in an attempt to topple one of the twin towers onto the other to kill thousands, an act clearly in the spirit of a weapons of mass destruction event. In fact, it has been reported that those behind the 1993 World Trade Center bombing were also gathering the ingredients for a chemical weapon that could have brought the death toll into the tens of thousands. Some reports indicated that the bomb might have been laced with cyanide, but the poison burned up in the detonation.[38]

In early 2000, United States and Israeli intelligence sources reported that Hamas, a militant Palestinian terrorist group that the Palestinian Authority denies responsibility for, was experimenting with chemical weapons in their rocket attacks against Israeli targets.[29] Although the radical Islamic group has not yet used chemical or biological agents in their terror attacks on Israel, the potential for such acts certainly exists. With the increasing availability of high-tech weapons and nuclear materials from former communist countries and the ease with which some chemical and biological agents can now be manufactured, there is growing concern that sub-state groups will now actively cross over into the weapons of mass destruction domain. Indeed, the fear also exists that one of the world's dictators might simply give weapons of mass destruction to a sub-state terrorist group.

1.7 Individual Terrorism

Perhaps the most troubling aspect of weapons of mass destruction terrorism is one not often heard in the War on Terror. It is the prospect of an individual setting off a weapon of mass destruction in a major urban area. Because they operate on their own, without affiliation to any known group or state, individuals who engage in "lone-wolf" terrorism are far harder to predict, track, or deter.

To demonstrate the seriousness of individual terrorism, on March 3, 1999, William C. Patrick, III, a leading American expert on biological warfare, walked through the security check system at the Rayburn House Office Building in downtown Washington D.C., carrying 7.5 grams of powdered anthrax, enough to kill everyone in the building, in a small plastic bottle.[39] Not only was he rubricating the ease with which a single determined terrorist could breach security systems and target, in this case, a major federal government installation, Patrick's action certainly should have provided the needed wake up call to United States government officials and the public at large. Unfortunately, it did not.

Patrick told a Congressional committee that he was trying to show how a hostile or aggressor state could smuggle powdered anthrax in to the United States in a secure diplomatic pouch.[40] What Patrick was really demonstrating, however, was the ease with which any individual terrorist—domestic or international—could unleash untold weapons of mass murder horror, almost at will. In his testimony, Patrick related that he had also carried other similar deadly materials and, "like Sherman went through Georgia," had "been through all the major airports, and the security systems of the State Department, the Pentagon, and even the CIA, and nobody [has] stopped me."[41]

The most notorious example of an individual terrorist attack in the United States occurred in April 1995 with the bombing of the Murrah Federal Building in Oklahoma City by Timothy McVeigh.[42] The bomb killed 167 people, including women and children. Although McVeigh did not employ a weapon of mass destruction in his attack, his actions clearly raised the issue of individual domestic terrorism in the context of weapons of mass destruction.[43] While one can ponder the bizarre "anti-government" sentiments that motivated McVeigh, the greater issue really revolves around individual access to material which can cause widespread damage of life and property.

Furthermore, not all individual terrorism can be associated with hardcore political or religious ideologues. Individual terrorism can be committed by persons seeking personal rather than political gain, or even by individuals who are mentally ill. Considering the number of "Timothy McVeighs" in any given open society, the prospect of individuals obtaining access to weapons of mass destruction is chilling, and, unfortunately, will continue to grow with time.

1.8 Al-Qa'eda-Styled Terrorism

The War on Terror is predominantly focused on defeating the al-Qa'eda terrorist network. The al-Qa'eda organization is a new type of terrorism that combines all of the forms of terror identified in this chapter. They were, at one time, state-sponsored by the Taliban government of Afghanistan and continue to be state-supported by any number of radical regimes including Iran, Iraq, the Palestinian territories, Syria, and so on. They also qualify as a sub-state terrorist organization because they have secretly infiltrated and established "sleeper" terrorist cells in various nations throughout the world to include the United States, Britain, France, England, Spain, Italy, and Germany. In addition, the al-Qa'eda also influences individual terrorism. Their ideology of hate has reached the minds of individuals who, although not directly tied to the organization, choose to commit terrorist acts because they have adopted the general theme and goal of the al-Qa'eda mindset. This certainly occurred in the shooting murder of several innocent civilians in California at Los Angeles International Airport on July 4, 2002, by Hesham Mohamed Hadayat; although law enforcement officials did all they could to downplay the impact that terrorist ideology had to play in the attack.

Some have described the al-Qa'eda as an entirely new type of entity in the world—not just a terrorist group but a "virtual state." The virtual state description is fundamentally valid. This virtual state exhibits many of the characteristics of the classic nation-state, but is able to walk in the shadows of international law because it has no fixed national boundaries. The al-Qa'eda virtual state has a military, a treasury, a foreign policy, and links to other nations-states. Indeed, because the United States is at war with a virtual state, the rules for fighting that war are facing challenges not yet fully appreciated by the law of war.

Finally, the War on Terror demands that the United States fully come to grips with the *modis vivendi* of the al-Qa'eda. Again, America must know the enemy if it is to defeat him. There are four basic reasons why the al-Qa'eda virtual state is vastly different from all previous terror groups that civilized nations have had to cope with.

First, threatened by the normative values of democracy, freedom, and human rights, the al-Qa'eda are dedicated to the destruction of the West and all those who adopt Western ideals, including the so-called moderate Muslim and Arab governments. Second, al-Qa'eda members have learned to use the super highway of modern technology to establish ties across the globe and provide logistical support for terror cells in practically any country in the world. Third, they have shown an intense desire to obtain any and all forms of weapons which can inflict mass casualties on civilians, including weapons of mass destruction. Fourth, they are willing to die in the furtherance of their cause. Making suicide the method of choice to inflict terror, a dedicated terrorist can target almost any public place. Tragically, these new terrorists have successfully used the openness of the democratic society to attack from within, placing great strains on civil liberties.

Endnotes

1. The lawyer Maximilien Robespierre is most often identified as the chief figure during the "reign of terror," in which the revolutionary leaders of the state engaged in the indiscriminate execution of thousands by the guillotine. The

height of the reign of terror occurred from 1793–1794. Ironically, Robespierre was a victim of the guillotine in 1794.

2. See, e.g., *The Complete Works of Flavius Josephus,* William Whiston trans. (Grand Rapids, MI: Kregel Pub., 1981). The Hebrew Zealots conducted random acts of assassination against the occupying Romans in Judea prior to Jerusalem falling to the Roman legions under Titus in 70 A.D.

3. USA/Patriot Act of 2001, 115 Stat. 272; Pub. Law 107-56 §411 (Oct. 26, 2001) [hereinafter Patriot Act].

4. See John Norton Moore, Frederick S. Tipson, and Robert F. Turner, *National Security Law*, (Durham, NC: Carolina Academic Press, 1990) [hereinafter *National Security Law*]. Chapter 10 of the text provides an overview of the historical development of terrorism and discusses the proposition that "the causes of terrorism or the political motivation of the individual terrorists are relevant to the problem of definition." Under this proposition, many have argued that acts of violence against "colonialism" or in wars of "national liberation" fall outside of the definition of terrorism. Hence, the dilemma of "[o]ne man's terrorism is another man's heroism."

5. See, e.g., James Bennet, "Israelis Declare Arab Woman Was In Fact a Suicide Bomber," *New York Times*, Feb. 9, 2002, at A6. The Israelis have suffered hundreds of suicide attacks by Palestinian terrorists. This particular suicide attack was the first such attack against Israel carried out by a female.

6. See U.N. Sec. Coun. Res. 1368 (Sept. 12, 2001) [hereinafter SC 1368]. The Security Council resolution uses the word terror or terrorism six times in the short one page document. Like all other United Nations efforts in this area, SC 1368 uses the term terrorism but offers no definition of terrorism other than to affirm that the September 11, 2001, attack on the United States was a "horrifying terrorist attack[s]."

7. There have been several draft proposals over the years by various United Nations Commissions and Sub-Commissions regarding the definition of terrorism. See e.g., 1954 Draft Code of Offenses Against the Peace and Security of Mankind, 9 U.N. GAOR Supp. (no. 9) at 11-12, U.N. Doc. A/2693 (1954).

8. See U.N. Doc. E/CN.4/Sub.2/2001/31.

9. United Nations Charter art. 51.

10. U.N. Definition of Aggression, G.A. Res. 3314, 29 U.N. GAOR, Supp. No. 31, U.N. Doc. A/9631 (1957), at 142.

11. See Jim Meenan, "Clinton: Terrorists Misjudged America," *South Bend Tribune*, Oct. 12, 2001, at A1. Former President Bill Clinton touched on this issue in a speech at Mendel Center at Lake Michigan College and also reminded the audience that the United States government had engaged in terrorism against slaves and American Indians. Perhaps the most infamous example of an American solider employing terror against women and children, in the context of war, was union general William T. Sherman in his march across the Deep South in 1864–1865. Sherman's war crimes were in violation of the Lieber Code, adopted by the United States in 1863 as General Orders No. 100. Richard Shelly Hartigan, *Lieber's Code and the Law of War* (Chicago, IL: Precedent Pub., Inc., 1983).

12. There are numerous federal statutes that offer slightly different definitions of terrorism. See, e.g., 28 C.F.R. §85 where the Dept. of Justice defines terrorism as "the unlawful use of force and violence against persons or property to intimidate or coerce a government, the civilian population, or any segment thereof, in furtherance of political or social objectives." 18 U.S.C. §2331 offers a slightly different definition of international terrorism.

13. Patriot Act.

14. Id.

15. Id. at §802.

16. Id.

17. See Sun-tzu, *The Art of War*, Ralph D. Sawyer (trans.) (New York: Barnes & Noble, Inc., 1994).

18. See Joshua Hammer, "Another Lebanon," *Newsweek*, Mar. 4, 2002, at 28. Some Palestinian militants urge that only Israeli soldiers should be targeted in the current conflict, as they are "legitimate" targets.

19. See H. H. Cooper, *Evaluating the Terrorist Threat, Principles of Applied Risk Assessment: Clandestine Tactics and Technology Series* (Gaithersburg, MD: Int. Ass. of Police Chiefs, 1974), at 4. Terrorism can be defined as "a purposeful human activity primarily directed toward the creation of a general climate of fear designed to influence, in ways destined by protagonists, other human beings, and through them, some course of events."

20. See David Noonan, "Danger: Handle with Care," *Newsweek*, Oct. 22, 2001, at 38; Jennifer Barrett, "The Year of Living Dangerously," *Newsweek*, Jan. 8, 2002, at 10. From September to November 2001, five United States citizens

were killed by ingesting the Anthrax virus sent through the United States postal system.

21. Caleb Carr, *The Lessons of Terror: A History of Warfare Against Civilians, Why It Has Always Failed and Why It Will Fail Again* (New York: Random House Inc., 2002).

22. "Combating Terrorism: Threat and Risk Assessments Can Help Prioritize and Target Program Investments," *U.S. GAO Report to Congressional Requesters*, Apr. 1998.

23. See, e.g., Robert Jay Lifton, *Destroying the World to Save It: Aum Shinrikyo, Apocalyptic Violence, and the New Global Terrorism* (New York: Henry Holt & Co., Inc., 2000).

24. Lou Michel and Dan Herbeck, *American Terrorist: Timothy McVeigh and the Tragedy at Oklahoma City* (New York: Harper Collins Pub. Inc., 2001).

25. Vernon Loeb, "Anthrax Vial Smuggled In To Make A Point At A Hill Hearing," *Washington Post*, Mar. 4, 1999, at 1.

26. William C. Chasey, *The Lockerbie Coverup* (New York: Bridger House, 1995).

27. See Ruth Wedgewood, "Responding to Terrorism: The Strikes Against bin Laden," 24 *Yale J. Int'l L.* 599 (1999). Wedgewood advocates that terrorism may need to be incorporated into a new legal view of what qualifies as warfare.

28. Id.

29. Paul Bedard, "Danger Zone," *U.S. News & World Report*, Mar. 6, 2000, at 10.

30. See Report of the International Law Commission on the Work of its Thirty-Eighth Session, U.N. Doc. A/41/10 (1986).

31. The Vienna Convention on Diplomatic Relations was entered into force for the United States on Dec. 13, 1972. The U.S. ratification appears at 111 Cong. Rec. 23, 733 (1965).

32. Secretary of Defense Caspar W. Weinberger, Address to the American Bar Association's National Conference on Law in Relation to Terrorism (June 5, 1986).

33. Id.

34. See FBI Director Louis J. Freeh, Statement before the Senate Select Committee on Intelligence (Jan. 28, 1998): "The ease of manufacturing or obtaining biological and chemical agents is disturbing. Available public source material makes our law enforcement mission a continuous challenge."

35. William Nelson, "Opening Pandora's Box: The Status of the Diplomatic Bag in International Relations," 12 *Fordham Int.'l L. J.* 494 (1989).

36. An early pattern was set regarding the use of force to counter state-sponsored terrorism under the Reagan Administration. On April 14, 1986 the United States conducted bombing strikes on various targets in Libya. This was in response to the Libyan ordered bombing of a discotheque in West Berlin on April 5, 1986.

37. Ian O. Lesser, Bruce Hoffman, John Arquilla, David Ronfeldt and Michele Zanini, *Countering the New Terrorism* (Santa Monica, CA: RAND, 1999), at 17.

38. William S. Cohen, "Preparing for a Grave New World," *Washington Post*, July 26, 1999, at A19.

39. Vernon Loeb, "Anthrax Vial Smuggled In To Make A Point At A Hill Hearing," *Washington Post*, Mar. 4, 1999, at 1.

40. Id.

41. Id.

42. An accomplice, Terry Nichols, was also convicted. Tim Kelsey, "The Oklahoma Suspect Awaits Day of Reckoning," *The Sunday Times* (London), Apr. 21, 1996.

43. Id.

Chapter 2

The War on Terror

As we gather tonight, our nation is at war ... and the civilized world faces unprecedented dangers.[1]

—George W. Bush

Synopsis
2.1 September 11, 2001
2.2 An Act of War
2.3 The Rule of Law—Use of Force
2.4 NATO
2.5 Congressional War-Making Power
2.6 The Employment of Lawful Violence
Endnotes

By definition, the traditional approach to combating terrorism is encompassed in two terms—antiterrorism and counterterrorism.[2] Antiterrorism involves all those steps and actions taken by authorities to decrease the probability of a terrorist act occurring. The proactive, preventative stage to stopping terrorism, antiterrorism includes techniques designed to harden potential high profile targets (e.g., government buildings or military installations), as well as actions taken to detect a planned terrorist attack before it occurs. For example, to assist in the battle against future terrorist attacks the Pentagon is experimenting with video surveillance, modeling techniques and commercial technologies such as those used to identify automatic teller machine customers by scanning their faces.

One of the facets of the War on Terror is the realization that antiterrorism relies heavily on the efforts of ordinary citizens who, when observing suspicious behavior, are willing to notify law enforcement. Sometimes the suspicions prove profitable, as with the September 2002 arrest of six members of the "Lackawanna" sleeper terrorist cell in New York, and sometimes the suspicions prove incorrect, as in the case of three men of Middle Eastern descent that were overheard "joking" at a Georgia restaurant about a terrorist plot to be conducted in Miami, Florida. The three were subsequently stopped in Florida and, after a day-long investigation, were released. Antiterrorism, then, is very much a bottom-up approach. Ordinary citizens are the best first line of defense.

America allows free speech in most circumstances, but never allows illegal violence. Another innovative antiterrorism program is designed to ease tensions between the government and antigovernment organizations. In the wake of the Oklahoma bombings, for example, this approach saw Federal Bureau of Investigation (FBI) agents talking directly to various militia leaders. From Montana to Indiana, federal agents opened dialogues with leaders of several militia organizations to provide a forum for discussion in the hope that these channels of communication would help prevent acts of violence.[3]

Counterterrorism measures are those tactical actions taken by authorities in response to an actual terrorist incident. In this vein, planning and training will have a great impact on the success or failure of real world counterterrorist measures. While the Department of Justice, through the FBI, is still the lead agency in the event of a terrorist attack with a weapon of mass destruction, the expected mass casualties, physical damage, and potential for civil disorder resulting from such an incident will undoubtedly see a shift to the Department of Defense (DOD) as the *de facto* lead federal agency for many counterterrorism issues.

2.1 September 11, 2001

The War on Terror began for the United States on September 11, 2001, with coordinated suicide attacks using hijacked domestic airplanes by nineteen members of a sophisticated international "paramilitary" terrorist network known as al-Qa'eda ("the Base").[4] The simultaneous attacks occurred in New York, Washington, D.C. and Pennsylvania, killing over 3,000 people and destroying billions of dollars in property.

Al-Qa'eda is an umbrella organization founded in 1989 by a Saudi Arabian named Osama (or Usama) bin Laden. Osama bin Laden formed the group out of elements of the Maktab al-Khidamat, an organization founded by Osama bin Laden and Abdallah Azzam (a member of a group called the Palestinian Moslem Brotherhood) in the early 1980s to provide

Chapter 2: The War on Terror

money, equipment, and manpower to the Afghan resistance against the Soviet Union's occupation of Afghanistan. With the withdrawal of the Soviets in 1989, bin Laden started al-Qa'eda in order to redirect his efforts to "attack the enemies of Islam all over the world."[5]

From the early 1990s until the end of 2001, the al-Qa'eda operated openly in the country of Afghanistan with the complete support of the Pashtun-dominated Taliban government.[6] During the tenure of the Taliban regime, the relationship between the Taliban and the al-Qa'eda terrorist organization provided a seminal example of state-supported terrorism.[7] In fact, under the Taliban, Afghanistan became a terror training ground for thousands of Arab and non-Arab al-Qa'eda militants including Kashmirs, Chechens, Uzbeks, Uighurs, and others (including a number of Americans).[8] These training camps sent cells of well-trained terrorists into numerous countries where they were encouraged to recruit additional membership and carry out terrorist attacks on command. While al-Qa'eda has thousands of supporters and low-level operatives worldwide, only carefully selected Muslim males are offered full membership. Interestingly, the al-Qa'eda leadership does not allow volunteers to join the group. Instead, al-Qa'eda seeks out candidates for full membership. These recruits must sign an oath of allegiance called a *bayat,* swearing to carry out the dictates of al-Qa'eda leaders on penalty of death. They are then indoctrinated and trained extensively in assassination, kidnapping, explosives, small arms, hijacking, and torture.

Any reasonable doubts as to the involvement of Osama bin Laden's terrorist network in the attacks of September 11, 2001, were dispelled by the December 13, 2001, public release of the so-called "bin Laden videotape." The tape established that bin Laden (1) knew when the hijackers would strike, (2) knew that the hijackers understood that they were on a "martyrdom operation," but had no details until shortly before the attacks, (3) was pleasantly surprised by the total collapse of the two towers of the World Trade Center in New York, (4) listened with anticipation to radio broadcasts to confirm the terror attacks, and (5) expressed joy and amusement as he detailed the story of the attacks. Perhaps the most damning segment of the thirty-nine-minute tape occurred when bin Laden stated to an unidentified Shaykh:

We calculated in advance the number of casualties from the enemy who would be killed based on the position of the tower. We calculated that the floors that would be hit would be three or four floors. I was the most optimistic of them all. Due to my experience in this field, I was thinking that the fire from the gas in the plane would melt the iron structure of the building and collapse the area where the plane hit and all the floors above it only. This is all that we had hoped for.[9]

Almost a year to the day after the attack of September 11, the al-Qa'eda terrorist organization released another videotape claiming full credit for the attacks. The video specifically mentioned the World Trade Center attack, the Pentagon attack, and the attempted attack on the United States Capitol, which did not occur.[10]

2.2 An Act of War

In a speech delivered in 1984, Jeanne J. Kirkpatrick spoke of a coming "terrorist war [against the United States], [that] is part of a total war which sees the whole society as an enemy, and all members of a society as appropriate objects for violent actions."[11] Her words became reality on September 11, 2001, and the world community came to understand terrorism as "an act of war." Indeed, viewing terrorism as an act of war is a new manifestation of the changing nature of armed conflict. As such, it poses a new challenge for the historically fixed international rules relating to armed conflict.

Apart from the enormity of the al-Qa'eda attack, what made the events of September 11, 2001, so vastly different from all previous incidents of terror[12] was that the United States and the North Atlantic Treaty Organization (NATO) both specifically characterized the attack as an "armed attack" on the United States. The unprecedented armed attack determination was significant because it, in turn, immediately signaled that the United States intended to frame the terror attack as an event equivalent to an "act of war"[13] under international law.

The use of the terms "war" or "act of war" traditionally refers to the use of aggressive force against a sovereign state by another state in violation of the United Nations Charter and customary international law. Historically, such illegal acts most often occur without a formal declaration of war. The aggressive act itself triggers the ensuing war.

Accordingly, a "use of force" joint resolution was passed by the United States Congress; the President labeled the attack "an act of war;" and, for the first time in its history, NATO invoked its collective self-defense clause, should a NATO member suffer an armed attack. Thus, from its inception the War on Terror was legally couched by the United States in terms of traditional law of war terminology, even though the actual attack was carried out, strictly speaking, by a non-state actor.[14]

Understanding the need for international approval for prosecuting the War on Terror under the rule of law, the United States turned to the United Nations Security Council on the day after the attack in hope of obtaining a strong use of force resolution.[15] Instead, the United States received what might be deemed as a very strong statement of support in United Nations Security Council Resolution 1368:

The Security Council,
Reaffirming the principles and purposes of the Charter of Nations,
Determined to combat by all means threats to international peace and security caused by terrorist acts,
Recognizing the inherent right of the individual or collective self-defense in accordance with the Charter,
1. Unequivocally condemns in the strongest terms the horrifying terrorist attacks which took place on 11 September 2001 in New York, Washington, D.C. and Pennsylvania and regards such acts, like any act of international terrorism, as a threat to international peace and security;
2. Expresses its deepest sympathy and condolences to the victims and their families and to the people and Government of the United States of America;
3. Calls on all States to work together urgently to bring to justice the perpetrators, organizers and sponsors of these terrorist attacks and stresses that those responsible for aiding, supporting or harbouring the perpetrators, organizers and sponsors of these acts will be held accountable;
4. Calls also on the international community to redouble their efforts to prevent and suppress terrorist acts including by increased cooperation and full implementation of the relevant international anti-terrorist conventions and Security Council resolutions, in particular resolution 1269 (1999) of 19 October 1999;

5. Expresses its readiness to take all necessary steps to respond to the terrorist attacks of 11 September 2001, and to combat all forms of terrorism, in accordance with its responsibilities under the Charter of Nations;
   6. Decides to remain seized of the matter.[16]

Because of the structured magnitude of the terrorist attack, Resolution 1368 specifically recognized America's "inherent right of individual and collective self-defense in accordance with the Charter"[17] and specifically called on "all States to work together urgently to bring to justice the perpetrators, organizers, and sponsors of these terrorist attacks." Resolution 1368 further addressed the issue of responsibility for those states who supported or sponsored the terrorist attacks by "stresses[ing] that those responsible for aiding, supporting or harboring the perpetrators, organizers and sponsors of these acts will be held accountable." Taken as a whole, it can be argued that Resolution 1368 provided the United States and its allies with the legal authority necessary to respond to the terrorist attack through the use of military force in self-defense should a state[s] who supported, sponsored, or harbored the terrorists refuse to cooperate in bringing those responsible to justice.

2.3 The Rule of Law—Use of Force

If the mark of a civilized state is measured by how well it follows the rule of law, it is necessary to understand what that term means, particularly in the realm of waging war. The concept rule of law was first coined by Western legal scholars in the late sixteenth century.[18] The term was initially used to refer to the common law system of jurisprudence with particular emphasis on equality before the courts. However, the more modern and common meaning is directly associated with all of those rules and legal standards of behavior recognized and practiced between states in the context of the community of nations.

In this setting, one can logically trace the origins of the rule of law back to the 1648 Peace of Westphalia, which concluded the Thirty Years' War in Europe. At that time a number of Christian European states officially recognized themselves as being in a community of sovereign nation-states and guided by certain rules of international and social intercourse.[19] The utility of the concept of the nation-state soon spread throughout Europe, typified by the colonial powers of Europe holding themselves out as the "self-appointed executive committee of the family of nations."[20] With the Treaty of Paris in 1856, non-Christian nations were also admitted and periodic international conferences were held in such international cities as Vienna and Geneva.[21]

In early days, this community of nations was not deemed to be anything other than a loose association bound together by only a few international agreements and the thinnest of diplomatic threads. Although the primary purpose of this association was to promote world peace and to mitigate, when necessary, "the miseries of war,"[22] independent sovereignty reigned supreme since the association lacked any legal character or corporate personality. Thus, the rule of law remained a concept with little viability behind it.

After World War I reflected the total impotence of the association to deter those nations bent on aggression, the victorious European nations created the first international organization with legal parameters, the League of Nations.[23] Formed in large part with the direct assistance of President Woodrow Wilson, the much-heralded League of Nations was the first truly international organization specifically directed toward the curtailment of war. As laudable as that goal might be, the League of Nations' efforts to maintain the peace were totally ineffective. In fact, they were actually counterproductive.

First, accepting the false premise that World War I had somehow been caused by a combination of misunderstandings and entangling collective security alliances, the League of Nations naively adopted a series of procedural requirements focused on third-party dispute settlement processes.[24] The framers assumed that wars, like all disputes, could be settled through negotiation and arbitration. This approach is best reflected in Article 12 of the Covenant of the League of Nations:

> The members of the League agree that if there should arise between them any dispute likely to lead to a rupture, they will submit the matter either to arbitration or to inquiry by the council, and they agree in no case to resort to war until three months after the award by the arbitrators or the report of the Council.[25]

Second, the League of Nations concentrated almost solely on disarmament as the best guarantee of world peace. Somehow the founders of the League of Nations believed that there existed a direct correlation between the number of weapons in existence and the probability of armed conflict. In short, they naively believed that the threat of war could be reduced if the League of Nations implemented international agreements which called for the destruction of weapons and the reduction of military forces.[26] In the next two decades, disarmament treaties such as the London Naval Conferences (1930) saw England, France and the United States completely emasculate their military while Germany and her allies (Japan and Italy) embarked on a massive buildup of their armies, navies and air forces.

During this rush to disarm, other international agreements which related to armed conflict were drafted and adopted by the world community, of which the Geneva Conventions of 1929 was the most prominent. Perhaps, the most controversial document that came out of the post-World War I era was the Kellogg-Briand Pact.[27] Signed by almost all of the major world powers, the Pact wishfully prohibited war for the solution of international disputes or as an instrument of national policy.[28]

Although the Kellogg-Briand Pact was viewed by many as an idealistic proscription against war, the abolition of war did not mean that states gave up the inherent right of self-defense; all signatories strongly asserted that the defensive use of military force was absolutely legitimate under the Pact.[29] Paradoxically, the Pact, spawned by a sincere desire to rid mankind of the scourge of war, was actually a dramatic and positive shift in the focus of the rule of law pertaining to war.

The Kellogg-Briand Pact shifted the emphasis from procedural and moral issues[30] related to the legitimacy of war to simply prohibiting all *aggression* under "any circumstances." In effect, a red line of distinction was made between the aggressive use of force, which was always prohibited, and the defensive use of force in response to aggression, which was always lawful. Unfortunately, the Pact did not specifically spell out what it so strongly implied concerning self-defense. The Kellogg-Briand Pact did not devote a single word to the traditional and inherent right of self-defense.

In summation, most of the League of Nations' activities were rooted in the sincere but naive assumption that war was intrinsically irrational and that rational man could solve his differences simply through negotiation and reason. Many nations thought this philosophy, coupled with a massive disarming effort, would lead to the abolition of war.

In the first major application of this philosophy of negotiation and so-called reason, Neville Chamberlain, Prime Minister of England, tried to appease the Nazi dictator Adolf Hitler by traveling to Munich, Germany, in October of 1938. The resulting Munich Agreement prompted Chamberlain to foolishly remark, "I believe it is peace for our time . . . peace with honor."[31] Of course, the fruits of appeasement produced the exact opposite. The clear signal given to the aggressor—peace at any price—prompted the Axis powers to launch the most destructive war in the history of mankind.

When World War II ended in 1945, the international community once again sought to create a new methodology to reduce or to eliminate armed international conflict, just as they had done following World War I. Work quickly began on a series of international agreements and instruments designed to accomplish this ideal. Many of the efforts produced widespread and immediate acceptance throughout the world,[32] which ranged from the creation of the United Nations in 1945 to the 1949 Geneva Conventions. In this regard, the civilized world recognized the necessity of anchoring its desire for world peace on ideas that would inhibit both the external and, to a lesser degree, the internal dimensions of state sovereignty. The unfettered power of member states to pursue activities and policies that threatened international peace and security had to be squarely addressed. In addition, great concern was voiced about the acts of states in regard to the treatment of their own citizens.

Since the sovereignty of each state would serve as the basis for the new world organization, internationally recognized legal constraints and attendant enforcement mechanisms had to be placed on those nations who threatened the peace. In leading the effort to create such an organization, the United States held out to the world community the vision of a world order based on four essential human freedoms. These four freedoms were first articulated in President Franklin Roosevelt's major speech before Congress on January 6, 1941: freedom of speech, freedom of religion, freedom from want, and freedom from fear. Echoing these ideals, the victorious powers formed the United Nations.

With the emergence of the United Nations and the principles of international behavior embodied in the Charter of the United Nations, the deficiencies in the Kellogg-Briand Pact were largely corrected. Along with the prohibition of all forms of armed aggression, the U.N. Charter specifically recognized a nation-state's inherent right of self-defense if attacked.[33] Today, in the search for a workable model to address conflict management, the U.N. Charter is considered by many to be synonymous with the international rule of law.

As embodied in Articles 2(3) and 2(4) of the U.N. Charter, the maintenance of "international peace and security"[34] is, in fact, the very purpose of the United Nations. Since all members of the United Nations are recognized as sovereign equals,[35] no nation may resort to "threat or [the] use of force against the territorial integrity or political independence of any state"[36] to settle any form of dispute. This, and the clear prohibition in Article 1 against any nation committing "acts of aggression or other breaches of the peace,"[37] resulted in a workable, legal framework dedicated to curtailing unlawful aggression. It established a concrete legal framework by which behavior could be gauged.

Recognizing that even the most brilliantly crafted legal framework is useless without an enforcement mechanism, the drafters of the Charter also established an extensive and flexible international framework for responding to those rogue nations which might choose to violate the provisions of the Charter and engage in unlawful aggression. Chapter VI of the Charter authorizes the Security Council to investigate any situation that might endanger the maintenance of international peace and security and to make recommendations for the peaceful resolution of such disputes. Chapter VII of the Charter authorizes the Security Council to determine the existence of a threat or breach of the peace, or act of aggression, and to take appropriate measures in response. Even though Article 43 provides for the mechanism for member nations to make troops available on the call of the Security Council, no such agreements have ever been concluded. Instead, to enforce the peace the Security Council relies on the forces of member nations, contributed and organized on an ad hoc basis for each situation.

Finally, recognizing the utopian absurdity of outlawing war, but building upon the framework of the Kellogg-Briand Pact, the U.N. Charter does not restrict all uses of force; it only restricts the unlawful use of force; that is, aggression.[38] Thus, the final element in this legal structure, and the one that is of immeasurable value in the real world, rests upon the U.N. Charter's recognition of the lawful use of force to deter unlawful armed aggression.

Explicitly acknowledging the long-standing customary right of self-defense, Article 51 states that "nothing in the present Charter shall impair the inherent right of individual or collective self-defense if an armed attack occurs against a Member of the United Nations . . . ."[39] While there still exists lingering controversy over such matters as what constitutes an armed attack and the utility of the term inherent, the modern rule of law specifically recognizes the fundamental distinction between unlawful aggression and lawful self-defense. In the overall picture, the rule of law has evolved from a vision "in the minds of some men, of an ideal aspiration towards universal values of law,"[40] to the reality of a world that acknowledges the existence and validity of established legal norms. If a nation operates in accordance with this rule of law, it can rightly claim the legal and moral high ground in any conflict.

In summary, there are four primary provisions of the U.N. Charter under which the use of force is analyzed. The starting point, of course, requires a firm understanding that the U.N. Charter does not outlaw the use of force; it only outlaws the use of aggressive force.

First, Articles 2(3) and (4) set out the general obligations of member states to settle disputes in a peaceful manner and to refrain from "the threat or use of force." U.N. Charter Article 2(3) requires that, "[a]ll Members shall set their international disputes by peaceful means in such a manner that international peace and security, and justice are not endangered." U.N. Charter Article 2(4) states, "[a]ll Members shall refrain in their international relations from the threat or use of force against the territorial integrity or political independence of any state, or in any other manner inconsistent with the Purposes of the United Nations."

Second, if a state engages in the use of aggressive force, Article 24 of the U.N. Charter actually gives the Security Council the "primary responsibility for the maintenance of international peace and security." Then, Article 27 requires that all permanent members of the U.N. Security Council must agree on enforcement provisions, i.e., the use of armed force. These permanent members are listed in Article 23 of the U.N. Charter. They are China, France, Russia, the United States and Britain. Still, even if the Security Council issues an enforcement ruling, there is no standing U.N. military force to enforce it. Historically, the United States has provided the lion's share of military muscle to back up the Security Council.

The third element of the analytical framework is Article 51 of the Charter, which sets out the codification of the "inherent right of self-defense." The inherent right of self-defense refers to the right of a country to unilaterally engage in acts of self-defense; regardless of what any other nation or organization, to include the United Nations, may or may not do. This is a well-known and ancient component of international law.

Article 51 of the U.N. Charter states:

> Nothing in the present Charter shall impair the inherent right of individual or collective self-defense if an armed attack occurs against a Member of the United Nations, until the Security Council has taken measures to maintain international peace and security. Measures taken by Members in the exercise of the right of self-defense shall be immediately reported to the Security Council and shall not in any way affect the authority and responsibility of the Security Council under the present Charter to take at any time such action as it deems necessary in order to maintain or restore international peace and security.

Finally, to complete the analysis, one must determine what is meant by the term "armed attack." In order to clearly define when an unlawful use of force in violation of Articles 2(3) and (4) occurs, international law looks primarily at the definition of aggression as adopted by resolution of the U.N. General Assembly. A state engages in aggression in the following ways according to the U.N. Definition of Aggression:

> **Article 1**
> Aggression is the use of armed force by a State against the sovereignty, territorial integrity, or political independence of another State, or in any manner inconsistent with the Charter of the United Nations . . . .
> **Article 2**
> The first use of armed force by a State in contravention of the Charter shall constitute prima facie evidence of an act of aggression . . . .

Article 3
   Any of the following acts, regardless of a declaration of war, shall . . . qualify as an act of aggression:
   (a) The invasion or attack by the armed forces of a State . . . of another State or part thereof;
   (b) Bombardment by the armed forces of a State against the territory of another State . . .
   (c) The blockade of the ports or coasts of a State by the armed forces of another State;
   (d) An attack by the armed forces of a State on the land, sea, or air forces, or marine and air fleets of another State;
   (e) The use of armed forces of one State . . . in contravention of the conditions provided for in the agreement or any extension of their presence in such territory beyond the termination of the agreement;
   (f) The action of a State in allowing it territory, which it has placed at the disposal of another State to be used by that other State for perpetrating an act of aggression against a third State;
   (g) The sending by or on behalf of a State of armed bands, groups, irregulars, or mercenaries, which carry out acts of armed force against another State of such gravity as to amount to the acts listed above, or its substantial involvement therein.[41]

2.4 NATO

NATO, of which the United States is a full member, also viewed the attacks of September 11 as an "armed attack" under international law. NATO invoked its collective self-defense clause under Article 5 of the NATO Charter where "an armed attack on one or more of [its members] shall be considered an attack on all," and that the members may exercise the right of self-defense which includes the "use of armed force, to restore and maintain the security of the North Atlantic area."[42] The real significance of invoking Article 5, of course, rested more in the European recognition that the terrorist attacks were, in fact, tantamount to an armed attack or act of war against the United States,[43] and not simply criminal acts of terrorism.

Armed with the Congressional Joint Resolution, U.N. Resolution 1368 and the NATO Resolution, President George W. Bush exercised his authority as the commander in chief,[44] under Article 2, Section 3, of the Constitution, and quickly set about gathering the necessary evidence to find those who committed the attacks and to establish linkage to the state or states that may have provided support to the terrorists.

2.5 Congressional War-Making Power

Congress was also quick to address the attacks. Although Congress elected not to exercise it's power to "declare war"[45] under Article 1, Section 8, of the Constitution,[46] they did issue a strongly worded joint resolution which left no doubt as to their desire to authorize the President to use military force if necessary to respond to the attacks.[47] The joint resolution is cited as the "Authorization for Use of Military Force."[48] In an unprecedented show of unity of support, this resolution was passed by every member of the Senate and every member of the House of Representatives, save one. Among other things, the Congressional Resolution recognized the authority of the President:

> Under the Constitution to take action to deter and prevent acts of international terrorism against the United States . . . [and] authorized [the President] to use all necessary and appropriate force against those nations, organizations, or persons he determines planned, authorized, committed, or aided the terrorist attacks that occurred on September 11, 2001, or harbored such organizations or persons, in order to prevent any future acts of international terrorism against the United States by such nations, organizations or persons.[49]

Even without a Congressional resolution, the president's authority to order the military to action is unquestioned under the terms of the United States Constitution. In fact, there is a long history of American presidents utilizing military forces abroad in situations of armed conflict or potential conflict to protect United States citizens or promote United States interests. The number of instances where the president has used military forces abroad without, for example, a Congressional declaration of War, well exceeds 250 in number. Selected instances include: 1798–1800, undeclared naval war with France; 1801–1805, the First Barbary War (Tripoli declared war but not the United States); 1806, Mexico Incursion; 1806–1810, Gulf of Mexico Incursion; 1810, West Florida Incursion; 1812, Amelia Island in Florida; 1813, West Florida; 1813–1814, Marquesas Islands; 1814–1825, Caribbean (engagements between pirates and Ameri-

Chapter 2: The War on Terror

can war ships in response to over 3,000 pirate attacks on merchantmen between 1815–1823); 1815, Second Barbary War; 1950–1953, Korean War; 1958, Lebanon; 1962, Cuba; 1962, Thailand; 1964, Congo; 1964–1973, Vietnam War; 1965, Dominican Republic; 1980, Iran; 1981, El Salvador; 1982, Lebanon; 1983, Honduras; 1983, Chad; 1983, Grenada; 1986, Libya; 1989, Panama; 1989, Andean Region; 1991, Persian Gulf War; 1993, Bosnia; 1993–1995, Somalia; 1993–1995, Haiti; 1997, Serbia; and 2001, Afghanistan. In fact, the last time Congress declared war was in December 1941.

Nevertheless, the president's authority to use the armed forces and the authority of Congress to declare war or to otherwise share in the process of war making has been the source of much debate over the life of the Republic. Clearly the framers gave each branch of government war making powers in furtherance of their vision of a government of "checks and balances." This check also ensured a built-in source of friction between the two branches.

The most well known source of contention between the Congress and the executive branch led to the War Powers Resolution, enacted over President Richard Nixon's veto in 1973. The War Powers Resolution seeks to curtail or limit the power of the executive in the employment of American forces abroad. It requires the president to consult with Congress if American forces are introduced into hostilities or into situations where hostilities are imminent and, after a time set at a maximum of ninety days, either obtain Congressional approval of any continued military action or withdraw. Needless to say the War Powers Resolution raises serious separation of powers issues which, to date, the United States Supreme Court has not squarely addressed. In any event, no American president from either political party has directly complied with the War Powers Resolution. At most, when presidents have employed United States armed forces in hostile situations or in places where conflict was imminent, Congress has simply been notified in writing "consistent with the War Powers Resolution."

One power that Congress clearly has in war making is over "the purse." Ultimately, Congress has the power to cut off funding to any protracted use of military forces.

2.6 The Employment of Lawful Violence

In the days immediately following the September 11 attacks, a conclusive body of evidence pointed directly to the al-Qa'eda terrorist organization as the perpetrators of the attacks and to Afghanistan's Taliban as the state-supporter of the terrorist al-Qa'eda organization. Determined to respond if necessary under the inherent right of self-defense, the Bush administration offered the Taliban government a time certain ultimatum to turn over the al-Qa'eda leaders and to shut down all terrorist camps in Afghanistan.[50] President Bush issued the ultimatum in a solemn speech given to a joint session of Congress on Sept. 20, 2001. The pertinent part reads:

> And tonight, the United States of America makes the following demands on the Taliban: Deliver to the United States authorities all the leaders of al-Qa'eda who hide in your land . . . [c]lose immediately and permanently every terrorist training camp in Afghanistan, and hand over every terrorist, and every person in their support structure, to appropriate authorities. Give the United States full access to terrorist training camps, so we can make sure they are no longer operating. These demands are not open to negotiation or discussion. The Taliban must act, and act immediately. They will hand over the terrorist, or they will suffer their fate.

When the Taliban leadership refused to comply with any aspect of the demand, the United States exercised, in conjunction with NATO and its other allies,[51] the lawful use of military force to accomplish those aims. Numerous nations contributed assistance to the American led effort including Pakistan, Saudi Arabia, Britain, Russia, Germany, Australia, France, Canada, Japan, and so on. In addition, much of the actual ground combat was borne by indigenous Afghan trial fighters, primarily the so-called Northern Alliance under the guidance and support of United States Army Special Forces and other United States Special Operations Forces conducting direct action and unconventional warfare missions. The military campaign to dislodge the Taliban and al-Qa'eda took approximately three months, from October 7 to December 23, 2001. Approximately 6,500 air combat missions were flown which attacked over 120 fixed targets. Four hundred vehicles were destroyed and an undetermined number of combatants were killed (some have put the figure as high as 10,000).

In tandem with the removal of the Taliban regime from power the United States and its allies were able to destroy the al-Qa'eda camps and dismantle much of the infrastructure of the terrorist group in Afghanistan by the end of December 2001. By any account, the Bush strategy[52] of using American air power, American Special Operations Forces and the ground forces of various Afghan resistance groups worked brilliantly in terms of mitigating the loss of life[53] to American forces and reducing civilian suffering.[54] Early critics of the Bush approach incorrectly predicted that the United States could not achieve victory without the use of massive American ground forces and an attendant heavy loss of life. This same pessimism was seen in exaggerated predictions of American lives that would be lost in the Gulf War should the United States attempt to expel Iraq from Kuwait in accordance with U.N. Resolution 678.[55]

Since the fall of the Taliban government, the al-Qa'eda no longer operates with the open support of a state, but has been forced to revert to clandestine operations primarily as a sub-state terror group.[56] As of September 2002, states throughout the world have arrested well over 1,500 members of the al-Qa'eda network on a variety of terror related charges.

At the close of 2002 there were 12,000 coalition troops on the ground in Afghanistan, including 7,000 Americans. The coalition soldiers are assisting in improving security, tracking down al-Qa'eda holdouts, and most importantly, assisting in building a new democratically based Afghan army.

Endnotes

1. President George W. Bush, State of the Union Address (Jan. 23, 2002).

2. "Countering Terrorism on U.S. Army Installations," *TC 19-16*, Apr.1983, at 1–2.

3. Kevin Johnson, "FBI's Uneasy Alliance," *USA Today*, Nov. 29, 1999, at 1.

4. See Anthony H. Cordesman, *Transnational Threats from the Middle East: Crying Wolf or Crying Havoc?*, (Carlisle, PA: Strategic Studies Inst., 1999), at 91-92 [hereinafter Crying Wolf or Crying Havoc].

5. Id. at 92.

6. See, e.g., Christopher Dickey, "Training for Terror," *Newsweek*, Sept. 24, 2001, at 42.

7. But see Ali A. Jalali, "Afghanistan: The Anatomy of an Ongoing Conflict," *Parameters*, Spring 2001, at 89. Some commentators have argued that the Taliban regime was not a recognized government. Only three nations officially recognized the Taliban as the legitimate government of Afghanistan—Saudi Arabia, Pakistan, and Iran. Jalali writes "neither the Taliban-led 'Islamic Emirate of Afghanistan' nor the 'Islamic State of Afghanistan' headed by ousted President Rabbani has the political legitimacy or administrative efficiency of a State."

8. At least two Americans were trained in al-Qa'eda terror camps in Afghanistan and joined the Taliban forces, the most notorious individual being John Walker who was sentenced to twenty years by a federal district court.

9. See James M. Dorsey, "Some Fear Bin Laden Video Will Strain Relations Between U.S. and Saudi Arabia," *Wall Street Journal*, Dec. 17, 2001, at A13 [hereinafter "Bin Laden Video"]; Neil King, Jr., Bush, "Tough Talk Shakes Up Diplomatic Stance," *Wall Street Journal*, Jan. 31, 2002, at A20.

10. Neil MacFarquhar, "Tapes Show Plans for Attacks Evolved Over 2 Years," *New York Times*, Sept. 10, 2002, at A16.

11. Jeanne J. Kirkpatrick, Speech at the Jonathan Institute's Conference on International Terrorism, Washington, D.C. (June 25, 1984).

12. See http://nsi.org/Library/Terrorism/profterr.txt. The lethality of terrorism has only increased over the years, with the United States the most frequent target of terrorism.

13. George Petrochilos, "The Relevance of the Concepts of War and Armed Conflict to the Law of Neutrality," 31 *Vand. J. Transnat'l L* 575 (1998).

14. The distinction of whether an event qualifies as an act of war is more important in terms of civil law. See, *Pan American World Airlines, Inc. v. Aetna Cas. & Sur. Co.*, 505 F.2d 989 (2d Cir. 1974). The court found that the hijacking of an aircraft by a non-state actor did not qualify as an "act of war" for the purpose of activating an exclusionary clause in the insurance policy.

15. The United States was seeking a resolution similar in tone to U.N. Security Resolution 678 which allowed all members to push Iraq out of Kuwait "by all means necessary."

16. SC Res. 1368.

17. U.N. Charter, art. 51.

18. Lord Lloyd of Hampstead and M. D. A. Freeman, *Lloyd's Introduction to Jurisprudence* (London: Stevens, 1985), at 1054–60.

19. See, generally, William H. McNeill, *The Pursuit of Power* (Chicago: University of Chicago Press, 1982), at 120–25.

20. Charles G. Fenwick, *International Law* (New York: Appleton-Century-Crotts, 1965), at 122.

21. Id.

22. Id. at 123.

23. League of Nations Covenant, Treaty of Versailles, 2 U.S.B.S. 43.

24. See *National Security Law,* supra Chapter 1, note 4, at 65.

25. League of Nations Covenant, at Part I. art. 12. See also Leon Freidman, *The Law of War, A Documentary History* (1972), at 424–25.

26. Id. at 423–24.

27. Kellogg-Briand Pact of Aug. 27, 1928, 2 U.S.B.S. 732 (1930).

28. Id. at art. I.

29. *National Security Law,* supra Chapter 1, note 4, at 69–70.

30. See Hugo Grotius, *Prolegomena to the Law of War and Peace* (New York: Francis W. Kelsey trans., 1957).

31. See Justin Wintle (ed.), *The Dictionary of War Quotations* (London: Hodder & Stroughton, 1989), at 121.

32. See, generally, *National Security Law,* supra Chapter 1, note 4, at 71–81.

33. See Gerhard Von Glahn, *Law Among Nations* (New York: MacMillan, 1992), at 130.

34. U.N. Charter art. 2 ¶1.

35. U.N. Charter art. 2 ¶1. "The Organization is based on the principles of the sovereign equality of all its Members."

36. U.N. Charter art. 2 ¶4.

37. U.N. Charter art. 1, ¶1.

38. U.N. Definition of Aggression, at 142.

39. U.N. Charter art. 51.

40. *Lloyd's Jurisprudence*, supra note 18, at 1060.

41. U.N. Definition of Aggression.

42. Article 5 of the North Atlantic Treaty reads:

    The Parties agree that an armed attack against one or more of them in Europe or North America shall be considered an armed attack against them all; and consequently they agree that, if such an armed attack occurs, each of them, in exercise of the right of individual and collective self-defense recognized by Articles 51 of the Charter of the United Nations, will assist the Party or Parties so attacked by taking forthwith, individually and in concert with other Parties, such action as is deemed necessary, including the use of armed force, to restore and maintain the security of the North Atlantic area. North Atlantic Treaty, 63 Stat. 2241, T.I.A.S. 1964 (1949).

43. See, e.g., William Drozdiak, "Attack on U.S. is an Attack on All, NATO Agrees," *Washington Post*, Sept. 13, 2002, at A25.

44. United States Constitution, Article II, §2. "The President shall be Commander in Chief of the Army and Navy of the United States and the Militia of the Several States . . . ."

45. Certain statutory consequences attach to a congressionally declared war. For example 50 U.S.C. §21 provides that "[w]henever there is a declared war . . . all natives, citizens, denizens, or subjects of the hostile nation or government . . . shall be liable to be apprehended, restrained, secured, and removed as alien enemies."

46. United States Constitution Art I §8. "The Congress shall have power . . . To declare War, grant Letters of Marque and Reprisal, and make Rules concerning Captures on Land and Water. To have and support Armies . . . ."

47. See Authorization for Use of Military Force Joint Resolution, Public Law 107-40, 115 Stat. 224.

48. Id.

Chapter 2: The War on Terror 37

49. Id.

50. "Bush Issues Ultimatum to the Taliban, Calls Upon Nation and World to Unite and Destroy Terrorism," *Congressional Quarterly*, Sept. 22, 2001, at 2226.

51. For an excellent overview of the roles and missions of the Army's elite Special Forces see Hans Halberstadt, *Green Berets, Unconventional Warriors* (Navato, CA: Presidio Press, 1988).

52. See, e.g., Dan Balz, "Bush Confronts a Nightmare Scenario: Crisis Looms as Refining Test of President's Leadership," *Washington Post*, Sept. 12, 2002, at A2.

53. See Michael R. Gordon, "A Nation Challenged: The Debate; Gauging the Use of Ground Troops and the Scale of the Afghan War," *New York Times*, Nov. 4, 2001, at A3.

54. But see Barry Bearak, Eric Schmitt, and Craig S. Smith, "Unknown Toll in the Fog of War: Civilian Deaths in Afghanistan," *New York Times*, Feb. 10, 2002, at A1. The article discusses the issue of collateral damage to civilians and civilian property caused by the United States air strikes. The average estimate ranges between 1,000 to 1,300 civilian deaths. See also Jonathan Weisman, "Rumsfeld Admits Allies were Killed," *USA Today*, Feb. 22, 2002, at A4.

55. See U.N. Resolution 678 (Nov. 29, 1990).

56. See "Bin Laden Video," supra note 9.

Chapter 3

Expanding the War on Terror

The United States of America will not permit the world's most dangerous regimes to threaten us with the world's most destructive weapons.[1]

—George W. Bush

Synopsis
3.1 Why They Hate
3.2 Weapons of Mass Murder
3.3 Future Battles and the Rule of Law
3.4 Power versus Words—The Rule of Law
Endnotes

With the establishment of an interim Afghan government under the leadership of Hamid Karzai, the United States-led coalition continues to track down the remnants of the al-Qa'eda and Taliban now in hiding.[2] More importantly, from a foreign policy stance, the United States is clearly attempting to parlay the resounding success it achieved in removing the renegade Taliban government from power into a deterrence signal to other states who either support or sponsor terrorism. In his State of the Union Address on January 29, 2002, President Bush cautioned the American people that even though Afghanistan was no longer a supporter of terrorist organizations that the War on Terror was not over. Indeed, the use of armed force against any state that harbored al-Qa'eda would pose little legal debate.

In a visionary shift in direction, President Bush signaled that renegade regimes who either possessed or were seeking to acquire weapons of mass destruction posed "a grave and growing danger" to world peace that could no longer be ignored. President Bush specifically labeled Iraq, Iran and North Korea as "an axis of evil"[3] because of their continuing support and sponsorship of terrorist groups.[4] Beyond these three states, the yearly United States State Department official list of nations considered as either states who support or sponsor terrorism currently includes Libya, Syria, Sudan, and Cuba. If nothing else, the president's key point in the message to the nation signaled his resolve that the "United States of America will not permit the world's most dangerous regimes to threaten us with the world's most destructive weapons."

President Bush's remarks raised much debate—both as a policy matter and as a legal matter. Considering that the use of armed force can only be justified under international law when used in "self-defense," can the United States go beyond the rhetoric and actually carry the War on Terror to those rogue nations who are identified so closely as supporters and sponsors of terrorist activities, but have not actually physically engaged in a specific act of aggression against the United States? Furthermore, even if the United States has legal justification to employ its military force against, for example, Iraq, there are practical matters which must be carefully weighed.[5] At a minimum, the United States must demonstrate from the particular circumstances that the use of armed force will not create an even greater danger to international peace and security. Vice President Cheney has repeatedly argued that "Deliverable weapons of mass destruction in the hands of a terror network or a murderous dictator, or the two working together, constitutes as grave a threat as can be imagined. The risks of inaction are far greater than the risk of action."[6]

The question of whether the War on Terror should be expanded involves two disturbing trends which in and of themselves pose a direct challenge to the peace and stability of the world and stand at odds with the central goals of the U.N. Charter to "maintain international peace and security" [Article 1(1)] and to "promot[e] and encourag[e] respect for human rights and for fundamental freedoms for all without distinction as to race, sex, language, or religion" [Article 1(3)]. The first aspect relates to the radical ideological beliefs of the new breed of terrorists and the totalitarian states which either harbor them or, as President Bush feared, provide "arms to terrorists, giving them the means to match their hatred." The second aspect relates to the willingness of these al-Qa'eda-styled terrorists to use weapons of mass destruction[7] in their desire to carry out grandiose schemes to kill multitudes of civilians. Taken together, the mix is lethal and a clear and present danger to the international peace and security of the global community. Because of the murderous nature of the terrorists, it is not enough to look for the needle in the haystack; the haystack must be destroyed.

3.1 Why They Hate

First, the ideological motivations of many al-Qa'eda styled terrorist organizations appears to be focused on the advancement of cult-like "religious" objectives rather than the more typical aspirations of traditional old-styled terrorist groups who are primarily concerned with the achievement of political or territorial goals.[8] Driven by extremist Islamic apocalyptic visions these new breed of terrorists are bent on destroying through violence those individuals and things which are deemed to be outside of a very narrow *weltanschauung* (world view). There are numerous al-Qa'eda-styled terrorist organizations that fit this mold: Abu Nidal Organization, a.k.a. Fatah Revolutionary Council; Armed Islamic Group; al-Gama'at al-Islamiyya; Islamic Resistance Movement (Hamas); Hezbollah, a.k.a. Party of God, Islamic Jihad; International Islamic Jihad against Jews and Crusaders; Jamaat ul-Fuqra; al-Jihad, a.k.a. Islamic Jihad; the Palestine Islamic Jihad, Abu Sayyaf; al Aqsa Martyrs Brigade; and so forth. As previously noted, a 1995 RAND-St. Andrews Chronology of International Terrorism study revealed that "25 of 58, or 42 percent of known, active, international terrorists groups had a predominately religious component or motivation,"[9] most often associated with radical Islamic fundamentalism.

Perhaps the most chilling revelation of this vicious mindset is found in the "bin Laden videotape," released to the public on December 13, 2001. The tape clearly illustrates the twisted religious machinations of the al-Qa'eda terrorists and their like who use religion to justify the mass murder of innocent civilians. In the conversation between bin Laden and an unidentified Shaykh regarding the attacks of September 11, 2001, numerous references are made to "Allah," "Muhammad," the "*fiqu* [holy war] of Muhammad," and so on. At one point, bin Laden boasts that the attacks were beneficial to a "true" understanding of Islam. [The attacks] "made people think (about true Islam), which benefited them greatly." The video closes with the guest praising bin Laden in the name of Allah, "By Allah my Shaykh [bin Laden]. We congratulate you for the great work. Thank Allah." In fact, in the case of many of the militant Islamic terrorist organizations, direct links have been established to various *Deobandi* religious schools of hate or *madrassas*,[10] which openly advocate the most violent forms of terrorism against Western interests.[11]

Osama bin Laden and his followers are not simply another sub-state isolated religious terror cult like Japan's Aum Shinriko. According to a thought provoking special report from *Newsweek* entitled, "Why Do They Hate Us," these terrorists "come out of a culture that reinforces their hostility, distrust and hatred of the West—and of America in particular."[12] Incredibly, a Gallup poll taken in late February 2002 indicated that a majority of the Arab world condemned the attack on the United States, but believed that Arabs did not carry it out.[13] This opinion is shared through the region despite the fact that all nineteen of the hijackers were Arabs.

The al-Qa'eda has cited numerous grievances against the United States which justifies their use of terror to include American support of "puppet" Arab governments, importation of oil, support for Israel, Westerners living in Arab lands, morally corrupt Western culture, and so on. These complaints are hollow. Like all enemies of freedom and pluralism, be it the German Nazis or the Stalinist Communists, the radical Islamic terrorists attack the West for what it *is*, not for what it has done. In a nutshell, whether the anti-Americanism is motivated by religious enmity, radical idiosyncrasies or just blind hatred, these al-Qa'eda styled terrorist groups have no regard or respect for human life let alone the human rights and fundamental freedoms of others. To be sure, the U.N. Charter's rule of law and expression of human rights are viewed as hateful concepts of Western domination.

Related to the inherent dangerousness of al-Qa'eda styled terrorist groups, is the fact that states that provide support to these people suffer from the scourge of totalitarianism and open hostility to America and the West. This is an important phenomenon not only because terror groups could probably not flourish into sophisticated networks without the overt support of a state, but because, as President Bush warned in his State of the Union speech, "time is not on our side." Renegade regimes will sooner or later provide weapons of mass destruction to these radical disciplines of hate. The rogue state does not require a sophisticated delivery system—the suicide terrorist is the delivery system.

Conversely, a topic covered in depth in Chapter 6 argues that democracies do not sponsor or support terrorism, dictatorships do. There exists an abundance of empirical evidence that democracies do not engage in international terrorism, instigate war, engage in democide (genocide and mass murder),[14] or abuse the human rights of their people.[15] As Anthony Lake, a former Clinton administration special assistant to the president for national security affairs, related in an address at John Hopkins University: "Democracies tend not to wage war on each other and they tend not to support terrorism—in fact, they don't. They are more trustworthy in diplomacy and they do a better job of respecting the . . . human rights of their people."[16] Certainly, in the preamble to the U.N. Charter and in Article 1 of the Charter, it is evident that the drafters also understood that nations who respect human rights and fundamental freedoms do not support or engage in terrorism. This truth is axiomatic.

3.2 Weapons of Mass Murder

The world must wake from its millenary sleep and recognize the real possibility that weapons of mass destruction will be used against large civilian population centers. Clearly, the terror attacks of September 11, 2001, have demonstrated that international terrorism has now "broke us across the threshold" of creating mass casualties. The al-Qa'eda-styled terrorist is not content to kill in the tens or twenties, he aggressively seeks access to weapons of mass destruction in order to murder in the thousands and tens of thousands. While nuclear weapons may be beyond the reach of international terrorists at this time,[17] biological and chemical weapons are not. Biological and chemical agents are inexpensive, easy to obtain, hard to trace and capable of killing thousands upon thousands.

Add into the equation the fact that al-Qa'eda terrorists have demonstrated a clear desire to use weapons of mass murder if possible and Bush's call for expanding the War on Terror to any state (e.g., Iraq) that exhibits a willingness to support terror makes fundamental sense. Congress has agreed, issuing a use-of-force resolution in October, 2002.

Even without being supplied by a renegade state with weapons of mass murder, terrorists can acquire them in the following ways. According to a *Public Agenda Special Report: Terrorism*, there are four general scenarios regarding the terrorist use of nuclear devices: (1) the terrorist makes a crude nuclear bomb using smuggled uranium or fissile material; (2) an unstable nation falls into the hands of terrorists (e.g., Pakistan is said to have dozens of nuclear weapons); (3) a conventional bomb is employed to explode radioactive materials (so-called "dirty bomb"); or (4) a nuclear power plant is attacked.[18] Accordingly, a doomsday scenario becomes a central consideration of whether or not the War on Terror should be expanded. Researchers at Stanford University have compiled a "database of lost, stolen and misplaced nuclear material—depicting a world awash in weapons grade uranium and plutonium that is not publicly accounted for."[19] Even one or two dedicated suicide bombers armed with a chemical, biological or nuclear weapon could inflict catastrophic death and destruction in an urban environment.

The problem, of course, is how does one deal with an ideology steeped in pseudo-religious fanaticism which compels its foot soldiers of terror to gladly commit suicide in order to kill innocent civilians?[20] If it seems obvious that third party dispute mechanisms will bear no fruit with terrorists who are filled with such hate, one is left with the unpleasant truism voiced by the ancient Romans—*oderint dum metuatant* ("let them hate us as long as they respect us").[21] In the short term the United States was not able to reason with the al-Qa'eda and the Taliban regime to comply with the principles of peace embodied in the U.N. Charter. Fortunately, America was able to employ the proper application of force under the rule of law to, as President Bush pledged in his first major speech following the September 11, 2001, attack, "bring them to justice or bring justice to them."[22]

In addition, America was extremely fortunate that the War on Terror began prior to the al-Qa'eda gaining access to weapons of mass murder. September 11, 2001, could have happened at any time, but at least now the United States has embarked in a worldwide War on Terror without having suffered the devastation of a true weapons mass destruction event. Clearly, the use of the military arm of the United States must not cease until the states that support al-Qa'eda styled terrorism have been neutralized.

3.3 Future Battles and the Rule of Law

The troubling question for the United States and the entire civilized world is how to legally frame a rule of law that speaks to preventing future attacks by sophisticated state-supported or state-sponsored terrorist groups, particularly in light of their use of weapons of mass destruction and the existence of renegade states. If the employment of a weapon of mass murder is on the near horizon, do the current international rules related to the use of force (i.e., only used in self-defense) actually work in the new real world? In other words, must a state wait for a catastrophic state-sponsored or state-supported terrorist attack before it can respond,[23] or does a threatened state have the right to engage in anticipatory self-defense,[24] or even, perhaps, in a controversial legal theory known as "counterproliferation self-help,"[25] against a regime it believes capable of such acts?

The concept of anticipatory self-defense is also termed alternatively as "preemption self-defense" or "preventative self-defense," and has been used by the Israelis against another state, as illustrated by Israel's preemptive air strike on Arab airfields in the 1967 War and against individuals, as illustrated in the ongoing Palestinian conflict.[26]

The United States has long recognized the right of anticipatory self-defense to counter threats to its national security. In the United States, scholars regularly cite the famous Caroline Doctrine, which domestically defines the circumstances that permit forcible self-help, or self-defense. The Caroline Doctrine grew out of an 1837 raid by Canadian troops in New York. In justifying the Canadian military response to Canadian rebels who had entered American territory, United States Secretary of State Daniel Webster set down the rules for acts of self-defense. Under the Caroline Doctrine a nation may resort to necessary and proportional acts of self-defense if such acts arise out of an instant and overwhelming necessity, leaving no choice of means and no moment of deliberation.

The problem, of course, is that some states may claim the right of anticipatory self-defense as a pretext for aggression. To weigh the validity of the concept of anticipatory self-defense, international law views the employment of this doctrine in the context of an "imminent" armed attack and as a part of the inherent right of self-defense of Article 51 of the U.N. Charter. Traditionally, the analysis was fairly clear cut; imminent was viewed in terms of the actual mobilization by the aggressor state of its conventional military forces in preparation for an armed attack. In the War on Terror, however, the enemy does not rely on conventional forces. The rogue state and al-Qa'eda-styled terrorists rely on the use of weapons of mass murder which, in their hands, may very well satisfy the rule-of-law requirement of "imminent." Regardless, the use of force in preemption must be reasonably proportionate to the specific danger that is to be averted.

The United States Deputy Secretary of Defense, Paul Wolfolwitz, was an early and vocal proponent of anticipatory self-defense speaking with approval of the Israeli military's use of preemptive force in regards to the killing of known Palestinian terrorists,[27] and embracing the idea as a necessary instrument of United States policy in the War on Terror: "Our approach has been to aim at prevention and not merely punishment. We are at war. Self-defense requires prevention and sometimes preemption."[28] In September 2002, the White House issued the *National Security Strategy of the United States of America* which clearly spelled out America's intention to employ the concept of preemption:

> The United States has long maintained the option of preemptive actions to counter a sufficient threat to our national security. The greater the threat, the greater the risk of inaction—and the more compelling the case for taking anticipatory action to defend ourselves, even if uncertainty remains as to the time and place of the enemy's attack. To forestall or prevent such hostile acts by our adversaries, the United States will, if necessary, act preemptively.[29]

The *National Security Strategy* document spells out a three part approach to weigh the use of preemption.

> We will always proceed deliberately, weighing the consequences of our actions. To support preemptive options, we will:
>
> - build better, more integrated intelligence capabilities to provide timely, accurate information on threats, wherever they may emerge;
> - coordinate closely with allies to form a common assessment of the most dangerous threats; and
> - continue to transform our military forces to ensure our ability to conduct rapid and precise operations to achieve decisive results.[30]

The concept of counterproliferation self-help takes the matter of anticipatory self-defense to the next level, although in the 2002 *National Security Strategy*, the distinction has essentially been swallowed under preemption. Counterproliferation self-help is focused specifically on rogue totalitarian States who seek to acquire weapons of mass destruction. The concept argues that when the threat of a totalitarian state or terrorist group

Chapter 3: Expanding the War on Terror

using a weapon of mass destruction directly threatens the national survival of another state, that a new international legal regime should allow for the threatened state to engage in "preventive or preemptive use of force to either deter acquisition plans, eliminate acquisition programs, or destroy illicit weapons of mass destruction sites at any stage in the proliferators acquisition efforts."[31]

The 1981 Israeli air attack on Iraq's Osiraq nuclear reactor is the best illustration of this emerging and much-needed doctrine.[32] Although the international community condemned the Israelis as violating the rule of law regarding the use of force in self-defense, history and common sense proved their actions were entirely justified. Israel has been defending itself in its own War on Terror for a long time.

The argument that the War on Terror must be enlarged because of the overwhelming danger to the global community is the only reasonable position to advance in the era of terrorism and weapons of mass destruction. Again, the reason that Iraq is a target for a preemptive military strike is not because Saddam Hussein cannot be deterred. It is because Saddam may provide weapons of mass murder to an al-Qa'eda-styled terrorist organization, which cannot be deterred. Again, the delivery system for a weapon of mass destruction is a terrorist seeking martyrdom. Any rogue nation that exhibits the potential to pass on weapons and support to the new breed of terrorist is a target for swift military action.

Finally, a less-discussed legal basis for military intervention against a rogue nations falls under the evolving legal theory known as humanitarian intervention. For example, although conducted with the specific approval of the United Nations, the December 1992 United States military intervention into Somalia[33] was motivated purely on humanitarian grounds to aleviate human suffering and, even without United Nations sanction, would appear on its face to be a proper exercise of the developing customary legal theory of humanitarian intervention.

The theory of humanitarian intervention, recognized by many modern international scholars, holds that when the government and infrastructure of a country has disintegrated to the point that its people are being subjected to a widespread pattern of gross human rights violations over a prolonged period of time, another nation may intervene to stop the loss of life and to assist in the restoration of law and order. The caveat to the theory, of course, is that once the loss of life has stopped and law and order has been restored, the intervening force must immediately depart.[34]

3.4 Power versus Words—The Rule of Law

The argument is sometimes made, rather cynically, that what really matters in achieving a particular goal is the possession of the necessary power to influence the desired outcome. Accordingly, since the overriding goal of the War on Terror is the protection of American interests and the maintenance of global stability by preventing terrorism and unlawful aggression, the United States should depend upon dispositions of effective power without concern for the rearrangement of authoritative words to color that power. In weighing the use of force in the War on Terror, some argue that concentration should simply rest on the use of power, downplaying the necessity or impact of words. This approach might be termed a power versus word argument, a phenomenon which rests particularly well with totalitarian regimes, but is also periodically raised by members of democratic societies.

Thus, when Iraq invaded and conquered the sovereign nation of Kuwait in 1990, no amount of words, treaty obligations or diplomacy halted their exercise of total and brutal aggression against the territory, people or environment of Kuwait. Exercising what was termed the law of the jungle, Iraq simply took what it wanted. The fact that Iraq was a member of the United Nations and bound by the principles relating to dispute settlement through means other than the use of force had no effect whatsoever on its activities. In this regard, the words and ideas contained in the U.N Charter deterred neither Iraq's open and brutal aggression of Kuwait, nor Saddam Hussein's lust for power and territory.

In fact, throughout the entire Gulf crisis, Iraq made no real attempt to even conceal, let alone justify, its violations of the U.N. Charter, the Geneva Conventions or other applicable treaties. In the end, it was only the application of power through the superior military might of the allied coalition headed in chief by the United States, which succeeded in halting Iraq's aggression.

Other examples of the apparent disconnect of power *vis-à-vis* words can be found in the arena of human rights. The willingness of many states to eagerly endorse numerous human rights covenants that are never put into practice shows that this cynical model finds some basis in fact. If power is all that ultimately counts, then what use do words have in the real world of dealing with international conflict?

Casting the use of power as the dominant factor in the use of force captures only a portion of the issue at hand. Because words without corresponding force have little effect in the deterrence of unlawful activities, the model incorrectly dismisses the role of words in the process. Of course, aggression can never be halted by words alone, no matter how much those words reflect accepted norms. However, the deficiency of this reasoning rests on misunderstanding the critical role which clearly defined norms play in the process of deterrence. Clearly defined norms actually provide stimulus and sinew for subsequent action. Such norms are the very building blocks necessary to generate the support to defeat unlawful activities.

If words are the basis for viable action, words must impart unambiguous understanding. A basic tenet of providing instruction is simplicity, appropriately known in the vernacular of the military as KISS (keep it simple stupid). To be efficacious to a wide audience, concepts should be kept as simple as possible. Additionally, since each discipline of study has its own unique system of terminology, effective communication mandates that the more complex the body of material to be learned, the greater one must rely on shorter concepts which take the place of longer chains of thought.

Along with simplicity, concepts must be thoroughly inculcated to be retained. Repetition is also key to all learning; it alone can ensure comprehension and, hence, meaningful communication. Thus, the more complex the body of learning, the greater the need for repetition.

In the War on Terror the Bush administration has demonstrated a high level of sophistication concerning the need to couch actions in simple, yet meaningful terminology. And, more importantly, that terminology is largely cemented in the rule of law as it pertains to the use of force.

> One of the lessons of contemporary science about human behavior is that it helps in creating the conditions necessary for the achievement of a goal to have the goal more sharply delineated. The clarification in detail of distinctions between lawful and unlawful coercion will not, of course, of itself establish all the necessary conditions for restraint of unlawful coercion. But it may perform the very necessary task of outlining the

major contours of the effects sought—in terms of which alternative choices in the rearrangement of effective power and in the adoption of new modalities in practice must be appraised.[35]

As previously outlined, when President George W. Bush formed the allied coalition against the Taliban, he firmly rooted the campaign in the norms of the U.N. Charter and under the domestic law of the United States. The subsequent force applied by the United States and its allies had the full backing of a universally recognized set of lawful standards contained in Article 51 of the U.N. Charter. Similarly, the primary Security Council resolution dealing with the attack on America was based upon the lawful authority of the U.N. Charter. Conversely, the Taliban regime had no legal basis in which to frame its aggression and, apart from a few radical Islamic states, almost no supporters within the community of nations.

As the crisis over weapons inspections in Iraq has also demonstrated, power applied without the framework of words is almost as counterproductive as words issued without the necessary power to enforce them. Thus, to emphasize power in the power-versus-words analysis fails completely in the long run because words are the very basis for establishing acceptable norms of agreed behavior which, in turn, distinguish lawful actions from unlawful actions.

Furthermore, most of the world can quickly grasp the idea of following the rule of law in halting an aggressor who has broken the law, or who threatens the employment of weapons of mass murder. In this light, America is only defending itself against rogue nations; *they* have been at war with the United States for a long time.

The rule of law has its problems, but those problems are more in the context of application rather than definition; the meaning is simply framed, the application is not. In its strict meaning, the rule of law has immediate association. The meaning of the rule of law will always refer to that body of accepted and well-recognized principles of international law, the most critical being in the context of the use of force. It is safe to say, in terms of international behavior, that the phrase rule of law will always bring to mind the illegality of the use of aggressive force. The struggle is not so much in meaning—the primary strength of the rule of law—it is

Chapter 3: Expanding the War on Terror 51

whether the rule of law will prevail as the means of justification in a given situation.

If respect for the rule of law is to survive as the measure of civilized behavior, it does not contribute to the discussion to advocate the use of force apart from legal parameters. The United States must abide by the international principles, as they now exist. While it is certainly prudent to sternly warn states that support or sponsor terrorism that they will be held absolutely accountable for any acts of aggression, anticipatory self-defense can only be used if the United States can reasonably make the case to the world that a significant attack by terrorists using weapons of mass murder is imminent.

Thus, even if the attacks of September 11, 2001, are considered an act of war by the al-Qa'eda and the Taliban, the United States cannot unilaterally expand the War on Terror to nations not directly linked to the September 11, 2001, assault unless it articulates a credible preventative self-defense argument. In considering whether the war should be expanded to Iraq, for example, there is evidence that Iraq has engaged in support for the al-Qa'eda terror network. The level of support, however, is conflicting and it remains for the Bush administration to make that case to both the American people and the rest of the civilized world.[36]

If one argues that Saddam Hussein is so dangerous that his regime presents an imminent threat *ab initio*, it is prudent for America to follow the pattern it has set for itself since the end of the Cold War and seek specific U.N. Security Council approval for the use of armed force in preventative self-defense. Historically, the United Nations has only authorized armed force on two occasions; both instances related to stopping clearly defined acts of aggression. In a stunning show of world solidarity immediately following the Cold-War era, President George H. Bush was able to obtain a clear "use of force" resolution from the U.N. Security Council, prior to using lawful violence to expel the 1990 illegal Iraqi invasion and occupation of Kuwait.[37] Resolution 678 reads in relevant part:

> The Security Council . . .
> Authorizes member states cooperating with the government of Kuwait, unless Iraq on or before January 15, 1991 fully implements . . . the foregoing Resolutions, to use all necessary means to uphold and implement

the Security Council Resolution 660 and all subsequent relevant Resolutions and to restore international peace and security in the area . . . .[38]

The only parallel to the Security Council's authorization for the use of force in the Gulf War was in the Korean War. On July 7, 1950, responding to North Korea's armed aggression into South Korea, the Security Council authorized the creation of a unified command under the authority of the United States. The resolution was passed, however, only due to the temporary absence of the Soviet Union.[39]

Considering the new threats which the War on Terror presents in terms of rogue terrorist states, American policy makers can and must develop an active global-based strategy designed to deter and defeat future al-Qa'eda styled terror attacks. At a minimum, this means new thinking in three areas. First, the United Nations must be energized to immediately address the issue of reaching consensus on a definition for terrorism, which should also include language regarding when a particular act of terrorism should be considered as an act of war.

Second, the United States must insist that the concept of counterproliferation self-help be placed on the table as a viable addition to the international rule of law regarding the use of force against a radical state that seeks access to weapons of mass destruction. Most certainly the United States will do well to obtain the direct assistance and input of the major powers, particularly the Russians.

Third, juxtaposed to pressing the international community for concrete definitions and new legal approaches on how to fight terrorism in the new era, the United States should also earnestly promote the spread of democratic values as the absolute best avenue to promote war and terrorism avoidance over the long term. Democracy is not an American value; democracy and human rights are normative world values. The world community has wisely made assistance to the new Afghan government to build roads, schools, factories, homes, and so forth, contingent on its movement towards the adoption of democratic values; more must be done in this region of the world. The totalitarian ponds that foster terrorism must be drained. The cost of inaction is too great.

Finally, as set out in Chapter 5, whatever the future may hold, the United States must continue to reinforce the basic truism that a democracy

Chapter 3: Expanding the War on Terror

never answers terror with terror in the context of the employment of military force in self-defense. The United States is absolutely obligated under international law to follow the law of war as codified in the Geneva Conventions of 1949 and as set out in custom. By all accounts, the American military did an outstanding job in the combat activities in Afghanistan in abiding by the law of armed conflict while caring for basic humanitarian needs of civilians caught up in the conflict.[40] As the world's leading democracy, it is imperative that the United States continue to exercise the lawful use of military force in accordance with the letter and spirit of the rule of law or face the possibility that it will be battling the children of hate and terrorism in the next generation.[41]

Endnotes

1. President George W. Bush, State of the Union Address (January 29, 2002). David E. Sanger, "Bush, Focusing on Terrorism, Says Secure U.S. is Top Priority," *New York Times*, Jan. 30, 2002, at A1.

2. The al-Qa'eda core leadership killed as of November 2002 includes Mohammed Atef, Abu Hafs and Qaed Salim Sinan al-Havethi.

3. The term "axis" is commonly associated with the alliance between Japan, Germany, and Italy in World War II. In the case of Iraq, Iran, and North Korea there is no similar treaty alliance, only a shared willingness to support or sponsor international terrorism.

4. David E. Sanger, "Bush, Focusing on Terrorism, Says Secure U.S. is Top Priority," *New York Times*, Jan. 30, 2002, at A1.

5. Such practical matters include the moral and proportionality factors set forth in the Catholic "just war" tradition. See "Living with Faith and Hope After September 11," U.S. Conference of Catholic Bishops, Dec. 2001. Pub. No. 5-491 USCCB Pub. Wash. D.C.

6. Richard Bendeho, "Cheney Urges Action on Iraq," *USA Today*, Aug. 27, 2002, at A1.

7. According to §1403 of the National Defense Authorization Act for FY 1997, a weapon of mass destruction is defined as: "Any weapon or device that is intended, or has the capability to cause death or serious bodily injury to a sig-

nificant number of people through the release of toxic or poisonous chemicals or their precursors, a disease organism, or radiation or radioactivity."

8. But see *Crying Wolf or Crying Havoc?* supra Chapter 2, note 4. Cordesman stresses that all religions have their extremists, but believes that Islam itself is a powerful stabilizing force in most of the Middle East.

9. Ian O. Lesser et al., *Countering the New Terrorism*, (Santa Monica, CA: RAND, 1999), at 17. The RAND database includes all terrorist incidents since 1968.

10. But see, e.g., Alan Zarembo, "A Merger of Mosque and State," *Newsweek*, Oct. 15, 2001, at 28. Sheik Muhammad Raffaat Othman who teaches Islamic law at Cairo's Al-Azhar University believes that the Koran prohibits "attacking innocent, unarmed people." He stated that the "Prophet Muhammad demanded that we not kill women, children or the elderly. Attacks should be against soldiers and armed civilians."

11. Rick Bragg, "A Nation Challenged: Schools; Shaping Young Islamic Hearts and Hatreds," *New York Times*, Oct. 14, 2001, at A1.

12. Fareed Zakaria, "Why Do They Hate Us?," *Newsweek*, Oct. 22, 2001, at 24. However, Zakaria makes the point in the same article that "[e]very Islamic country in the world has condemned the attacks of Sept. 11. To many, bin Laden belongs to a long line of extremist who have invoked religion to justify mass murder and spur men to suicide."

13. Andrea Stone, "In Poll, Islamic World Says Arabs Not Involved in 9/11," *USA Today*, Feb. 27, 2002 at A1.

14. See, e.g., R. J. Rummel, *Death by Government: Genocide and Mass Murder in the Twentieth Century* (New Brunswick, NJ: Transaction, 1994). Rummel's exhaustive statistical research is considered to be the groundbreaking work in this area and points the way to a new paradigm on war avoidance. In short, if democracies do not fight each other, then it is in the interest of the global community to promote the spread of democratic behavior.

15. One of the most disturbing aspects of the Taliban was their systematic abuse of women. See Tim McGirk and Shomali Plain, "Lifting the Veil on Sex Slavery," *Time*, Feb. 18, 2002, at 8. "Of all the ways the Taliban abused women, this [systematic rape and slavery] may be the worst."

16. Anthony Lake, Special Assistant to the President for National Security Affairs, Address to Johns Hopkins University, School of Advanced International Studies, Oct. 21, 1993.

17. See Peter Eisler, Fred Bayules, and Dan Vergano, "U.S. Cities Brace for the Next Acts of Terrorism," *USA Today*, Sept. 24, 2001, at 5A [hereinafter Next Acts of Terrorism].

18. See, e.g., http://www.publicagenda.org/specials/teerrorism/terror.htm.

19. Andrew Quinn, "Loss of Nuclear Material Tabulated," *San Jose Mercury News*, Mar. 7, 2002, at A1.

20. For an excellent overview of this issue, see Fareed Zakaria, "Why Do They Hate Us?" *Newsweek*, Oct. 15, 2001 at 21.

21. See Arthur Ferrill, *The Fall of the Roman Empire* (New York: Thames & Hudson Ltd., 1986); Margaret Lyttelton and Werner Forman, *The Romans* (London: Orbis Pub. Ltd., 1985). But see, Caleb Carr, *The Lessons of Terror: A History of Warfare Against Civilians, Why It Has Always Failed and Why It Will Fail Again* (New York: Random House Inc., 2002). Carr argues that as long as Rome exercised its military power in a way that did not terrorize civilians it was highly successful. The Roman practice of offering Roman citizenship to tribes who agreed to serve in the Roman army as auxiliary troops greatly benefited the expansion of the empire. For example, the *Honariani Atecotti Seniores* were formed from captured pirates from the Scottish Atecotti tribe circa 300 A.D. and served in the *Auxilium Palatinum* (the author is a descendant of this tribe). On the other hand, the later Roman practice of slaughtering civilians only stiffened resistance amongst the barbarians who eventually conquered Rome.

22. See, e.g., Jeanne Cummings, "Bush Says Our Nation Saw Evil, But Isn't Frightened Into Chaos," *Wall Street Journal*, Sept. 12, 2001, at A6.

23. The concept of self-defense is not created by the U.N. Charter. U.N. Charter art. 51 simply recognizes the "inherent right of self-defense." See William McHugh, "Forcible Self-help in International Law," *Naval War College Review*, No. 25, 1972.

24. See Myers S. McDougal and Florentino P. Feliciano, *Law and Minimum World Public Order* (New Haven: Yale University Press, 1961). For an opposing view see Kume, "Individual and Collective Self-Defense in Article 51 of the Charter of the United Nations," 41 A.J.I.L. 872, 878 (1947). Regardless, the use of force in self-defense must be reasonably proportionate to the

specific danger that is to be averted. See Gerhard Von Glahn, *Law Among Nations* (6th ed.) (Macmillian Pub. Co., 1992).

25. See, e.g., Guy B. Roberts, "The Counterproliferation Self-Help Paradigm: A Legal Regime for Enforcing the Norm Prohibiting the Proliferation of Weapons of Mass Destruction," *Denver Journal of International Law and Policy*, Summer 1999, at 485 [hereinafter "Counterproliferation Self-Help"].

26. The Israelis have long used the concept of first strike to target known terrorists fighters before they commit future acts of terrorism.

27. See Steven Erlanger, "A Nation Challenged: Diplomacy; Russian Aide Warns U.S. Not to Extend War to Iraq," *New York Times*, Feb. 4, 2002, at A10, col. 6.

28. Id.

29. *The National Security Strategy of the United States of America*, The White House, September 17, 2002, p. 15.

30. Id. p. 16.

31. See "Counterproliferation Self-Help," supra note 25.

32. See Louis Rene' Beres and Yoash Tsiddon-Chatto, "Reconsidering Israel's Destruction of Iraq's Osiraq Nuclear Reactor: Aggression or Self-Defense?" *Vanderbilt J. Transn'l L*, No. 75, (1982), at 417.

33. U.N. Security Council Resolution 794, U.N. SCOR, 3101 mtg., U.N. Doc. S/RES/794 (Dec. 3, 1992) [SC Res. 794].

34. See, generally, Richard Lillich, *Humanitarian Intervention and the United Nations* (Boston: Little, Brown & Co., 1973). Law and Minimum World Public Order, at 63.

35. David Roger and Carla Robbins, "U.S. Steps Up Case Against Iraq, Both in Congress and at the U.N.," *Wall Street Journal*, 27 Sept., 2002, at A1.

36. On August 2, 1990, with absolutely no basis in international law and in complete disregard of the principles embodied in the United Nations Charter, massive Iraqi armored forces unlawfully invaded and occupied the sovereign nation of Kuwait. See "The Iraqi Invasion; Invading Iraqis seize Kuwait and Its Oil; U.S. Condemns Attack, Urges United Action," *New York Times*, Aug. 3, 1990, at A1. On August 8, 1990, Iraq annexed Kuwait. See "Confrontation

in the Gulf: U.S. may Send Saudis a Force of 50,000; Iraq Proclaims Kuwait's Annexation; Bush Draws 'Line'," *New York Times*, Aug. 9, 1990, at A1.

37. S.C. Res. 678 (Nov. 29, 1990), reprinted in 29 I.L.M. 1565 (1990).

38. See Bruce Russett and James S. Sutterlin, "The U.N. in a New World Order," 70 *Foreign Affairs* 69, 73.

39. See Patrick E. Tyler, "A Nation Challenged: The Aide," *New York Times*, Sept. 28 2001, at B2. In conjunction with the military campaign, the United States military air-dropped tons of food to Afghan civilians.

40 See, e.g., Jeffrey F. Addicott, "U.S. Must Follow the Law of War or Battle Enemy's Children," *Birmingham News*, Oct. 28, 2001, at C5.

Chapter 4

Civil Liberties and the War on Terror

The boisterous sea of liberty is never without a wave.
—Thomas Jefferson

Synopsis
4.1 Past Efforts to Address Terrorism
4.2 Federal Courts and Military Tribunals
4.3 Investigating Terrorist Suspects
4.4 Use of the Military in Domestic Law Enforcement
4.5 Immigration
4.6 New Information-Gathering Technologies
4.7 Assassination
4.8 Increased Security Measures in Public Places
4.9 The Constitution and the War on Terror

The probability that terrorist organizations like al-Qa'eda may employ chemical, nuclear, or biological weapons of mass destruction in suicide attacks poses not only a direct threat to the well being of tens of thousands of innocent people, but raises new controversies regarding the possible curtailment of long recognized civil liberties.[1] In creating greater domestic security from future terrorist attacks, the United States government must not trample on American liberties in the name of preserving them. This concern speaks to the matter of "due process." The term due process is most commonly used to describe the rights that American enjoy as spelled out in the Fourteenth Amendment to the United States Constitution,

> All persons born or naturalized in the United States and subject to the jurisdiction thereof, are citizens of the United States and of the State wherein they reside. No State shall make or enforce any law which shall abridge the privileges or immunities of citizens of the United States; nor

shall any State deprive any person of life, liberty, or property, without due process of law; nor deny to any person within its jurisdiction the equal protection of the laws."[2]

The term also has come to be associated with American values of fairness and reasonableness in the treatment of others.

Currently, there are seven main areas of concern that have been voiced in the public square as the government and law enforcement develop new approaches to deal with future terrorist threats. They involve: (1) the use of military tribunals; (2) the power of the United States to investigate, detain and question terrorist suspects; (3) the expansion of the use of the United States military to enforce domestic law; (4) immigration; (5) the use of new information-gathering technologies; (6) the presidential executive order on assassination; and (7) the increase in security measures at public airports and other public facilities.

4.1 Past Efforts to Address Terrorism

As the world watched helplessly while hijacked planes smashed into the World Trade Center and the Pentagon, the attack exposed gaping vulnerabilities in both United States military and law enforcement strategies to guard the nation against a full-fledged international terrorist assault. Although the threat of a significant terrorist attack on United States soil was not an unknown topic of discussion prior to the events of September 11, 2001,[3] very little was done by the federal government in the area of anti-terrorism.[4] Actions to address the threat of organized terrorism were piecemeal and misguided. After the dual bombings of two American embassies in Africa in the summer of 1998 left more than 300 people dead, then President Clinton vowed that "[n]o matter how long it takes, or where it takes us, we will pursue terrorists until the cases are solved and justice is done." Militarily, President Clinton launched seventy-five cruise missiles at some al-Qa'eda terrorist training camps in Afghanistan and a suspected VX nerve gas production facility at the Shifa Pharmaceuticals plant in Khartoum, Sudan. Nancy Soderberg, a former National Security Council senior aide in the Clinton administration admitted: "In hindsight, it wasn't enough, and anyone involved in policy would have to admit that."[5] In the kindest light to all administrations before September 11, 2001, action by the government was mistaken because the United States had no frame of reference in which to gauge the magnitude of the threat.[6]

In the international sphere, a brief survey of the American approach to global terrorism prior to September 11, 2001, reveals that America was content to enter into a handful of specific international conventions aimed at encouraging multilateral cooperation in punishing certain narrowly defined acts of terrorism such as hostage taking and hijacking of aircraft. Some examples of specific antiterrorist conventions include: The Convention on Offenses and Certain Other Acts Committed on Board Aircraft (Tokyo Convention, 1963); Convention for the Suppression of Unlawful Seizure of Aircraft (Hague Convention, 1971); Convention for the Suppression of Unlawful Acts Against the Safety of Civil Aviation (Montreal Convention, 1973); Convention on the Prevention and Punishment of Crimes Against Internationally Protected Persons, Including Diplomatic Agents (New York Convention, 1976–1977); and the International Convention Against the Taking of Hostages (Hostages Convention, 1979). As impressive as the titles sound for these ad hoc conventions, the general position of the United States[7] was simply a mirror of the world community's ineffective approach to the problem of global terrorism. Washington seemed content to react to incidents.[8]

In the domestic arena, apart from various criminal reforms making terrorist acts abroad a crime under United States domestic law,[9] most of the attention of the executive branch and Congress was focused on passing various domestic counterterrorism[10] legislation, such as the 1996 Defense Against Weapons of Mass Destruction Act, commonly referred to as NLD Act after its sponsors' names, Senators Nunn, Lugar and Domenici. This legislation was limited in scope and designed primarily to assist in planning and training efforts for the use of emergency personnel responding to a major terrorist incident involving a weapon of mass destruction.[11] Early on these initiatives received much deserved criticism as a band-aide approach to the real world problem of a major terrorist attack.[12]

In most areas of management, meaningful reorganizations of bureaucracies are the product of some form of crisis. Counterterrorism initiatives are no exception. Since the 1980s there have been numerous legislative initiatives that address terrorist activities, most enacted on the heals of some type of terrorist attack. The central focus of any umbrella security program must involve the coordinated efforts of key federal and state agencies designed to protect United States personnel and property.[13]

The Bush administration has taken two major steps to fulfill its obligation to protect the American people from future attacks by international terrorists. The first is the creation of a new cabinet-level department entitled Office of Homeland Security[14] and the second is the passage of an exhaustive piece of anti-terror legislation known by short title as the Patriot Act. The bill passed in the Senate by a vote of 98-1. The House of Representatives passed their version by a vote of 377-56.[15]

4.2 Federal Courts and Military Tribunals

In the wake of the military campaign in Afghanistan, the vast majority of the Taliban fighters were processed and released in Afghanistan. Approximately 1,000 al-Qa'eda and Taliban fighters were turned over to American forces for disposition. Those turned over to the United States military were deemed to be either too dangerous to parole or suspected of committing war crimes. As of the close 2002, over 500 had been transported to Guantanamo Bay, Cuba, for temporary internment.[16] They are currently being held in custody until either hostilities cease or until specific charges are levied against them for associated war crimes.

Two questions immediately arose regarding due process concerns for these individuals. First, were they entitled to treatment as prisoners of war under the Geneva Conventions?[17] Second, if criminal trials were to be pursued by the United States should these individuals be tried in a United States federal district court or by means of a United States military tribunal?[18]

An analysis of the first question regarding the status of al-Qa'eda and Taliban fighters under international law begins with the fact that the United States has long incorporated in its laws the international law of war, both customary and codified.[19] After some internal debate, the Bush administration correctly affirmed that the Geneva Conventions of 1949 did apply to the conflict in Afghanistan and, hence, the Taliban government. However, President Bush also determined that the captured al-Qa'eda and Taliban fighters were not eligible for prisoner of war status.[20]

Since the al-Qa'eda fighters belong to a terrorist organization[21] and are not recognized members of an armed force,[22] they are unlawful belligerents under the laws of war. *Army Field Manual (FM) 27* codifies

Chapter 4: Civil Liberties and the War on Terror

the law of land warfare. FM 27-10, paragraph 60(b) indicates that "[p]ersons who are not members of the armed forces as defined in [the Geneva Conventions], who bear arms or engage in other conduct hostile to the enemy thereby deprive themselves of many of the privileges attaching to the members of the civilian population." This means that they are responsible for breaches of the law of war, but are not entitled to the status of prisoners of war.[23] In the view of the Bush administration, the al-Qa'eda engaged in acts of war both in the September 11, 2001, attacks and in fighting alongside the Taliban forces in the internationally recognized armed conflict in Afghanistan. Actually, it can be argued that the al-Qa'eda have been engaged in acts of war against the United States government since 1996, since they have been linked to the 1996 bombing of the United States military barracks at Khobar Towers, Saudi Arabia, the 1998 United States Embassy bombings in Kenya and Tanzania, and the 2000 suicide boat attack on the U.S.S. *Cole* in Yemen.

As to the captured Taliban fighters, the United States determined that they were likewise not entitled to prisoner of war status under the Geneva Conventions because of their failure to comply with the Conventions' criterion which requires lawful combatants to wear distinctive military insignia, i.e., uniforms which would make them distinguishable from the civilian population at a distance.[24] In finding that the Taliban "have not effectively distinguished themselves from the civilian population," the United States also added that the Taliban fighters had further forfeited any special status because they had "adopted and provided support to the unlawful terrorist objectives of the al-Qa'eda." While the later finding would not necessarily indicate that the Taliban fighters would not be entitled to prisoner of war status, the former finding would.[25] Still, the Bush administration has repeatedly indicated that all detainees were to be treated in accordance with the humanitarian concerns[26] set out in the Geneva Conventions even though they were not entitled to the additional protections the Geneva Conventions gives to prisoners of war.[27]

Second, if the al-Qa'eda and Taliban detainees are not prisoners of war and it is determined that there is sufficient evidence to believe that a particular individual has committed war crimes, what is the appropriate forum for prosecution? Again, FM 27-10 is considered as the embodiment of the United States Army's interpretation of the law of war in the field. FM 27-10, paragraph 498 indicates that

[a]ny person, whether a member of the armed forces or a civilian, who commits an act which constitutes a crime under international law is responsible therefore and liable to punishment. Such offenses in connection with war comprise: a. Crimes against peace. b. Crimes against humanity, and c. War crimes.

FM 27-10, article 499 defines war crimes as "the technical expression for a violation of the law of war by any person or persons, military or civilian. Every violation of the law of war is a war crime." The United States policy is that American soldiers accused of violations of the law of war will be prosecuted under the provisions of the Uniform Code of Military Justice (UCMJ) for the substantive offense. For example, killing unarmed civilians is a war crime and also a substantive crime of murder. A deliberate attack on noncombatant civilians clearly violates the law of war and the customary law of war. Indeed, the law of war was designed to protect innocent civilians.

Ostensibly, the United States has four options which it may pursue against the detainees—turn the accused over to an appropriate foreign jurisdiction (e.g., the new government in Afghanistan); turn the accused over to an International Tribunal; try the accused in a United States federal district court; or try the accused in a United States military tribunal. If one is only concerned with expediency, the first option is probably the most attractive and needs little discussion. Likewise, the use of an International Tribunal is attractive but probably not workable due to concerns over such issues as the absence of a death penalty, possible security comprises of "sources and techniques" for gathering intelligence and reduced levels of due process provided to the accused.[28]

As to prosecuting these individuals in a federal district court of the United States, it is well settled that said courts have the legal authority under both domestic and international law to prosecute nonresident aliens for terrorist crimes committed on foreign soil as well as for war crimes. A widely cited precedent which amplifies just how far the jurisdictional reach extends in this regard is the case of *U.S. v. Yunis*.[29] The *Yunis* case involved the criminal trial of an Arab terrorist by the name of Fawaz Yunis who participated in the hijacking of a Royal Jordanian Airlines airplane at Beirut International Airport in June 1985.[30] The only connection the act had with the United States was the fact that the plane contained some

American citizens on board.[31] After reviewing the pertinent international agreements relating to hostage taking and hijacking the federal district court denied a defense motion to dismiss for lack of jurisdiction and Yunis was convicted of conspiracy, hostage taking and air piracy.[32]

On appeal of his conviction, the Court of Appeals for the D.C. Circuit said the following about the concept of customary international law as it applied to certain criminal acts: "Nor is jurisdiction precluded by norms of customary international law. The district court [correctly] concluded that two jurisdictional theories of international law, the 'universal principle'[33] and the 'passive personal principle,'[34] supported assertion of United States jurisdiction to prosecute Yunis on hijacking and hostage-taking charges."[35] According to the appellate court, the "universal principle" of jurisdiction allows states to prosecute those "offenses recognized by the community of nations as of universal concern, such as piracy, slave trade, attacks on or hijacking of aircraft, genocide, war crimes, and perhaps certain acts of terrorism." Under the passive personal principle, a state may prosecute non-nationals for crimes committed against its nationals outside of its territory.

In summary, then, United States federal district courts have jurisdiction to try individuals for terrorist related offenses under a variety of statutes and, in at least one case involving a foreign national who tried to commit an in-flight bombing of an American Airlines flight from Paris to Miami on December 22, 2001,[36] that power has been exercised.[37] However, instead of charging suspected al-Qa'eda war criminals with violations of the law of war, the federal courts would simply apply parallel statutes related to the *malum in se* crime[38] or apply the appropriate terrorist statute.

The final forum which is available to prosecute those individuals taken from Afghanistan who are suspected of committing war crimes is the military tribunal. On November 13, 2001, President Bush signed an executive (military) order which authorized the creation of military tribunals to try certain "non-citizens" for engaging in terrorist acts against the United States or aiding or abetting in terrorist acts against the United States [39] Because military tribunals have not been used since the end of World War II, the efficacy of using this forum to prosecute the al-Qa'eda and Taliban fighters for war crimes mandates analysis from both legal and historical perspectives.

Military tribunals are non-Article III courts.[40] They derive their basic grant of authority from Articles I and II of the United States Constitution. Respectively, Congress has the power to "define and punish . . . offenses against the Law of Nations,"[41] and the president is the "Commander in Chief of the Army and Navy."[42] Furthermore, Congress has specifically provided for the use of military commissions in Article 21 of the UCMJ.[43]

Historically, military commissions have been used in a variety of situations associated with urgent government needs related to war. In *Madsen v. Kinsella*, the Supreme Court spoke at some length on the history of military tribunals, saying: "Since our nation's earliest days, such commissions have been constitutionally recognized agencies for meeting many urgent governmental responsibilities relating to war."[44] In addition, the Courts have recognized the fact that military tribunals have been used without Congress specifically "declaring war."[45] For example, military tribunals were used in the War with Mexico, even though Congress never formally declared war. The Mexican war lasted from 1846–1848. The war broke out when Texas, an American settled province of Mexico that had broken away in 1836, was annexed as a state by the United States in 1845. Congress passed the Act of Congress of May 13, 1846, which did not declare war, but recognized "a state of war as existing by the act of the Republic of Mexico."[46]

A military tribunal consists of a panel of military officers who are authorized to render a verdict and sentence. The historical concern in this instance is not whether military tribunals can be used to prosecute United States citizens who may or may not be belligerents, but whether tribunals are constitutionally able to prosecute non-citizen belligerents for offenses in violation of the law of war. Regarding the use of military tribunals to try United States citizens who are not belligerents, the Supreme Court rendered its opinion in 1866 in *Ex Parte Milligan*,[47] where it held that as long as the civilian courts were operating, the use of military tribunals to try United States citizens who were not actual belligerents was unconstitutional.[48] In December of 1866, the United States Supreme Court granted a writ of habeas corpus to a civilian noncombatant named Lambdin P. Milligan, a pro-Confederate Indiana resident who was convicted in October 1864 by a military tribunal convened in Indianapolis, Indiana. Milligan was convicted of treason and sentenced to be hanged. The lower federal court had denied his petition for habeas corpus. In granting the

Chapter 4: Civil Liberties and the War on Terror 67

writ for review, the Supreme Court held that although the American Civil War was still in progress at the time of the trial, the circumstances in Indiana, a union state not in control by Confederate forces, did not justify the use of a military tribunal to prosecute a United States citizen because the civil courts were open and free to function. As to the use of military tribunals to prosecute noncitizen and citizen belligerents for offenses in violation of the law of war, the standard is set out in the World War II case of *Ex Parte Quirin*.[49]

In *Ex Parte Quirin*, the United States Supreme Court upheld the convictions of eight German saboteurs who had been captured in the United States and tried by a military tribunal ordered by President Franklin Roosevelt.[50] The Germans had been sent to attack public and government facilities. At least one of the Germans claimed American citizenship. The Court upheld the jurisdiction of the military tribunal against all the Germans, stating: "By the Articles of War, and especially Article 15, Congress has explicitly provided, so far as it may constitutionally do so, that military tribunals shall have jurisdiction to try offenders or offenses against the law of war in appropriate cases."[51] The Court easily distinguished the case from *Ex Parte Milligan*, holding that offenses against the law of war by actual belligerents were constitutionally authorized to be tried by military commission.[52] Besides the trials of the German saboteurs during World War II, subsequent military tribunals were used to prosecute approximately 2,600 members of the Axis for violations of the law of war,[53] to include the murder of captured American soldiers at the Battle of the Bulge.[54] The surviving high-ranking war criminals in the German military and government were tried by a special international tribunal in Nuremberg, Germany, at the so-called Nuremberg trials.[55] The Japanese leaders were tried at the International Military Tribunal for the Far East.

Although the Supreme Court has long held that the Constitution's Fifth[56] and Sixth Amendment[57] protections apply to non-United States citizens,[58] such protections do not extend to belligerents subject to trial in military tribunals for war crimes. Seemingly, the use of military tribunals has deeply seated historical and legal precedent as long as the accused are actual combatants charged with violations of the law of war. In *Application of Yamashita*,[59] the Court traced the history of military tribunals and concluded: "By thus recognizing military commissions in order to preserve their traditional jurisdiction over enemy combatants . . . Congress gave sanction, as we held in *Ex Parte Quirin* to any use of military commissions contemplated by the common law of war."[60]

While issues remained to be worked out, challenging the constitutionality of military tribunals to try the al-Qa'eda terrorists for war crimes will prove a difficult task.[61] In its January 2002 report on the lawfulness of using military tribunals, the American Bar Association (ABA) Task Force on Terrorism and Law found that the terror attacks of September 11, 2001, were arguably violations of the law of war that would justify the use of military tribunals to prosecute accused terrorists.[62] Similarly, in February 2002, the ABA House of Delegates supported the President's use of military tribunals, but recommended that the implementing regulations afforded to "an accused in any military tribunal be raised to the level that would satisfy the requirements of fundamental fairness.[63]

A more fertile area for discussion is associated with the rules and procedures by which the military tribunals will operate.[64] After months of speculation, [65] on March 21, 2002, the Secretary of Defense promulgated Military Commission Order No. 1, entitled *Procedures for Trials by Military Commissions of Certain Non-United States Citizens in the War on Terrorism.*[66] As expected, the rules and procedures generally contain many of the same provisions found in the Manual for Courts-Martial,[67] which applies to United States military personnel when tried under the UCMJ.[68] Specifically, the rules provide the following rights for the accused who is charged with a violation of the law of war:

- a copy of the charges in English and a language he understands;
- a presumption of innocence for the accused;
- guilt must be proved by the government beyond a reasonable doubt;
- access to evidence that the prosecution plans to present at trial;
- access to evidence known to the prosecution tending to exculpate the accused;
- right to remain silent;
- right to testify subject to cross-examination;
- right to obtain witnesses and documents for defense;
- right to present evidence and cross-examine witnesses;

- the appointment of interpreters to assist defense;
- right to be present at every stage of trial (except when proceedings are closed by the Presiding Officer) unless disruptive;
- access to sentencing evidence;
- cannot be tried again by military commission once verdict is final;
- right to submit a plea agreement;
- two-thirds of the military officers on the panel must agree on findings of guilt;
- unanimous decision of a seven member panel for death sentence;
- right to a free military attorney or to hire a civilian attorney;
- trial would be open to public (exceptions recognized for physical safety of participants, protection of classified information).

The military commission itself will be appointed by the secretary of defense or his designee and will contain a panel of three to seven members, all of whom are commissioned officers in the United States military. A presiding officer (PO) will be appointed to preside over the proceedings. The PO will be a judge advocate and will also serve as a voting member of the panel. The prosecutor will be a judge advocate although the attorney general may provide special trial counsel to assist. The military commission is authorized to summon witnesses, administer oaths, require document production, and to designate special commissioners to take evidence.

Two areas of remaining tension associated with the use of military commissions concern the matters of post-trial review and evidence.[69] The rules state that the record of trial will be transmitted to a review panel of three officers, one of whom has experience as a judge (the rules do provide that the review panel can contain civilians appointed by the president). The review panel will review the record of trial and within thirty days, forward the case to the secretary of defense with a recommendation or remand the case for further proceedings. If the review panel sends the record of trail to the secretary of defense, he will then conduct an independent review and either remand the case for further proceedings or forward it to the president with his recommendation for a final decision (the rules do provide that the president can grant the secretary of defense the authority to approve the findings and sentence).

In regards to the issue of admissible evidence at trail, the rules allow that the military tribunal will operate in the traditional manner of all previous tribunals and consider hearsay evidence and information gathered without a search warrant.[70] The standard for admissible evidence is that it would have probative value to a reasonable person. In addition, witnesses may testify by telephone or audiovisual means, evidence from previous trials may be considered, and the panel may take conclusive notice of facts not subject to dispute.[71] Obviously, these "relaxed" provisions are necessary due to the exigencies of war.

4.3 Investigating Terrorist Suspects

One of the first issues of concern to draw the attention of the public following the terrorist attacks of September 11, 2001, was the possibility that other al-Qa'eda terrorist cells were at large on American soil.[72] Federal, state and local law enforcement personnel were put on the highest alert and an immediate search for suspected terrorists associated with the attacks on America began under the direction of the Department of Justice.[73]

The violation of immigration laws served as the primary authority for the FBI and immigration officials to detain well over 1,000 individuals across the United States in the wake of the terrorist attacks. Within four months about two-thirds of those detained accepted voluntary departure orders or were deported. As of the end of 2002, approximately 150 individuals were still being detained or prosecuted for possible terrorist connections. How many of those illegal aliens who were deported were terrorists is unknown. However, the FBI has broken up at least three major sleeper cells in the United States. One major radical Islamic terrorist cell operating in the Detroit area was broken up in late August 2002 and four extremists were charged.[74] In September 2002, another terrorist cell in New York was broken up by the FBI with the arrests of six Arab-Americans who had trained in al-Qa'eda terror camps in Afghanistan in the summer of 2001. In October 2002, six more terrorists were arrested in Oregon and Michigan. Four members were indicted in federal court in Oregon on charges of trying to join or help Taliban and al-Qa'eda in Afghanistan wage war on the United States.

Chapter 4: Civil Liberties and the War on Terror

To better assist law enforcement to prevent future acts of terrorism against the United States, Congress passed the Patriot Act which contains a variety of criminal procedure provisions. Because almost all of the provisions in the Patriot Act amend or add language to existing federal statues, it will be some time before the meaning and impact of many of the provisions can be fully evaluated in terms of constitutionality. For example, Section 203 of the Act amends the Federal Rules of Criminal Procedure (FRCP)[75] to allow the sharing of grand jury information with other interested federal agencies if it relates to foreign intelligence; Section 219 amends the FRCP[76] to authorize nationwide search warrants for terrorism cases; and Section 213 adds a subsection to 18 U.S.C. Section 3103a in order to authorize a delayed notice of execution of a search warrant (under specific conditions).

Although an in-depth analysis of the new changes authorized by the Patriot Act is beyond the scope of this book, the provision giving the attorney general broad powers to take into custody and detain illegal aliens suspected of terrorism will most likely prove to be the most controversial and bears analysis here. The power to indefinitely detain illegal aliens raises at the very least a constitutional due process issue under the Fifth Amendment, a matter which will most certainly require resolution by the federal judiciary.[77]

Specifically, Section 412(a) of the Patriot Act adds Section 236A to the Immigration and Nationality Act,[78] allowing the attorney general to take into custody any alien certified to be inadmissible or deportable on one of six grounds: (1) espionage, (2) sabotage, (3) export restrictions, (4) attempt to overthrow the United States Government; (5) terrorist activities, and (6) any other "activity that endangers the national security of the United States."[79] Section 412(a)(5) then requires the government to either begin criminal or deportation proceedings within seven days of the detention.[80] Ostensibly, however, Section 412(a)(6) empowers the government to indefinitely detain certain certified illegal alien terrorists who are not likely to be deported in the foreseeable future due to the continuing nature of the investigation.[81] The question of concern regards the matter how long a certified individual terrorist may be detained and under what conditions?[82]

The United States Supreme Court has yet to rule on the constitutionality of Section 412(a)(6). Nevertheless, because of a 2001 decision entitled

Zadvydas v. Davis,[83] it seems likely that the Court will probably find that Section 412(a)(6) is constitutional. In *Zadvydas*, the Court was concerned with the constitutionality of whether the government could detain a removable illegal alien beyond the removable period (i.e., indefinitely, or "only for a period reasonably necessary to secure the alien's removal from the country").[84] The Court construed the applicable section of the Immigration and Nationality Act[85] narrowly, firmly disapproving the indefinite detention of aliens who were not likely to be deported.[86] However, the Court in *Zadvydas* did recognize in the opinion that suspected terrorists could be held for indefinite periods in preventive detention.[87] The Supreme Court understood that illegal aliens detained for "terrorism or other special circumstances where special arguments might be made for forms of preventive detention," should not be affected by the general rule disapproving the indefinite detention of resident aliens not likely to be deported.[88] *Zadvydas* seemingly exempted suspected alien terrorists as a "small segment of particularly dangerous individuals" that the government could subject to indefinite detention.[89]

The Patriot Act's provision on indefinite detention for certified detainees is likely to pass constitutional muster because it actually exceeds the *Zadvydas* standard regarding suspected terrorists held on an indefinite basis. First, Section 412(b) specifically provides that judicial review of detentions of suspected alien terrorists is via habeas corpus.[90] Second, the new law proscribes fixed time limits for review of the attorney general's certification. Section 412(a)(6) provides that an alien whose "removal is unlikely in the reasonably foreseeable future, may be detained for additional periods of up to six months if release threatens national security or the safety of an individual or the community."[91] Furthermore, Section 412(a)(7) requires the attorney general to review said certification every six months and allows the suspected illegal alien terrorist to request a reconsideration of the certification every six months.[92] If these provisions are satisfied, the said terrorist suspect may be held indefinitely.

4.4 Use of the Military in Domestic Law Enforcement

There have been a number of new developments associated with the War on Terror that impact on the use of the United States military. Recognizing the need to increase military preparedness to fight the War on Terror, Congress has increased defense spending by ten percent over last year to $343 billion dollars (and $355 billion for next year).[93] More importantly, the Pentagon issued its long-awaited Quadrennial Defense Review (QDR) on October 1, 2001.[94] The QDR is the official strategic policy of how the United States armed forces should be utilized. The new QDR eliminates the long-standing vision of structuring the United States military to fight two simultaneous wars[95] and now envisions a military that is based on a "capabilities-based model" flexible enough to fight asymmetrically and to deal with, among other things, international terrorism. In short, the 2001 QDR now holds homeland security as the primary mission of the Department of Defense. In addition, the creation of a new four-star general combatant command[96] responsible for coordinating military support for defending the territory of the United States has been created.[97] The command is called Northern Command and is based in Colorado. But even with these changes, the United States has yet to cross the mental bridge from waging conventional warfare on foreign soil to developing action-oriented tactics and strategies to combat international terrorism in the homeland.[98]

One of the areas that is being looked at in the context of new missions for the American military is the question of whether a long standing law prohibiting the use of the active military to support domestic law enforcement within the borders of the United States should be revoked or modified.[99] This law is the 1878 Posse Comitatus Act which prohibits the use of the military to execute the civil laws of the United States. In full text, the Posse Comitatus Act states:

> Whoever, except in cases and under circumstances expressly authorized by the Constitution or Act of Congress, willfully uses any part of the Army or the Air Force as a posse comitatus or otherwise to execute the laws shall be fined under this title or imprisoned not more than two years, or both.[100]

Posse comitatus is Latin for "the force of the country" and refers to the English common law doctrine which empowered the local sheriff to summon able-bodied men to help enforce the law in an emergency situation. With end of Reconstruction, federal troops employed as a standing army of occupation were finally withdrawn from the South in 1877. In 1878, Congress passed the Posse Comitatus Act which stopped the practice of local or federal civilian law enforcement from being able to conscript military troops into their posses. The Act came about due to the use of federal troops in the Southern states to assist civilian law enforcement of the Reconstruction Act of 1867 following the American Civil War. It originally only applied to the United States Army, but was extended in 1947 to the Air Force. Nevertheless, the Department of Defense views the Act as applying to all services. However, the Posse Comitatus Act does not apply to a member of the Reserve component when not on active federal duty, nor to a member of the state National Guard when not in federal service.[101] Finally, the Act does not apply to the Coast Guard, which is an arm of the Department of Transportation.

Several laws grant specific exceptions to the application of the Posse Comitatus Act. United States Code, Title 18, Section 831, provides that if nuclear material is involved in an emergency, the secretary of defense may provide assistance to the Department of Justice, notwithstanding the Posse Comitatus Act.[102] The Posse Comitatus Act does not prevent the President from using the military in cases of civil disorders or emergencies. In fact, the military has been used hundreds of times in such domestic operations. The Act also does not apply to the use of United States armed forces personnel who either arrest or assist in the arrest of international criminals outside of the territory of the United States.[103] A variety of United States courts have held that military support to domestic law enforcement short of actual search, seizure, arrest, or similar confrontation with civilians does not violate the Act.[104] Specific examples of permitted support to domestic law enforcement include traffic direction and the provision of information, equipment, and facilities.[105]

With the creation of the United States Northern Command, the issue of the Posse Comitatus Act is sure to be raised again.[106] Arguments that the Posse Comitatus Act is a Congressional statute and can be repealed in toto does not rest well with the long national tradition of excluding the military from domestic law enforcement.[107] Americans clearly have an aversion to the use of soldiers as a policing force. In a letter sent to Defense Secretary Rumsfeld in October of 2001, Senator John Warner (R-VA) asked if the Posse Comitatus Act should "now be changed to enable our active-duty military to more fully join other domestic assets in this war against terrorism?"[108] For now, the answer appears to be no.

One alternative to the use active duty military force to conduct law enforcement or to respond to a major terrorist attack would be the use of

National Guard and Army Reserve to create a rapid deployment force for each state with the attendant funding to develop and train the necessary personnel. Following the 1991 war with Iraq, this idea was quickly put into full force in Israel, where a Home Defense Command was set up. Composed of 97 percent reservists, Israel has established sixty-seven stations throughout the nation in order to better deal with the aftermath of a weapons of mass destruction event. This same idea has not taken hold of policymakers in the United States.

The primary hindrance to a weapon of mass destruction rapid response force in each state rests in the massive amount of funding and training. One way to help reduce costs for developing such a force comes from the state defense forces model. United States Code, Title 32, Section 109, provides: "In addition to its National Guard, if any, a state or territory may, as provided by its laws, organize and maintain defense forces."[109] State legislatures in twenty-four states and Puerto Rico have created state defense forces to perform a wide variety of functions from light infantry duties (the Virginia Defense Force) to military police functions (Ohio Military Reserve).

Of particular interest, in looking at the mechanics of creating rapid-response forces (RRF) to deal with weapons of mass destruction, is the example set by the Texas State Guard. During 1998, for example, units of the Texas State Guard rapid reaction force "participated in 122 events, which involved 1,865 members who contributed 24,663 man-hours and saved the state's cities $490,860."[110] Activities included crowd control, traffic control, and search-and-rescue operations—just the type of activities sorely needed in the aftermath of a weapon of mass destruction terrorist attack.

4.5 Immigration

Concerns for security measures have caused the United States to revisit the issue of immigration laws regarding who is allowed into the country and under what conditions they are allowed to remain. According to the latest statistics released by the Immigration and Naturalization Service, over 30 million visas were granted to foreign nationals in 1998 to enter the United States.[111] The reason for entry into the United States generally includes reasons related to study, teach, travel, or to conduct business. Of paramount concern in weighing this figure is the fact that about 40 percent of the nation's undocumented immigrants have overstayed their visas[112] and the government has done little to correct the problem.

In the final analysis, whatever new changes Congress may make to existing immigration law, it is painfully obvious that a far better job has to be done. This critique extends from screening and background checks of individuals seeking visas to enter the borders of the United States[113] to tracking the millions of illegal aliens who have overstayed their visas. Nevertheless, concerns must be voiced in the public square that an inordinate tightening of immigration laws may promote "racial profiling,"[114] or encourage an atmosphere of bigotry and fear in the general population. Changes in the law should not negatively affect the vast majority of law-abiding aliens; no American wishes to see a return to the poisoned atmosphere that occurred when President Franklin Roosevelt ordered the internment of American citizens of Japanese descent[115] during World War II.[116]

4.6 New Information-Gathering Technologies

If the ability to engage in preventive measures to defeat terrorism are to be realized the government will most certainly seek to employ new information gathering technologies which will include at the very least the increased use of video surveillance in public places, image-recognition modeling to scan faces,[117] and eavesdropping on electronic message traffic.[118] Within days after September 11, 2001, the Attorney General proposed a laundry list of new wiretap and electronic eavesdropping powers to enable law enforcement officials to "act more quickly in fast-moving cases [of terrorism]."[119] Many of these requests, such as a revision of wiretapping laws pertaining to cell phones and so on, have already been enacted into law; many more issues are sure to be debated as the balance between privacy and security is stretched to the limit. While there exists no specific constitutional right to privacy in public places,[120] some privacy advocates fear that the next wave of government requests might "short-circuit constitutional safeguards under the guise of counterterrorism."[121] A survey of some of the new proposals for combating terrorism clearly adds to the discussion of where the line should be drawn between privacy and security.[122] Two new ideas currently in the mill involve electronic profiling and electronic eavesdropping.

Chapter 4: Civil Liberties and the War on Terror

Since the War on Terror, the Pentagon has stepped up its tests of various image-recognition technology hardware through the Defense Advance Research Projects Agency (DARPA).[123] DARPA is developing sophisticated technology that is superior to new automatic teller machines which can scan a customer's face for positive identification. This technology has already been tested in England where over 200 outdoor cameras are used in the London Borough of Newham to keep watch on "pedestrians and passerby, employing a facial-recognition system that can automatically pick out known criminals and alert local authorities to their presence."[124] These cameras can compare hundreds of thousands of faces on file against a particular subject face within seconds.[125]

An even more Orwellian advance is found in the FBI's sophisticated eavesdropping technology which uses electronic message traffic as a possible tool to track terrorists.[126] One piece of hardware is called "Carnivore" and is installed at the Internet service provider such as America Online.[127] Once installed, Carnivore can capture all messages to and from a given account, functioning as a type of wiretap that traces all calls and eavesdrops on all conversations.[128]

4.7 Assassination

In the days immediately following the terrorist attacks, serious discussions were revived concerning presidential Executive Order No. 12,333 which bans assassination.[129] The origin of the ban is traced to 1977, when President Gerald Ford issued the first executive order which prohibited political assassination.[130] In 1981, President Ronald Reagan issued his own Executive Order No. 12,333 which reads: "No person employed by or acting on behalf of the United States government shall engage in, or conspire to engage in, assassination."[131] Subsequent presidents have not changed the Reagan order banning assassination, but some senior lawmakers believe that the matter warrants reconsideration because it might impede the War on Terror.[132] This view is mistaken.

There are two interlocking principles that argue against overturning Executive Order No. 12,333. The first regards the definition of assassination and the second relates to the rule of law. Taken together, those who advocate that the ban should be lifted in order to allow the United States to engage in assassination are essentially advocating that the United States should be able to engage in "unlawful killing," or "murder."

Executive Order No. 12,333 provides no definition of assassination. A comparison of most dictionary definitions reveals that the most common definition associated with assassination is that it is "murder by surprise."[133] Since murder is per se an illegal act, the definitional problem automatically defeats any reasoned advancement of the proposition that murder should somehow be made lawful.[134] In other words, if murder is a violation of both domestic United States law[135] and international law, the executive order really does not make "illegal" something that was not already illegal.

America certainly employs violence, but only in self-defense. The use of force is rooted in the Article 51 of the U.N. Charter and can only be justified if exercised in self-defense. On several occasions, the United States has lawfully exercised the inherent right of self-defense against individuals or states.[136] President William Clinton, for example, sent cruise missiles against several al-Qa'eda terror training camps in Afghanistan following the 1998 al-Qa'eda attack on two United States' embassies in Africa. This military action was permitted under the rule of law regarding self-defense and was certainly not an act of assassination.

Similarly, the rules associated with the law of armed conflict describe lawful targets which can be destroyed in the proper context of combat operations. An enemy combatant—whether part of an organized military or a civilian who undertakes military activities—is a legitimate target at all times and may be lawfully killed, even if by surprise. On the other hand, the law of armed conflict absolutely prohibit the killing of noncombatants, except as a matter of collateral damage where civilians may be killed ancillary to the lawful attack of a military objective. In turn, civilians specifically targeted as a military objective in time of war is illegal and criminal. Thus, during the international armed conflict with the Taliban in 2001, the killing of the leader of the enemy would not be assassination as he is the "commander in chief" of the military and would be a legitimate target at all times (unless he surrendered).[137]

In short, assassination is an unlawful killing in violation of the rule of law. Assassination would be absolutely forbidden under international law even in the absence of an executive order supposedly banning the practice. The concerns about assassination as an American policy are misplaced in the War on Terror; the al-Qa'eda terrorists are legitimate military targets.

4.8 Increased Security Measures in Public Places

The final area of interest has little to do with civil rights although it is often seen as a severe restriction on the freedom of movement which Americans have long enjoyed. It has, however, much do to with inconvenience and cost to the public. Acting primarily through the rule-making power delegated to administrative agencies[138] such as the Federal Aviation Administration (FAA), the United States is steadily increasing the security of various public transportation facilities with particular emphasis on airports. Congress has passed a number of new pieces of legislation including the 2002 Aviation Transportation and Security Act[139] which requires increased airport screening through the use of advanced detection devices, physical searches and positive passenger bag match. This new law will prove a burden to both passengers and to the industry in general.[140] For instance, a proposed 12 billion dollar expansion to LAX International Airport in Los Angeles, California, was delayed until a new baggage-inspection facility[141] and screening machines required by the FAA were built.[142]

The Office of Homeland Security has implemented a new Homeland Security Advisory System (HSAS) created by Presidential Directive 3.[143] Utilizing a color-coded warning system, HSAS is an advisory system for federal, state, and local authorities to improve coordination and communication among all levels of government and the public.

It appears that increased security at public facilities and other public places is rapidly becoming a part of the reality of the modern era. It is perhaps the most obvious signpost that Americans are living in a new time. Paradoxically, it is not only our elected representatives who will decide how much security Americans will receive. Those decisions will be made in part, and implemented in the main, by administrative agencies—the so-called headless "fourth branch" of government.[144]

4.9 The Constitution and the War on Terror

To some, the War on Terror portends a society in which the rights of the individual will more and more have to give way in favor of ever increasing security measures designed to vindicate the expanding desire of protecting the safety of the public from global terrorism. It may be a correct assessment that the continuing War on Terror places our civil rights *vulnerable* to erosion, but the so-called "slippery slope" argument which resists all changes in the law must be viewed against the clear and present threat of al-Qa'eda-styled terrorist organizations and their possible use of weapons of mass destruction. The all too real specter of mass casualties, billions of dollars in physical damage, and civil disorder absolutely demands that the federal government fulfill its primary mission of ensuring the safety of its citizens and the viability of its citizens. As Justice Robert Jackson once remarked, "The Constitution is not a suicide pact."

To date, the American people have overwhelmingly approved of the overall performance of the government in finding a working balance between defending their freedoms while protecting their freedoms. Nevertheless, as the federal government makes policy and moves the nation in the War on Terror, it is prudent to well recall the caution of George Washington, "the price of freedom is eternal vigilance." Accordingly, all measures employed to combat terrorism must be within the bounds of democratic principles and the rule of law, and, more importantly, so-called extraordinary laws should be proportionate to the terrorist threat and frequently reviewed, revised, and rescinded if no longer needed.

Endnotes

1. The term civil liberties generally refers to "freedom from undue governmental interference or restraint" as measured against the protections of the Constitution. See *Black's Law Dictionary* 7th ed. (Ed. Bryan A. Garner, WestGroup, 1999).

2. U.S. Const. amend. XIV.

3. See, e.g., Malcolm Gladwell, "At Least 5 Die, 500 Hurt as Explosion Rips Garage Under WTC," *Washington Post*, Feb. 27, 1993, at A1. The February 26, 1993 terrorist attack on the World Trade Center in N.Y. prompted much discussion on the topic but no action beyond the prosecution of those directly responsible. The terrorists exploded a homemade bomb in a parking garage of the World Trade Center.

4. Antiterrorism refers to proactive steps taken to decrease the probability of a terrorist incident, e.g., increased security measures at airports, concrete barriers used to block traffic from public buildings, etc.

5. See, e.g., Brian McGrory and Michael Kranish, "Clinton Aides Regret Letting bin-Laden Off," *Houston Chronicle*, Sept. 21, 2001, at 7A.

6. The closest analogy was the domestic terror bombing in Oklahoma City in 1995.

7. See *Terrorism at Home and Abroad: Applicable Federal and State Laws*, CRS Report 95-1050 (updated Sept. 24, 2001).

8. Steven Sloan, *Beating International Terrorism* 43 (Montgomery, AL: Air University Press, 1986).

9. For a discussion regarding debate on two such bills see Thomas M. Franck and Michael J. Glennon, *Foreign Relations and National Security Law* 198-207 (St. Paul, MN: West Pub. Co., 1993).

10. Counterterrorism refers to all those steps taken by authorities in response to a terrorist attack, e.g., mobilization of medical providers, rescue crews dispatched to the scene, activation of the National Guard, etc.

11. The central Clinton-era legislation was the 1996 "Defense Against Weapons of Mass Destruction Act," commonly called the NLD Act after the sponsors. See Defense Against Weapons of Mass Destruction Act, National Authorization Act for FY 1997, Title XIV, Pub. Law 104-201, Sept. 23, 1996. This act appropriated money for 8–12 person government training teams to conduct emergency training for the firefighters, police, and medical technicians of major cities in the United States. Approximately $300,000 was sent on each city.

12. See, e.g., Bradley Graham, "Anti-Terrorism Plans Termed Inadequate," *Washington Post*, Oct. 3, 1998, at A9.

13. See Raymond E. Heddings, *U.S. Roles in Providing Humanitarian Assistance Following NBC Accidents/Incidents: The Legal Considerations*, (Colorado Springs, CO: Institute for National Security Studies 1999).

14. See *Fed. Register*, vol. 66, Oct. 10, 2001, at 51812–51817. On October 8, 2001, President Bush issued Exec. Order No. 13,228 establishing the Office of Homeland Security as an agency within the Executive Office and named Tom Ridge as the Assistant to the President for Homeland Security. In the President's September 20, 2001, address to a joint session of Congress the mission of the office is to "lead, oversee, and coordinate a comprehensive national strategy to safeguard our country against terrorism and respond to any attacks that may come." See also, http://www.whitehouse.gov/homeland_security_book.html.

15. Patriot Act.

16. The United States Naval Station at Guantanamo, Cuba was established in 1903 following the United States' war with Spain in 1898. It is not considered United States sovereign territory. The initial detention facility was named Camp X-Ray.

17. Geneva Convention of August 12, 1949, Relative to the Treatment of Prisoners of War, 6 U.S.T. 3316, T.I.A.S. No. 3364, 75 U.N.T.S. 135 [hereinafter G.C. Relative to POWs].

18. The term military tribunal is synonymous with military commissions.

19. *The Paquete Habana*, 175 U.S. 677, 700 (1900).

20. Jess Bravin, "Bush Says No Taliban, Al Qaeda Fighters Are POWs Under Geneva Conventions," *New York Times*, Feb. 8, 2002, at A20.

21. See International Law Committee Report to ABA at 7–8. "The law of war applies to non-state [sic] actors, such as insurgents. Given the degree of violence in these attacks [September 11, 2001] and the nature and scope of the organization necessary to carry them out, it is much more difficult to argue that they are not acts of war than to argue that they are."

22. The United States is not a signatory to Protocol Additional to the Geneva Conventions of August 12, 1946, and Relating to the Protection of Victims of International Armed Conflicts, June 8, 1977, 1125 U.N.T.S. 3 [hereinafter Protocol I]. Protocol I seeks to extend coverage to non-international conflicts in which "peoples are fighting against colonial domination and alien occupation and against racist regimes in the exercise of their right to self-determination. See Abraham Sofaer, "The U.S. Decision Not to Ratify Protocol I to the Geneva Conventions on the Protection of War Victims," 82 *A.J.I.L.* 784 (1988).

23. The president's determination would apply to al-Qa'eda members who were actually engaged in combat. The matter is less clear for those members of al-Qa'eda who did not actively participate in the conflict as to whether they would be considered illegal belligerents.

24. FM 27-10 para 504(g) lists as a war crime in addition to the "grave breaches" of the Geneva Conventions, the "[u]se of civilian clothing by troops to conceal their military character during hostilities."

25. But see G.C. Relative to POWs at art. 5. The determination as to status should be made by a separate military board, not the president of the United States. The applicable provision reads: "Should any doubt arise as to whether persons, having committed a belligerent act and having fallen into the hands of the enemy . . . shall enjoy the protections of the present Convention until such time as their status has been determined by a competent tribunal."

26. But see Susan Sachs, "Group Reports Mistreatment of Detainees," *USA Today*, Mar. 15, 2002, at A11. Amnesty International issued a report alleging that the United States had violated detainee's right to humane treatment. The report cites no access to lawyers, no right to challenge the lawfulness of detention, lack of a presumption of innocence, solitary confinement, heavy shackling, and lack of exercise.

27. Id. and G.C. Relative to POW at arts. 13, 22. The Bush administration has repeatedly stressed that all of the detainees were treated in accordance with the humanitarian mandates of international law and the Geneva Conventions requirement that all "prisoners of war must at all times be humanely treated [art 13]." POWs shall be afforded "every guarantee of hygiene and healthfulness [art. 22]." Numerous international humanitarian groups have been allowed to visit the detainees to include the International Committee of the Red Cross.

28. For example, speaking strictly in terms of American due process, the accused Slobodan Milosevic is being tried in the U.N. generated international war crimes tribunal in the Hague for war crimes, genocide, and crimes against humanity. Under the tribunal rules, he can be convicted on any single charge by only a simple majority of the panel of judges. A United States military tribunal would at least require a two-thirds vote for guilt.

29. *United States v. Yunis*, 681 F. Supp. 896 (1988).

30. Ihsan A. Hijazi, "Beirut Highjackers Free Travelers, Blow Up Jet," *New York Times*, June 13, 1985, at A8.

31. Id.

32. Fawaz Yunis received concurrent sentences of five years for conspiracy, thirty years for hostage taking, and twenty years of air piracy. His conviction and the D.C. court's jurisdiction was upheld by the Court of Appeals for the D.C. Circuit. See, *United States v. Yunis*, 924 F. 2d 1086 (D.C. Cir. 1991).

33. See Restatement (Third) of the Foreign Relations Law of the U.S. §§404, 423 (1987).

34. See *United States v. Benitez*, 741 F. 2d. 1312 (11th Cir. 1984), *cert. denied*, 471 U.S. 1137 (1985).

35. *United States v. Yunis*, 924 F.2d 1086, 1089–1090 (D.C. Cir. 1991).

36. Alan Cowell, "A Nation Challenged: Shoe Bomb Suspect; Reports Narrow Down Movement of Man With Plastic Explosive," *New York Times*, Dec. 28, 2001, at B5.

37. See Michael Elliott, "The Shoe Bomber's World," *Time*, Feb. 25, 2002, at 46. Richard Reid, a.k.a. Abdel Rahim, is British citizen with direct ties to the al-Qa'eda network. He attempted to explode bombs hidden in his shoes while the aircraft was in flight over the Atlantic Ocean. Each shoe contained about 4 oz. of an explosive named pentaerythritoltetranitrate. The crew and passengers subdued him. On January 16, 2002, Mr. Reid was indicted by a federal grand jury on nine counts, including the use of a weapon of mass destruction and attempted murder. Admitting his ties to al-Qua'eda and hatred for America, Reid pled guilty in October 2002 to eight charges including attempted use of a weapon of mass destruction, attempted homicide and placing an explosive device on an aircraft.

38. The United States has apparently determined that those terrorists associated with the September 11, 2001, attacks that are captured in the United States will be tried in federal district courts. See Kevin Johnson and Richard Willing, "Array of Unknowns Still Troubling U.S.," *USA Today*, Mar. 8, 2002, at A4. Zacarias Moussaoui, the alleged "20" hijacker of September 11, 2001, is being tried in a federal district court in Alexandria, Virginia in a multi-count indictment.

39. See Military Order of November 13, 2001. The President specifically relied on his constitutional authority as the commander and chief, the Authorization for Use of Military Force Joint Resolution, and 10 U.S.C. §§821, 836. The presidential order applied both to those who were implicated in the September 11, 2001, attack and to individuals complicit in "acts of international terrorism." The issue of whether individuals not directly associated with violations of the laws of war could be tried via a military tribunal is unsettled.

40. U.S. Constitution art. 3.

41. U.S. Constitution art. 1 ¶8.

42. U.S. Constitution art. 2 ¶2.

43. 10 U.S.C. §821. Uniform Code of Military Justice (UCMJ). "The provisions of this chapter conferring jurisdiction upon courts-martial do not deprive military commissions, provost courts, or other military tribunals of concurrent jurisdiction with respect to offenders or offenses that by statute or by the law of war may be tried by military commission, provost court, or other military tribunal."

44. *Madsen v. Kinsella*, 343 U.S. 341, 346 (1952). "They [military tribunals] have been called our common-law war courts."

45. See *Talbot v. Seeman*, 5 U.S. 1, 28 (1801). Chief Justice John Marshall recognized the use of military force in "partial hostilities, in which case the laws of war, so far as they apply to our situation, must be noticed."

46. *Prize Cases*, 67 U.S. 365 (1862). See also, Spence J. Crona and Niel A. Richardson, "Justice for War Criminals of Invisible Armies: A New Legal and Military Approach to Terrorism," 21 *Oklahoma City University Law Review* 349 (1996).

47. *Ex Parte Milligan*, 71 U.S. (4 Wall) 2 (1866).

48. But see *Ex Parte Mudd*, 17 F. Cas. 954 (S.D. Fla. 1868) (No. 9,899). In September 1868, the U.S. District Court for the Southern District of Florida denied a writ of habeas corpus for Dr. Samuel Mudd, a civilian citizen of Maryland, a union state, who had been convicted by a military tribunal for his part in the Lincoln assassination of April 14, 1865. On June 30, 1865, the military tribunal convicted Dr. Mudd and sentenced him to life in prison. Dr. Mudd was transferred to a prison in Florida where he filed the writ of habeas corpus relying on *Ex Parte Milligan*. In denying the petition, Judge Thomas J. Boynton distinguished the murder of Lincoln as a military crime, even though the war had arguably ended prior to the assassination of Lincoln. The appeal of this decision reached the United States Supreme Court in February 1869, but was dismissed by Chief Justice Chase as moot due to the fact that President Andrew Johnson had pardoned Dr. Mudd and two other civilians.

49. *Ex Parte Quirin*, 317 U.S. 1 (1942).

50. President Roosevelt issued Proclamation 2561 and a military order appointing a military commission after the capture of the German saboteurs. 7 Fed. Reg. 5101, 5103 (July 7, 1942).

51. *Ex Parte Quirin*, at 28. Congress incorporated the Articles of War into the UCMJ in 1950. Article 15 is now contained in substantial part at Article 21,

UCMJ. There has been no use of Article 21 to date regarding military tribunals.

52. Id. at 45–46.

53. For an excellent historical development see H. W. Elliott, The Trial and Punishment of War Criminals in the "New World Order." (unpublished doctor of juridical science thesis 1996, rare book room U. of Va. School of Law) [hereinafter Elliott S.J.D. Thesis].

54. See Jan E. Aldykiewicz, "Authority to Court Martial Non-US Military Personnel for Serious Violations of International Humanitarian Law Committed During Internal Armed Conflicts," 167 *Military Law Review* 74 (2001).

55. The international tribunal was created, and the crimes within its jurisdiction spelled out, in the London Charter of August 8, 1945. The tribunal consisted of representatives from the major allied powers—the United States, the U.S.S.R., Great Britain, and France. The accused were charged with a combination of offenses labeled: crimes against humanity, crimes against peace ("the planning, preparation, initiation or waging of a war of aggression . . . .") and war crimes. The tribunal lasted from November 20, 1945 to October 1, 1946. Twelve of the twenty-two defendants were convicted and sentenced to death, seven were convicted and sentenced to terms in prison ranging from ten years to life and three were acquitted. For a critique of some aspects of the Nuremberg trials regarding standards of proof, rules of evidence, and so on, see, H. K. Thompson, Jr., and Henry Strutz, *Doenitz at Nuremberg: A Reprisal* (New York: Amber Pub. Corp., 1976).

56. U.S. Const. amend. V.

57. U.S. Const. amend. VI.

58. See *Wong Wing v. United States*, 163 U.S. 228 (1896). The case regards aliens present in the United States and charged with criminal offenses.

59. Japanese General Tomoyuki Yamashita was tried before a United States military commission for his failure to exercise command over 20,000 Japanese sailors who engaged in a rape and murder rampage in Manila in the closing days of World War II. The court did not prove that Yamashita ordered the war crimes, but convicted him under a "should have known standard."

60. *Application of Yamashita*, 327 U.S. 1 (1946).

61. See Paul Leavitt, "Judge Rejects Lawsuit Regarding Detainees," *USA Today*, Feb. 22, 2002, at 4A. A federal district judge dismissed a lawsuit filed by "civil rights" advocates to force the United States to bring the detainees into a federal district court for trial. The Court held that the U.S. naval station in Cuba is not United States territory.

62. See Anne Gearan, "ABA Panel Supports Limited Military Trials," *Washington Post*, Jan. 8, 2002, at A4. See ABA website for post of full report. http://www.abanet.org.

63. See http://www.abanet.org/leadership/2002/8c.pdf. In the summary:
    The recommendation proposes that military commissions . . . be structured and implemented . . . having procedures that conform to those established for general courts-martial conducted pursuant to the UCMJ, and being made subject to judicial review in an appropriate federal court. The Recommendation takes no position on any issue other than those stated, and assumes that the President has inherent authority to authorize military commissions.

64. See Evan J. Wallach, "The Procedural and Evidentiary Rules of the Post-World War II War Crimes Trials: Did They Provide An Outline for International Legal Procedure?," 37 *Colum. J. Transnat'l Law* 851 (1999). Wallach discusses the standards promulgated by the President.

65. See Toni Locy and Richard Willing, "Proposal Would Widen Defendants' Rights," *USA Today*, Dec. 31, 2001, at 9A.

66 Department of Defense Military Commission Order No. 1, March 21, 2002 [hereinafter MCO #1].

67. Manual for Courts-Martial (MCM), U.S. (1988).

68. UCMJ, 10 U.S.C. §801 et seq.

69. See Jess Bravin, "Military-Tribunal Defendants Get More Rights that Bush Indicated," *Wall Street Journal*, Mar. 22, 2002, at A4.

70. This is not an uncommon matter in criminal cases in civil law countries in Europe. A panel of professional judges decide all factual and legal issues and may consider information they consider relevant to the case (e.g., hearsay). Furthermore, judges may question the accused. See, e.g., Mary Ann Glendon, Michael Wallace Gordon, and Christopher Osakwe, *Comparative Legal Traditions* 2nd ed. (St. Paul, MN: West Group, 1994).

71. MCO #1, supra at note 66, at para D.

72. See, e.g., Kevin Johnson and Toni Locy, "Terror-Related Arrests Soar," *USA Today*, Nov. 1, 2001, at A1.

73. The Department of Justice (DOJ) is the lead agency for domestic terrorism. DOJ uses the FBI as its primary action organization in this regard.

74. Danny Hakim, "4 Are Charged With Belonging to a Terror Cell," *New York Times*, Aug. 29, 2002 at A1.

75. Federal Rules of Civil Procedure 6(e)(3)(C).

76. FRCP 41(a).

77. See *Foucha v. Louisiana*, 504 U.S. 71 (1992). Protection from detention by the government rests at the heart of Constitutional due process concerns.

78. Immigration and Nationality Act, 8 U.S.C. §1001 et seq. The changes codified as 8 U.S.C. §1226A.

79. Id. at (3).

80. Id. at (5).

81. Immigration and Nationality Act, 8 U.S.C. §1001 et seq. The changes codified as 8 U.S.C. ¶1226A(6).

82. A collateral question also arises in terms of the attorney general's power to determine who qualifies is a terrorist. This question will certainly be argued along the lines of how much deference is given by the courts to the political branches in matters of national security. See, e.g., *Cooler & Gell v. Hartmarz Corp.*, 496 U.S. 384, 400 (1990).

83. *Zadvydas v. Davis*, 121 S. Ct. 2491 (2001).

84. Id.

85. 8 U.S.C. §1231(a)(6).

86. *Zadvydas v. Davis*, at 2498.

87. Id. at 2499. See also *Kansas v. Hendrickss*, 521 U.S. 346, 368 (1997) which the *Zadvydas* Court cited with approval.

88. Id. at 2502.

Chapter 4: Civil Liberties and the War on Terror 89

89. Id. at 2499.

90. 8 U.S.C. §1126B. Actually, the section limits judicial review to habeas corpus without providing for a standard of review.

91. 8 U.S.C. §1126A(6)

92. Id. at (7).

93. Adam Uymer, "Democrats in Senate Back Down on Missile Shield Issue," *New York Times*, Sept. 22, 2001, at A3.

94. For an excellent synopsis of the QRD see Ann McFeatters, "Defense Plan Begins at Home: Pentagon Drops War Preparation to Focus on Terror," *Pittsburgh Post-Gazette*, Oct. 2, 2001, at A6.

95. Robert H. Scales, Jr., *Future Warfare*, (Carlisle, PA: U.S. Army War College, 1999). Scales argued early on for the adoption of a new strategic vision based on training a prepared force to handle a variety of contingencies.

96. Combatant commands are headed by four-star general officers and are responsible for coordinating all United States military forces within a specific geographic area of the world. For example, Central Command based in Tampa, Florida is responsible for the Middle East, while Southern Command is responsible for Latin America and the Caribbean.

97. See Honorable Ike Skelton (D-MO), *Proposal for Department of Defense Homeland Defense Command*, government press release by Federal Document Clearing House, January 28, 2002.

98. See Aaron Bank, *OSS to Green Berets*, (Navato, CA: Presidio Press, 1986). This tension in tactics and strategy regarding how to fight unconventional warfare has always existed between the regular Army and the United States Army Special Forces.

99. All recent government commissions on terrorism have recommended against using United States soldiers as a quasi police force.

100. Posse Comitatus Act, 10 U.S.C. 375; 18 U.S.C. 1385.

101. Thus, the use of state National Guard personnel to conduct security screening at airports is not a violation of the Posse Comitatus Act.

102. Title 10 U.S. Code, Chapter 18.

103. *United States v. Yunis*, 681 F. Supp. 896 (1988).

104. Paul J. Rice, "New Laws and Insight Encircle the Posse Comitatus Act," 138 *Military Law Review* 109, Spring 1984.

105. Carolyn W. Pumphrey (ed.), *Transnational Threats: Blending Law Enforcement and Military Strategies* (Carlisle, PA: Strategic Studies Institute, 2000), http://carlisle-www.army.mil/usassi/welcome.htm.

106. See Terry Badger, "War Prompts Debate on Military Law," *Houston Chronicle*, Nov. 11, 2001, at A39.

107. See Thomas Lujan, "Legal Aspects of Domestic Employment of the Army," *Parameters*, Fall 1997, at 90.

108. Id.

109. 32 U.S.C. §109.

110. Captain Valentine J. Belfiglio, "State Defense Forces: Part of the Total Force," *Officer Review*, Sept. 1999, at 12.

111. For an excellent overview of the issue see Sonja Garza, "Immigration Clampdown Expected to be Far-Reaching," *San Antonio Express-News*, September 2, 2002, at A20. The 40 percent figure quoted in the text equates to anywhere between 3–5 million people.

112. Id.

113. See Eric Schmitt, "Agency Finds Itself Under Siege, With Many Responsibilities and Critics," *USA Today*, Mar. 15, 2002, p. A11.

114. Laurie Goodstein, "American Sikhs Contend They Have Become a Focus of Profiling at Airports," *New York Times*, Nov. 10, 2001, at B6 [hereinafter Profiling]. Since the attacks of September 11, 2001, the Department of Transportation (DOT) has issued memorandums to workers in transportation centers that discrimination is prohibited. The official policy of all the DOT prohibits the use of racial profiling. There have been numerous complaints of racial or religious profiling filed against airport workers.

115. See William Dudley, *Japanese American Internment Camps*, (San Diego, CA: Greenhaven Press, 2002).

Chapter 4: Civil Liberties and the War on Terror 91

116. William Harrell, executive director for the ACLU's Texas chapter compared the "current political climate and hysteria to . . . when Japanese-Americans were interned in camps."

117. This technology will be focused on immigration matters. See Customs Border Security Act of 2001, H.R. Rep. No. 320, 107th Cong. 1st Sess. 2001 WL 1558423 (Leg. Hist.).

118. See, e.g., Daniel G. Dupont, "Seen Before," *Scientific American*, Dec. 1999, at 56.

119. See Guy Gugliotta and Jonathan Kim, "Push for Increased Surveillance Powers Worries Some," *Washington Post*, Sept. 25, 2001, at A4.

120. See Restatement Second of Torts, §652B, cmt. C. (1977). An exception to the right of privacy is granted by excluding a defendant from liability when said defendant observes or photographs an individual who is not in seclusion, but rather has placed himself for public gaze. The Supreme Court has recognized a citizen's right to privacy only within the ambit of the home, the family, marriage, motherhood, and child rearing. See *Paris Adult Theatre I v. Slaton*, 413 U.S. 49, 65–66 (1973).

121. Guy Gugliotta and Jonathan Kim, "Push for Increased Surveillance Powers Worries Some," *Washington Post*, Sept. 25, 2001, at A4.

122. The United States is also preparing so-called "information warfare," where terrorists will target the Internet for electronic destruction. See Michael N. Schmitt, "Computer Network Attack and the Use of Force in International Law: Thoughts on a Normative Framework," 37 *Columbia Journal of Transnational Law* 3, 1999.

123. Conversation with Pentagon official, March 1, 2002.

124. See Daniel G. Dupont, "Seen Before," *Scientific American*, Dec. 1999, at 56.

125. Id.

126. See Marcia Coyle and Bob Van Voris, "A New Landscape as U.S. Seeks to Protect Itself," *National Law Journal*, Sept. 24, 2002, at A4.

127. Id.

128. Id.

129. E.O. 12333.

130. E.O. 11905.

131. See E.O. 12333 para 2.11.

132. Chuck McCutcheon, "Flawed Intelligence: No Easy Fix," *Congressional Quarterly*, Sept. 15, 2001, at 2146. Rep. Bob Barr (R-GA) proposed a bill (HR 19) which would have nullified the executive orders banning assassination. In regard to the ban on assassination, Sen. Jesse Helms (R-NC) noted on Sept. 11, 2001: "I hope I will live to see the day when it will once again be the policy of the United States of America to go after the kind of sneaky enemies who created this morning's mayhem."

133. But see *Black's Law Dictionary* 109 (7th ed. 1999). "The act of deliberately killing someone, especially a public figure, usually for hire or political reasons."

134. Definitional problems regarding the lawfulness of killing another human can be traced back to the Biblical prohibition on this matter found in the Decalogue at *Ex.* 20:13 and *Deut.* 5:17, which most English translations incorrectly render as: "Thou shalt not kill." In fact, the correct translation into the English is, "Thou shalt not murder." The Hebrew word for kill is not used in the prohibition. The Hebrew word that is used is *lo tirtzach* and "refers only to the criminal act of homicide, not taking the life of enemy soldiers in legitimate warfare." See R. B. Thieme, Jr., *Freedom Through Military Victory*, (Houston, TX: R. B. Thieme, Jr., Bible Ministries, 1977) at 50.

135. See Richard Shelly Hartigan, *Lieber's Code and the Law of War*, (Chicago: Precedent, 1983). Section IX of the Lieber Code is entitled Assassination. Section IX agrees that assassination is murder. "The sternest retaliation should follow the murder committed in consequence of such proclamation, made by whatever authority. Civilized nations look with horror upon offers of rewards for the assassination of enemies as relapses into barbarism."

136. W. Hays Parks, "Memorandum of Law: Executive Order 12333 and Assassination," *Army Lawyer*. Parks cites the 1986 U.S. naval and air forces attack on terrorist targets in Libya.

137. The law of war absolutely prohibit the killing of any lawful combatant who had properly surrendered. See FM 27-10, para. 470–478.

138. See, e.g., Cornelius M. Kerwin, *Rulemaking: How Government Agencies Write Law and Make Policy*, (Wash. D.C.: Congressional Quarterly, 1999) [hereinafter *Rulemaking*].

139. Aviation and Security Act, Public Law 107-71, 16 Nov. 2001.

140. See, e.g., American Airlines memorandum dated Feb. 7, 2002. http//www.aa.com

141. Dan Cray, "The New Airport: Safety Over Speed," *Time*, Feb. 11, 2002, at 17.

142. See, e.g., Matthew L. Wald, "At Airports, New Watchdog is Taking Over," *New York Times*, Jan. 27, 2002, A16.

143. See http://HSAScomments@fbi.gov.

144. See *Rulemaking*, supra note 138, at 47. Critique revolves around the fact that agencies are not specifically mentioned in the Constitution.

Chapter 5

Necessity and Rationale for the Law of War— Lessons from My Lai

Nothing is new under the sun.

—*Ecclesiastes* 1: 9–10

Synopsis
5.1 The Law of War
5.2 Voices from the Past—My Lai
5.3 Facts of My Lai
5.4 My Lai Comes to Light
5.5 Impact of My Lai
5.6 Why Did My Lai Happen?
5.7 Leadership
5.8 Lack of a Grand Strategy on the Part of the United States
5.9 Lessons of My Lai
5.10 Lesson One—Rationale for the Law of War
5.11 Lesson Two—Soldiers Must Be Trained in the Law of War
5.12 Lesson Three—Preventing Violations of the Law of War in the War on Terror
Endnotes

It is often remarked that we learn from history that we learn nothing from history. This truism has been attributed to the German philosopher Georg Hegel but the principle is certainly one of ancient origins, reflecting the fact that the human race has generally exhibited a total inability to learn even the most elementary historical lessons. Of course, the tragedy is that this need not be so, mankind can learn from history. Indeed, if history teaches mankind anything about avoiding the mistakes and disasters of the past, it is that he must first understand the historical lessons—lessons often realized only after the expenditure of incredible amounts of human blood and treasure—and then inculcate those lessons in each succeeding generation.

In the War on Terror, the most critical lesson is that the application of lawful violence is a necessary ingredient in defeating those who employ, or seek to employ, violence in an unlawful manner. The concept of lawful violence, of course, refers to the requirement that the international law of war must be fully followed. Those who violate the law of war commit war crimes.

To a large degree, from Valley Forge (1778) to Panama (1989) to the Gulf (1991) to Afghanistan (2001), the United States military can take full credit for a commendable record in its adherence to the law of war. This is because of its commitment to institutionalizing certain truisms which might be encapsulated in the old saw that "[a] right thing must be done in a right way or it is wrong."

Thus, defeating the enemy—a right thing—must be done under the law of war—in a right way—or the entire activity is wrong. This assessment is not only true in a democratic society, it is fundamentally necessary for the continuation of that democracy. Accordingly, it is necessary to explore the law of war and the rationale and necessity for abiding by those rules. Because these lessons are timeless, the very best lesson plan for the United States flows from a notorious war crime committed by American forces in the Vietnam War—the My Lai massacre.

The War on Terror involves the use of traditional combat techniques last seen in the 1991 Gulf War against Saddam Hussein, where two armed groups of soldiers engaged in open combat, but it also involves the more troubling type of combat which Americans encountered in the Indo-China conflict, where the Viet Cong and their communist allies regularly violated the law of war by refusing to wear distinctive uniforms, hiding amongst the civilian population, torturing and murdering American prisoners of war, and murdering noncombatants by the thousands. Tragically, in the Vietnam War this led to several instances of abuse of the law of war by American soldiers, the most notorious being the massacre at My Lai. While American forces in Afghanistan have generally exhibited broad compliance with the law of armed conflict and an understanding that ethical conduct and military prowess go hand in hand, it is absolutely imperative that the significance of the lessons learned at My Lai are revisited and impressed on every American soldier as the nation once again faces an enemy who engages in the same tactics as the Viet Cong and views our adherence to the rule of law as a weakness.

For many Americans the knowledge of enemy violations of the law of war elicits a negative reaction to the United States being required to follow the law of war. If the terrorists and allies of the terrorists do not abide by the rules, why should America? For this reason it is imperative that individuals who are unfamiliar with the law of war understand both the basic rationale and necessity for the law of war. This applies to the American people in general and, more importantly, to the soldiers who actually fight the enemy in the War on Terror.

Again, while it may seem out of place to discuss the law of war in the War on Terror against the lessons learned at My Lai, there is no better model to serve as the perfect vehicle for learning or relearning the necessity and rationale for the rules of armed conflict. Furthermore, it is equally necessary that American forces impress on their allies the need to comply with the law of war. In fact, reports have filtered out of Afghanistan that some of our Afghan allies have engaged in violations of the law of war. One incident is said to have occurred in the case of the deaths of 200 Taliban prisoners of war who died while being transported in shipping containers from the battlefield to internment camps. Not only is America relentlessly scrutinized and judged on how it complies with the law of war, but the conduct of our allies is also factored into the assessment. Criminal behavior casts a cloud over both the forces and the new government of Afghanistan.

As a nation that is governed by the rule of law, it is vital that America validate—for itself and for the civilized world—the legitimacy of its War on Terror by the manner in which it conducts that war. Clearly, the United States cannot claim that its forces are the "good guys," unless the rules of armed conflict are meticulously observed. Enforcement of the rules of war is a demonstration to the world and the American people that America is waging a *jus in bello*. No doubt, the attention of the world has shifted from the murderous machinations of the al-Qa'eda and their like to an extreme focus on how well the United States and its allies adhere to all aspects of the rule of law. For better or worse, this phenomenon is a reality. No one shows interest regarding the fact that the "bad guys" behave in gross violation of the law of war. After all that is precisely why they are the bad guys. On the other hand the world has an intense interest in how the "good guys" perform. If a military claims that their cause is just, they must act accordingly.

5.1 The Law of War

Warfare is not a novel phenomenon: it is as old as human history itself. Even a cursory review of the practice reveals that all cultures and societies have participated in warfare, either in defense or in aggression. Prior to the adoption of the U.N. Charter, which mandates that the analysis for determining the legitimate use of force turn under the self-defense provisions of Article 51, the concept of waging a just war was known as *jus ad bellum*. *Jus ad bellum* encompassed several elements to include: (1) the nation had a just cause; (2) the nation was acting under the legitimate governing authority; (3) the nation had just intentions; (4) the nation issued a public declaration of the causes for the use of force and the intentions associated with the use of that force; (5) the nation considered the proportionality in the results; (6) the nation demonstrated that the use of force was only used as a last resort; and (7) there existed a reasonable hope of success.

As stated, international law no longer recognizes *jus ad bellum* as a viable legal tool in determining when military force is lawful. Nevertheless, as a practical matter *jus ad bellum* still has great moral weight in the context of demonstrating the validity of the use of force and ensuring the continuation of public support in a pluralistic society for the War on Terror.

In tandem with the concept of *jus ad bellum*, the term *jus in bello* refers to just conduct in war or abiding by the law of war. This means that the nation that goes to war engages enemy targets under the concepts of military necessity, proportionality and unnecessary suffering. In contrast to *jus ad bellum*, *jus in bello* is still a recognized concept in international law. As a matter of fact, as long as mankind has practiced war there have been rules to lessen and regulate the attendant sufferings associated with warfare.

To the uninitiated in the study of war, it seems somewhat incongruent that one of man's most violent activities should be governed by rules of conduct. Some writers, such as Leo Tolstoy, have even argued that the very establishment of rules which seek to regulate warfare are per se immoral because such rules wrongfully cloak war with a form of legitimacy and are therefore counterproductive to the goal of eliminating the scourge of war. Tolstoy advanced the notion that the waging of war should not be

Chapter 5: Necessity and Rationale for the Law of War... 99

regulated at all, "when it becomes too horrible, rational men will outlaw war altogether."[1]

Fortunately, most serious thinkers reject this utopian attitude, acknowledging the necessity of rules of conduct to mitigate the various categories of sufferings that are the natural consequence of war.[2] The law of war was never intended to be an idealistic proscription against war.[3]

The current corpus of the law of war consists of all of those laws, by treaty and customary principles that are applicable to warfare. Most nations have bond themselves by international agreements to follow the law of war. Those nations that have not signed these international agreements are nevertheless bound by them if the rules have reached the status of customary international law. Customary international law comes from observing past uniformities among nations of a norm or standard that has reached widespread acceptance in the international community. Evidence of customary international law may be found in judicial decisions, the writing of noted jurists, diplomatic correspondence, and other evidence concerning the practice of states.

The cornerstone of the law of war are the Geneva Conventions of 1949.[4] In the modern era, every nation on the planet is absolutely obligated to abide by the Geneva Conventions of 1949, whether they have signed the Conventions or not. The 1949 Geneva Conventions cover four categories:

- Geneva Convention of August 12, 1949, for the Amelioration of the Condition of the Wounded and Sick in Armed Forces in the Field;
- Geneva Convention of August 12, 1949 for the Amelioration of the Condition of the Wounded, Sick, and Shipwrecked Members of Armed Forces at Sea;
- Geneva Convention of August 12, 1949, Relative to the Treatment of Prisoners of War; and
- Geneva Convention of August 12, 1949, Relative to the Protections of Civilian Persons in Time of War.

In general, the rules of warfare are focused both on the proper targeting of military objectives and the treatment of enemy detainees, prisoners of war, and other noncombatants. Examples of the law of war include such common sense rules as the requirement to treat prisoners and detainees humanely; they may not be abused under any circumstances. Also, the probation on targeting for military attack civilians or protected places, such as hospitals and religious sites, and the duty to treat all noncombatants with dignity and respect are integral components of the law of war.

In the War on Terror, Congress has not declared war under the authority granted in Article I of the Constitution. This fact makes absolutely no difference in regard to America's obligation to follow the law of war. In fact, the law of war immediately applies whenever there is an international armed conflict involving two or more states, regardless of how the parties to that conflict care to label the conflict.

Mirroring the Geneva Conventions, the United States military has codified the law of war in FM 27-10. FM 27-10 affirms that the basic goal of the law of war is to limit the impact of the inevitable evils of war by

- protecting both combatants and noncombatants from unnecessary suffering;
- safeguarding certain fundamental human rights of persons who fall into the hands of the enemy, particularly prisoners of war, the wounded and sick, and civilians; and
- facilitating the restoration of peace.[5]

Violations of the law of war are called war crimes. In FM 27-10 defines "[t]he term war crime is the technical expression for a violation of the law of war by any person or persons, military of civilian. Every violation of the law of war is a war crime."[6] The definition in FM 27-10 would include both customary and treaty law within the parameters of the law of war. War crimes are categorized as either grave breaches or simple breaches. The term grave breaches is technically only related to those violations set out as such in the Geneva Conventions. Grave breaches would include the following acts committed against persons or property specifically protected by the Geneva Conventions: willful killing; torture or inhuman treatment, including biological experiments; or willfully causing great suffering or serious injury to body or health.[7]

Under the Geneva Conventions, each nation is under a strict obligation to search for all persons alleged to have committed war crimes. They must investigate the allegations of war crimes and if a grave breach of the law of wars is discovered, the nation must either prosecute or extradite those so accused. As previously related, it is the policy of the United

Chapter 5: Necessity and Rationale for the Law of War... 101

States that all American military personnel so accused are prosecuted by military courts marital under the substantive provisions of the UCMJ.[8]

5.2 Voices from the Past—My Lai

Every army has its own mythology, its symbols of heroism as well as its symbols of shame. The army of the United States is no exception. In the sphere of heroism the American military has an incredible reservoir of noble and fantastic figures to draw from—men whose military proficiency and ethical conduct in combat have maintained an impeccable American reputation for both battlefield excellence and strict adherence to the laws regulating warfare. More than any other army in modern history, the American army is able to proudly claim as its own some of the greatest soldiers in the history of warfare. Robert E. Lee and Douglas MacArthur certainly are two of the very best this country has ever produced and therefore the subject of much study in American military schools.

Unfortunately, the United States military also has its figures of shame; soldiers who have engaged in blatant violations of the most fundamental and civilized rules regulating behavior in combat. While American misconduct is certainly an aberration and not the norm, this fact does not lessen the severity of the shame. Without question, each and every grave breach of the law of war represents a horrible scar on the credibility of the American armed forces, as well as on the civilized democracy which they protect.

The greatest emblem of American military shame in the twentieth century occurred during the Vietnam War, a war few Americans have yet to properly understand.[9] While there were several cases of unlawful killings of unarmed civilians committed by American troops during the Indo-China War, by far the most violent, and hence the most infamous, has come to be called the My Lai massacre.

Of course, any discussion of the American violations of the law of war during Vietnam, in general, and at My Lai, in particular, must be viewed against the background of the enemy's activities. In this context, American violations absolutely pale in comparison to the thousands upon thousands of command directed slaughters that were committed by the communist regime of then, North Vietnam and their Viet Cong allies. With respect to the American presence in Vietnam, My Lai can certainly be characterized as an aberration. Professor Rummel noted:

> The American record in Vietnam with regard to observance of the law of war is not a succession of war crimes and does not support charges of a systematic and willful violation of existing agreements for standards of human decency in time of war, as many critics of the American involvement have alleged. Such charges were based on a distorted picture of the actual battlefield situation, on ignorance of existing rules of engagement, and on a tendency to construe every mistake of judgment as a wanton breach of the law of war.[10]

As was the case for the Taliban and al-Qa'eda in Afghanistan, blatant violations of numerous provisions of the law of war, to include murder, torture and intimidation, were the *modus operandi* for the communists. In the estimate of Rummel, North Vietnam sponsored the slaughter of over one and a quarter million of its own people from 1945 to 1987.[11] Included in this figure, since the fall of South Vietnam in 1975, are over 250,000 boat people and 250,000 other civilians who were either ruthlessly slaughtered outright or who perished in communist death camps set up to "re-educate" non-communists.[12] Sadly, these massive crimes have never been punished, much less acknowledged by numerous human rights groups. "In sum, re-education was a label for revenge, punishment, and social prophylaxes. But unlike the Khmer Rouge who were too public about their mass killing, the Vietnamese regime cleverly and at first hid it from the outside world."[13]

Nonetheless, the enemy's barbaric conduct offers little solace to the American conscience in the wake of My Lai. Misconduct by the enemy, be it the Communists of North Vietnam, the al-Qa'eda-styled terrorists, or the minions of Saddam Hussein, in no way justifies American violations of the law of war. For the Viet Cong and North Vietnamese, the strategy for a communist victory was intentionally predicated on terror and propaganda; for the United States, the massacre at My Lai was a horrible contradiction.

5.3 Facts of My Lai

The hard facts relating to the My Lai massacre are now fairly certain, thanks to a thorough criminal investigation aimed at the perpetrators of

Chapter 5: Necessity and Rationale for the Law of War . . .   103

the crime and a collateral administrative investigation ordered by the Secretary of the Army and headed by Lieutenant General W. R. Peers.[14] Despite an initial cover-up by some of those associated with the crime, the enormity of the atrocity made it unlikely that it could long be kept secret, although for well over a year the general public knew nothing of the incident.[15]

On March 16, 1968, an American combat task force of the 23rd Infantry Division (the American Division)[16] launched an airmobile assault into the village complex of Son My in the province of Quang Ngai, South Vietnam. As was the case for all such operations, the attack was executed only after the commander of the task force, Lieutenant Colonel Frank Barker (the task force was called Task Force Barker), had assembled the key junior commanders for a final review of the details of the combat operation. This briefing, which took place on March 15, 1968, involved discussions on the positioning of helicopters, artillery preparation and the specific assignments of the three companies that comprised the task force. While the other two companies provided blocking and support functions, Charlie Company, commanded by Captain Ernest Medina, would take the primary responsibility for battling any enemy resistance encountered in the village.

At the briefing the commanders were reminded that intelligence reports had indicated that the village complex was a staging area for the 48th Viet Cong local force battalion and that the Americans could expect an enemy force of up to two hundred and fifty soldiers.[17] In short, the United States soldiers anticipated that they would be outnumbered by the enemy. Still, having yet to engage any enemy forces in direct combat, the Barker Task Force saw the operation as an opportunity to finally fight the ever-elusive Viet Cong in the open.[18]

The intelligence regarding a large enemy force proved to be incorrect. When the American combat forces landed they soon found that the village was occupied almost totally by noncombatants.[19] Although the civilians offered no resistance whatsoever, some of the members of Charlie Company went on a command directed killing spree. Under the direct supervision of several company grade officers, First Lieutenant William L. Calley, Jr., being the most notorious, American troops murdered well over 200 unarmed South Vietnamese civilians.[20]

The largest killing of civilians occurred in the hamlet of My Lai, known to the Americans by the nickname of "Pinkville," a part of the Son My complex. Thus, the entire massacre came to be known as the My Lai massacre. The murdered consisted primarily of women, children and old men; some shot in groups, others as they fled. At My Lai proper most of the civilians had been methodically herded into large groups and then gunned down, primarily under the direct supervision of Lieutenant William Calley.

In addition to the unlawful killing of civilians, the soldiers engaged in the destruction of most of the homes and in the killing of the domestic animals in the village.[21] Several cases of rape were also reported to have taken place during the massacre.[22] When it was over, the statistics told the story: one American soldier in Charlie Company had been wounded by friendly fire[23] and hundreds of South Vietnamese women, children and old men were dead.

The only positive aspect of the incident was the fact that some of the American solders had either refused to participate[24] or had openly attempted to halt the killings. Chief Warrant Officer Two (CW2) Hugh C. Thompson, Jr., was one of those who took specific actions to halt the killings. Tasked with piloting one of the helicopters during the operation, CW2 Thompson testified that he noticed large numbers of "wounded and dead civilians everywhere."[25] Assuming that the Americans on the ground would assist those who were wounded—as was the standard procedure—CW2 Thompson began to mark the location of the wounded Vietnamese civilians with smoke canisters as he flew overhead. To his horror, he witnessed the exact opposite. Drawn to the smoke, American soldiers were shooting the wounded that CW2 Thompson had so accurately marked. Still only partially realizing the full impact of what was happening on the ground, CW2 Thompson immediately landed his helicopter into My Lai, near a large drainage ditch filled with dead and dying civilians. As he began to assist those Vietnamese who were still alive to leave the area, Lieutenant Calley and a handful of troops approached.

When CW2 Thompson asked for assistance in caring for the civilians, Lieutenant Calley made it clear that he intended to kill the remaining noncombatants. CW2 Thompson recalled that Lieutenant Calley said: "The only way you'll get them [the civilians] out is with a hand grenade."[26] However, instead of backing down from the clear designs of his superior officer, CW2 Thompson quickly ordered his M60 machine gunner, Private First Class Lawrence Colburn, to open fire on the American soldiers if they came any closer to the remaining civilians. CW2 Thompson then placed all the civilians he could on his helicopter and ferried them to safety.

5.4 My Lai Comes to Light
The initial attempts to cover up the crime could not quell the nightmares of those who had witnessed the murders. Rumors of the massacre persisted, coming to a boiling point when an ex-serviceman named Ron Ridenhour sent a second hand account of the massacre to President Richard Nixon, "twenty three members of Congress, the Secretaries of State and Defense, the Secretary of the Army, and the chairman of the Joint Chiefs of Staff."[27] Ridenhour had written a four-page letter that chronicled detailed information from several of the soldiers who had either taken part in the bloody killings or had witnessed it first hand.[28]

Ron Ridenhour's letter received prompt attention both in the media and in the legislative and executive branches of government. Needless to say, the initial military reaction was one of disbelief; no one believed that, (1) a massacre of that magnitude could have been committed by American soldiers, and (2) that the massacre "could have remained hidden for so long."[29]

As the horrible truth of the crime became known, the army quickly launched the comprehensive Peers Commission investigation, popularly known as the Peers Report.[30] At the same time the general public tasted the horror of the My Lai massacre through a series of gruesome photographs of the dead which had been taken by a former army photographer named Ronald Haeberle. The color photographs appeared in the December 1969 issue of *Life* magazine.

5.5 Impact of My Lai
In the subsequent judicial actions associated with the murders at My Lai, charges were preferred against four officers[31] and nine enlisted men.[32] Twelve other officers were charged with military type offenses associated with the cover-up.[33] Of these, only Lieutenant William Calley was convicted.[34] The other officers and enlisted men either had the charges against them dismissed or were found not guilty at their courts martial.

Tried before a military panel composed of six officers, Lieutenant Calley was found guilty of the premeditated murder of twenty-two noncombatants and of assault with intent to murder of a two-year-old child. Although Calley was sentenced to a dismissal and confinement at hard labor for life, the convening authority reduced this to a dismissal and twenty years at hard labor, and the Secretary of the Army further reduced the sentence to a dismissal and ten years at hard labor.[35]

Aside from the issue of individual culpability for those involved in the massacre, My Lai had a devastating impact on the outcome of the Vietnam War. Given the total lack of any semblance of a grand strategy on the part of the United States to win the war, it can be argued that this atrocity did as much to harm the survival of an independent South Vietnam as any other single event in the Indo-China War. The public revelation of this massacre not only solidified the anti-war movement in the United States, but it cast a pall of confusion and shame over the nation at large that significantly contributed to the eventual abandonment of South Vietnam to the Communist forces in the North. Beginning in 1969, a vocal and radical minority of war protestors incorporated opposition to the American ground solder to their general opposition to the War. For these people, the enemy was now the American soldier, not the Communists. The revelation of what happened at My Lai dealt a blow to the *esprit de corps* and professionalism of the United States Army that can still be felt today.

5.6 Why Did My Lai Happen?

Taken out of the context of the social and political climates that were brewing in the United States in the late 1960s and early 1970s and viewed from a purely objective perspective, the immediate focus in the aftermath of the crime was summed up in a single word: "Why?" Why did it happen? How could so many American boys have become involved in such a heinous war crime? And, more importantly, how could the officers in command of the operation have ordered such atrocities or participated in the attempt to cover them up? To realize that some civilians were killed as a collateral matter through military action against legitimate military targets was one thing, to have ground forces intentionally shoot innocent noncombatants in cold blood was incomprehensible.

The Peers Report did not cite any one factor as the cause for the massacre at My Lai. While the panel observed that "what may have influenced

Chapter 5: Necessity and Rationale for the Law of War . . .

one man to commit atrocities had had no effect on another,"[36] General Peers was determined that the final report should reflect some explanation as to why the massacre had occurred. Recognizing the inherent difficulty in finger pointing, the panel nonetheless identified several factors that seemed to be conducive to an environment which might have led to the violations of the law of war. In fact, the Peers factors are a witches' brew that would similarly apply to any war, particularly a war in which the enemy has no regard for the rule of law.

The lack of proper training in the law of war was a common theme in the interviews of the witnesses and subjects involved in My Lai. Perhaps the most graphic illustration of this factor was reflected at the trial of Lieutenant Calley, when he testified that the classes on the Geneva Conventions conducted during Officer Candidate School were inadequate.[37] In any event, the Peers Report entered specific findings that the soldiers that made up Task Force Barker had not received sufficient training in the "Law of War (Hague and Geneva Conventions), the safeguarding of noncombatants, or the Rules of Engagement."[38] Although the requirements set out in United States Army Republic of Vietnam (USARV) Regulation 350-1, dated 10 November 1967, made it clear that, at a minimum, all soldiers were required to have annual refresher training in the Geneva Conventions, in many cases there was no command emphasis on this requirement. Hence, to that degree, the individual soldier did not know what was required of him.

Pocket sized guidance cards, which were a mandatory issue item to all soldiers to assist in learning and abiding by the law of war, were usually never read and seldom lasted past the first monsoon rains.[39] In addition, Military Assistance Command Vietnam (MACV) Directive 20-4,[40] which required the immediate reporting of all violations of the law of war, was seldom stressed by the command structure.

Regardless of the deficiencies in providing training in the law of war, the Peers Report did not find this to be a significant reason for the grave breaches[41] of multiple murders which occurred at My Lai. Such deficiencies in training might excuse minor or technical breaches of the law of war, but not the grave *malum in se* breaches. The members of the Commission correctly noted that "there were some things a soldier did not have to be told were wrong—such as rounding up women and children and then mowing them down, shooting babies out of mother's arms, and raping."[42] It was patently obvious to the Commission that some of the members of the company were simply cold-blooded criminals dressed in military uniforms,[43] both enlisted and officers. Clearly these individuals found themselves in an environment where there was little if any deterrence to the overt expression of their criminal propensities.

A tendency by some of the members of Charlie Company to view the Vietnamese people as almost subhuman was thought to be another factor which may have contributed to the massacre. Of course, the use of derogatory terms to describe the Vietnamese as nothing but "gooks," "dinks," or "slopes" was not uncommon during the Vietnam War. In fact, soldiers in all wars have developed derogatory phrases to describe their enemies;[44] it is easier to dispatch an enemy who can be characterized as different. In the My Lai case, however, the Peers Report concluded that some of the members of Charlie Company had carried this tendency to dehumanize the enemy to an unreasonable extreme, viewing the "Vietnamese [people] with contempt, considering them subhuman, on the level of dogs."[45]

To discover the reason for this degree of hatred, the Peers Report had a detailed background analysis done on each individual in Company C. The results showed nothing unusual. The company was an average unit with 70 percent of the troops having high school diplomas and nineteen having some college credits. The reason for the hatred was a result of a combination of several factors, the greatest of these merely a reflection of the locked-in arrogance inherent in the criminal mind, the least, but more common, related to the frustration of having to fight an enemy who refused to abide by the law of war.

One of the most telling factors listed in the Peers Report dealt with examining the nature of the enemy that infested South Vietnam, with the implicit criticism that the United States military was never allowed to take the war to the real enemy—North Vietnam. In the South, the United States military was asked to carry out primarily defensive operations against a well trained and well-equipped guerilla force who could not be distinguished from the local population and who refused to abide by the established principles of the law of war.

> They would set up their bunkers in villages and attack from the midst of helpless civilians. Thus, surrounding themselves with and using innocent civilians to protect themselves is in itself a war crime and makes

them criminally responsible for the resulting civilian dead . . . . [T]hey would also directly attack villages and hamlets, kill the inhabitants, including children, in order to panic the civilians in the area and cause social chaos that the communist then could exploit.[46]

As the al-Qa'eda in Afghanistan, the Viet Cong and regular North Vietnamese Army soldiers knew every path, trail, and hut in their areas of operation. In addition, whether by brute force which included public torture and execution or psychological intimidation, the Viet Cong could count on the local support of the civilian population for shelter, food, and intelligence. As such, it was not uncommon for women and children to actively participate in military operations against American forces.[47] With women and children participating in combat activities, by laying booby traps, serving as scouts or actually bearing arms, the American soldier had to disregard the traditional indicators such as sex and age as criteria for categorizing the noncombatant and concentrate instead on the extremely difficult issue of hostile intent. The Peers Report recognized this dilemma:

> The communist forces in South Vietnam had long recognized our general reluctance to do battle with them among the civilian populace and had used that knowledge to our tactical and strategic disadvantage throughout the history of the war in Vietnam. Exploitation of that reluctance by . . . [the enemy] forces caused a distortion of the classic distinction between combatants and noncombatants.[48]

The difficulty of determining friend from foe was also woefully apparent in regards to the military-aged male Vietnamese. Having developed an incredible system of underground tunnels and caves, members of the Viet Cong and North Vietnamese Army were able to appear and disappear at will. Also, when under pressure, it took only seconds to remove all military insignia or equipment and to blend in with the local population.

Without question, the use of guerilla tactics, characterized by a heavy reliance on booby traps and hit-and-run missions, had a tremendous adverse psychological impact on the American commanders and their troops. In numerous interviews, the Peers Report noted that the general attitude of the soldier was one of extreme tension at engaging this unseen enemy; an enemy who hid behind women and children and would not come out in the open to do battle.[49]

Consequently, every civilian was viewed as a potential threat, every inch of ground as hiding a potential booby trap or mine. Descriptive terms such as "keyed up" were frequently used to describe the apprehension and frustration associated with going out on patrol or, in many cases, just being in friendly villages.[50] It was not uncommon for a friendly village to be visited by the Communists on any given night, setting landmines that would kill Americans the next day. Consequently, some of those who testified before the Peers Commission naturally assumed that the "effects of mines and booby traps were the main reason for the atrocities committed by the task force."[51] This view is incorrect. While such factors undoubtedly contributed to the extraordinary level of tension in the Barker task force, it would be far too simplistic to rely on the illegal warfighting tactics of the enemy as the primary reason for the atrocity. If this factor was the main cause for My Lai, one would have expected many massacres similar to My Lai to have taken place throughout Vietnam.

Taking strong note of the overall organizational problems throughout the Army structure in Vietnam, the Peers Report actually believed that certain specific organizational problems in Task Force Barker "played the most prominent part in the My Lai incident."[52] In focusing on Task Force Barker, it was apparent that the lack of staff personnel was a serious impediment to effective command and control. The task force "could hardly function properly, particularly in such matters as development of intelligence, planning and supervision of operations, and even routine administration."[53]

One of the dominant characteristics of the Vietnam War was the lack of effective organization in the United States Army's force structure. From brigades to platoons, shortages of personnel and frequent rotations resulted in ad hoc arrangements regarding the composition of military units. Adding to the organizational deficiencies was the influx of poorly trained or ill-disciplined troops who were on "short" tours of a year.[54] The short tour ensured problems in command and control; by the time the soldier had gained the necessary experience to be an effective member of the unit, he was eligible for transfer back to the "States." In the realm of directing combat operations, the lack of effective command and control can be disastrous.

Along with the general organizational problems in the task force, there was the lack of clear plans and orders concerning the operation into

Son My. Because the entire operation was based on intelligence that anticipated a large enemy force in the area, the American soldiers initially expected that they were going to be outnumbered by at least two to one. In addition, the task force leaders regularly employed the term "search and destroy"[55] without providing an adequate definition to the troops. The phrase search and destroy was never meant to provide license to kill whatever was encountered on an operation, despite the connotation of the term. In this regard, the Peers Report found that no instructions were ever given as to how to handle the civilians that might be encountered during the Son My operation.[56]

In the final analysis, the organizational problems outlined above contributed to an overall atmosphere that made the events at My Lai possible. But the real pin in the grenade was the most fundamental aspect of the command and control problem—lack of leadership at the ground level of the operation.

5.7 Leadership

The constant mental and emotional strain associated with combat conditions is certainly exacerbated by having to face enemies like the al-Qa'eda who engage in violations of the law of war, but the factor that weighed the heaviest in explaining the massacre at My Lai was none of the four discussed above. Rather, it was the lack of responsible leadership at the very level where it was most critical—at the junior officer level.[57] Although the Peers Report faulted all levels of command—"[i]t appears . . . that at all levels, from division down to platoon, leadership or the lack of it was perhaps the principal causative factor in the tragic events before, during, and after the My Lai operation"[58]—the direct underlying deficiency most certainly rested at the company and platoon level. One of the participants of the massacre, Private Paul Meadlo recalled the orders of his officer:

> "You know what to do with them," [Lieutenant] Calley said, and walked off. Ten minutes later he returned and asked, "Haven't you got rid of them yet? I want them dead. Waste them." . . . We stood about ten to fifteen feet away from them [a group of 80 men, women and children herded together] and then he [Lieutenant Calley] started shooting them. I used more than a whole clip—used four or five clips.[59]

By virtue of the chain of command structure of the military, the primary responsibility for ensuring adherence to the law of war rests on the officer corps, with particular professionalism demanded of those junior officers at the platoon and company level, where soldiers are most apt to encounter the vast majority of issues associated with the law of war. Simply put, soldiers are expected to obey the law of war and their officers are expected to see that they do.

The difficult issue is not in how to deal with those soldiers or officers who in their individual capacities violate the law of war—they are punished by military court martial. Rather, the real difficulty is presented by the officer who orders his soldiers to commit war crimes, or who knowingly fails to control those under his command who violate the law of war. Clearly, the difficultly at My Lai was a result of command-directed breaches of the law of war in the context of lawful versus unlawful orders. Beginning with the premise that all soldiers are expected to obey lawful orders, and are subject to courts martial if they do not, how should one expect the soldier to react to an unlawful order—assuming, of course, that the soldier can even recognize the order as unlawful?

In considering the question of whether a superior order constitutes a valid defense, military courts must take into consideration the fact that obedience to lawful military orders is the duty of every member of the armed forces; that the latter cannot be expected, in conditions of war discipline, to weigh scrupulously the legal merits of the orders received; that certain rules of warfare may be controversial; or that an act otherwise amounting to a war crime may be done in obedience to orders conceived as a measure of reprisal. At the same time it must be borne in mind that members of the armed forces are bound to obey only lawful orders.[60]

Furthermore, soldiers may not normally rely on the defense of superior orders should they obey an unlawful order; they are responsible for their own acts or omissions. When the defense of superior orders is raised, however, a two-tier test is applied. The first tier is a subjective one concentrating on whether or not the accused knew that the order was illegal. If the accused did not know that the order was illegal then the inquiry shifts to what the accused could reasonably have been expected to know regarding the legality of the order. "The fact that the law of war has been violated pursuant to an order of a superior authority . . . does not constitute a defense . . . unless [the accused] did not know and could not reasonably have

Chapter 5: Necessity and Rationale for the Law of War . . . 113

been expected to know that the act ordered was unlawful."[61] Although the objective tier of the two-part test draws upon the reasonable man standard, it is really a reasonable man under the stresses present in that particular combat environment.

Moreover, the job of distinguishing the legitimacy of the orders of a superior must be viewed against the backdrop of the entire concept of enforced discipline, extending from boot camp until discharge. The requirement for enforced discipline is absolutely essential to ensure that in the unnatural conditions of the combat environment soldiers will be able to function properly. No army could ever survive without a system promoting genuine and enforced discipline, which is firmly rooted in the requirement to obey the directions of superiors. It follows then, that if soldiers are expected to obey all lawful orders, they cannot be expected to scrupulously weigh the legal merits of orders received under the stresses of combat.[62]

Accordingly, this means that the officer corps of any army must be filled with only the finest available men and women. Nowhere is this requirement more essential than in the selection and placement of the men who serve as officers in combat units. Only men of the highest moral caliber and military skill should be assigned the responsibility of command. In commenting on leadership skills for officers, General George S. Patton, Jr., correctly stated: "If you do not enforce and maintain discipline, you [officers] are potential murderers."[63]

Under the concept of command responsibility or indirect responsibility, commanders can be charged with violations of the law of war committed by their subordinates if they ordered the crimes committed or knew that a crime was about to be committed, had the power to prevent it, and failed to exercise that power. In the United States, this standard has come to be called the Medina standard, so named for Captain Ernest Medina.

A second standard for indirect responsibility for commanders that has been the object of much debate and is recognized only in the United States is the Yamashita standard. The Yamashita standard is named for the World War II Japanese general, Tomoyuki Yamashita, who was tried before a military commission for war crimes committed by soldiers under his command. The primary charge against Yamashita revolved around the 20,000 Japanese sailors who went on a murder and rape rampage in Manila near the end of the war. Although the prosecution was unable to prove that

Yamashita ordered the crimes or even knew about them, he was convicted under a "should-have-known" standard. This should-have-known theory held that if, through normal events, the military commander should have known of the war crimes and did nothing to stop them, he is guilty of the actions of his soldiers. This should have known standard applies only when the war crimes are associated with a widespread pattern of abuse over a prolonged period of time. In such a scenario, the commander is presumed to have knowledge of the crime or to have abandoned his command.[64]

Herein is the underlying tragedy at My Lai and the lesson for the coming battles in the War on Terror: several of the junior officers on the scene were totally inadequate, not only in moral character and integrity, but also in basic military skills. As exhibited by their gross behavior, these officers were completely unworthy of the responsibility of command.

When one details the background of William Calley, the centerpiece of the command directed killings, it is not surprising to discover that he was not the type of individual who should have been charged with leadership responsibilities of any nature. Having flunked out of a junior college in Miami, Florida, Calley moved west before enlisting in the army in 1966.[65] Once in the army, Calley was somehow selected to attend Officers Candidate School, where he graduated despite poor academic marks.[66] Assigned to the field as a platoon leader in a combat unit, the soldiers under his command quickly discovered that Lieutenant Calley did not even understand basic military combat skills. As one rifleman in the platoon put it, "I wonder how he ever got through Officer Candidate School. He [Calley] couldn't read no darn [sic] map and a compass would confuse his ass."[67]

In summation, the factor that most directly resulted in the crimes at My Lai clearly rests on the shoulders of a few junior officers on the ground, Lieutenant William Calley being one of the worst. All the evidence suggests that it was Lieutenant Calley who initiated much of the murder, acting both in his individual capacity and, far more shamefully, in his capacity as an officer in charge of subordinates. Abusing the authority of his position, Lieutenant Calley directly ordered the soldiers under his command to commit murder; some of the men obeyed while a few did not. While no one can pardon the behavior of those who carried out the illegal

Chapter 5: Necessity and Rationale for the Law of War . . . 115

orders, the real tragedy of My Lai was the absence of competent and virtuous leadership.

Instead of setting the standard for moral conduct, Calley performed in the exact opposite fashion. He represented the antithesis of what a commander should be. As Sun Tzu laid out almost 500 years before Christ, "[t]he commander stands for the virtues of wisdom, sincerity, benevolence, courage, and strictness."[68]

5.8 Lack of a Grand Strategy on the Part of the United States

A final factor that must be explored in any war and one that few commentators on Vietnam have properly gauged: the full impact that the lack of a grand strategy by the United States had on the outcome of the Indo-China conflict. In this regard, My Lai was possible due to the total and complete absence of a strategy to deal with the communist sponsored aggression against South Vietnam. Fortunately, President George W. Bush has established clear objectives in the War on Terror and appears to be achieving those objectives in measured steps as American forces hold rogue nations like Iraq to account. His unequivocal vision for the total defeat of the Taliban government of Afghanistan could not have been clearer. The American military understood that vision and carried it out in a magnificent manner. In the War on Terror, it is imperative that the government continue to clearly define objectives as they appear and, just as important, to carefully ensure that those objectives are achieved.

If the concept of a grand strategy is defined as the use of a nation's full national power to achieve a particular objective, it is clear that at no time did the United States have a grand strategy in Vietnam for dealing with the communist aggression. On the other hand, it is just as obvious that the communists had from the very beginning a complete and dedicated grand strategy for conquering all of Indo-China through the use of revolutionary warfare.[69] Similarly, the al-Qa'eda certainly had a grand strategy to incite the whole of the Arab world in a crusade against the West and against "moderate" Arab rulers.

The basic mechanics of a sound grand strategy takes advantage of one's strengths and the enemy's vulnerabilities, while neutralizing the enemy's strengths and one's own vulnerabilities. In practically every category of factors associated with the art of waging war, the Communists in

Vietnam were able to fulfill this formula; the United States was not. Thus, while the communists mobilized all of the people under their control in a unity of effort—from the military to the political—the United States consistently sought to disassociate the American people from the war. Fortunately, in the War on Terror, the al-Qa'eda have failed to realize their grand strategy.

In the sphere of combat operations in Vietnam, the communists were particularly effective in drawing on their strengths. Conversely, the Americans typically refused to rely on their strengths. Aware that they were no match for the far superior power of American combat forces, the communists primarily employed small hit and run tactics against selected targets; they quickly discovered that engaging the United States military in conventional warfare was pure folly. Coupled with guerilla tactics deliberately focused on becoming the unseen enemy, the communists illegally took advantage of the American respect for the law of war. By hiding themselves in civilian populations the communists intentionally sought to blur the distinction between the combatant and the noncombatant, "hoping either for immunity from attack or to provoke . . . indiscriminate attack."[70]

Establishing well-stocked sanctuaries in neighboring Cambodia and Laos, they were immune from defeat as long as the United States refused to seriously attack these bases. In the War on Terror, the United States faces a similar situation with al-Qa'eda and Taliban forces taking sanctuary in various countries in the Middle East to include Pakistan, Iran, and Iraq. In the war in Vietnam, the United States never effectually used the overwhelming strength of its military to subdue and defeat North Vietnam. Instead, American measures were confined to patrolling efforts in reaction to communist attacks in the territory of South Vietnam. In the War on Terror, the Bush administration has targeted the enemy wherever they go. Whether through cooperation with friendly nations or on its own initiative, the United States seems correctly focused on going after the enemy—in the words of President Bush, to "smoke them out."

Finally, in tandem with their guerilla tactics, the Communists relied heavily on all forms of propaganda placing special emphasis on the ambiguity of words to erode the will of the United States to continue the war. For example, they falsely portrayed the conflict as a protracted war waged by agrarian reformers with no end in sight, while simultaneously promising a negotiated settlement at any moment. Al-qua'eda, on the other hand, has failed in its use of anti-Western propaganda.

In summation, the ultimate success of the communist strategy rested primarily in the fact that the United States never developed a coherent overall strategy of its own. Necessarily, this mandated that the communist's grand strategy would eventually prevail. What is surprising is that it was not until 1968 that the impact of not having a viable grand strategy became apparent to the American soldier. When it did, however, the painful beginning of the demoralization of the United States military quickly followed. As the attendant anti-war protests at home increased, many soldiers questioned the efficacy of their sacrifices in Vietnam. More importantly, the soldiers realized that the emphasis of the American leadership was not on achieving peace through a military victory, but on peace through negotiations—negotiations which constantly promised an end to the war at any time. As a consequence, no one wanted to be the last casualty in a war that was not supported at home and which the United States government refused to let the military win.

5.9 Lessons of My Lai

The massacre at My Lai cannot be undone. However, in developing a methodology for preventing future atrocities which could occur in the War on Terror, the images of the horror of My Lai perfectly illustrate the necessity for abiding by the law of war. In this regard, the Peers Report was a valuable tool in attempting to explain some of the factors that seemed to create an environment in which violations of the law of war were more likely to occur. Taken together, these factors can be reduced to three fundamental lessons.

One of the most troubling issues for American soldiers is the realization that in many of the wars that the United States has fought, the enemy has openly and repeatedly violated numerous provisions of the law of war.[71] In the Vietnam War, the communist forces regularly engaged in command-directed atrocities on a massive scale. Just in relation to the treatment of prisoners, for example, every single American prisoner of war was subjected to torture and maltreatment in flagrant violation of the Geneva Conventions.

For many American soldiers, knowledge of enemy violations presents an immediate negative response to the law of war. The realization that the enemy may often refuse to abide by the law of war prompts an immediate gut response—"Why should I care about the rules if the enemy doesn't?" Faced with such questions, it is not enough to simply inform the soldier that he will be punished for violations, it is imperative that the soldier understand the rationale for abiding by the law of war. Thus, it is critical that the soldier's question be answered so that he possesses a basic understanding of the entire concept of the development of rules regulating combat.

5.10 Lesson One—Rationale for the Law of War

Many people have some vague notion that rules regulating warfare came out of the aftermath of World War II or, at the most, World War I. Nothing could be further from the truth. As long as there have been wars there have been rules established to reduce the suffering to both the environment and to other humans. While some of these ancient rules would not be consistent with the modern humanitarian concepts reflected in the current law of war, it is interesting to note that many of the provisions in the modern law of war are derived directly from some of the earliest formulations of rules regulating warfare.

For example, in the book of Deuteronomy the ancient Hebrews were given specific instructions on the protections that were to be afforded to the persons and property of an enemy city under siege.[72] Generally, if the city surrendered, the inhabitants were not to be harmed. If the city refused to surrender, but was subsequently captured, no women or children were to be molested. In all cases, torture was absolutely prohibited. Similarly, protection for the environment was also codified; fruit trees located outside of a besieged city were protected from unnecessary damage; the fruit could be eaten but it was unlawful to cut down the trees.

To observe that the modern law of war rests firmly upon an ancient foundation of humanitarian concerns that are intrinsically acceptable is only one reason why the rules have enjoyed universal acceptance through time—the fact that such rules are morally valuable axioms only captures part of the truth as to their development and utility. Clearly, the historical development of rules regulating warfare also follows a general pattern of what might be termed pragmatic necessity. While many of the rules limiting suffering were undoubtedly based on humanitarian concerns, it can be

Chapter 5: Necessity and Rationale for the Law of War . . .   119

argued that the basic rationales for having a law of war are rooted in several collateral principles of self-interest.

First, under the concept of reciprocity, nations would develop and adhere to laws of war because they were confident that the enemy would also do the same under a quid-pro-quo theory. This mutual assurance theory has long been recognized as not only a primary motivator for establishing rules regulating warfare, but as the centerpiece in almost every other function of international intercourse.

The second element in the historical development of the law of war centers on a similar vein of self interest, reflected so aptly by Alexander the Great's[73] admonitions to his incredible army on the eve of practically every battle: "Why should we destroy those things which shall soon be ours?"[74] Under this reasoning, particularly in the context of securing limited amounts of spoil, the destruction of anything beyond military targets to subdue the enemy's military forces would be neither beneficial nor reasonable. Under modern principles, similar violations of the law of war would not contribute to the goal of the collection of legitimate reparations, a measure often employed against the aggressor nation.

A third line of reasoning draws on the related fact that abuses seldom shorten the length of the conflict and are never beneficial in facilitating the restoration of peace. The targeting of nonmilitary property usually produces unwanted effects for those who engage in such activities. The event in American history most often used to illustrate this point comes from the activities of Union General William T. Sherman during the American Civil War. General Sherman's widespread looting and burning of civilian homes and personal property, coupled with the deliberate slaughter of all domesticated animals on his march through Georgia and the Carolinas in the last two years of the War did not significantly contribute to the collapse of the Confederacy.[75] On the contrary, his brutal actions simply strengthened the resolve of Southerners to resist while sowing the seeds of hatred for generations to come.[76]

Clearly, the intelligent warfighter makes every effort to comply with and even exceed the requirements of the law of war, particularly in regards to the treatment of prisoners of war and noncombatants. Not only does humane treatment demonstrate the best evidence that your side is the one that is waging a *jus in bello*,[77] but it often serves as the best avenue to counter enemy propaganda concerning law of war violations. As the pragmatic Prussian soldier and author, Karl von Clausewitz observed: "If we find that civilized nations do not . . . devastate towns and countries, this is because their intelligence exercises greater influence on their mode of carrying on war, and has taught them a more effectual means of applying force . . . ."[78]

A fourth factor approaches the matter from a purely military perspective. Plainly put, the use of limited military resources for the destruction of civilian targets is a waste of assets and hence, detrimental to the goal of defeating the enemy's military. In short, such conduct is simply counterproductive, "it rarely gains the violator a distinct military advantage."[79]

The final rationale, albeit of greater impact in an era characterized by the widespread dissemination of information, rests in the very nature of the modern civilized nation-state. States that adhere to the principles of democratic institutions and fundamental human rights will not tolerate activities that are conducted in defiance of the rule of law. As brought out so strongly by the My Lai incident, civilized societies will not provide the necessary homefront support for an army that is perceived as acting in violation of the law of war. Although in the radical totalitarian regime this factor is generally ignored, in the United States, as in all democratic societies, this element of homefront support is absolutely essential to any deployment and sustainment of military forces. The basic minimum "standards of morality transcend national boundaries."[80]

The necessity of homefront support is not always easy for the military to sustain. In part the difficulty rests in the associated phenomenon of "imputed responsibility." With reference to any military in a democratic society, the term imputed responsibility recognizes the fact that the acts of a few soldiers who engage in egregious abuses of the law of war are immediately imputed to the entire military establishment. For instance, because Lieutenant Calley and a handful of others murdered babies at My Lai, large segments of the public might tend to view all American soldiers in Vietnam as baby killers. To a large degree the mass media feeds this phenomenon, as reflected by almost every Hollywood movie concerning the Vietnam War. In American cinema, the soldier is routinely depicted as engaging in abuses of the law of war or ingesting large quantities of illegal drugs. The fact that the vast majority of American soldiers did neither is not shown.[81] Accordingly, the best way for the military to combat the concept of imputed responsibility is to make every effort to see that abuses do not occur and, if they do, to promptly investigate and punish those proven to be guilty. Under no circumstances can a cover-up be justified—the light must be shed promptly and fully on all allegations of war crimes.

In the modern era, then, the law of war is based on a combination of rationales reflecting a mixture of pragmatism and moral concerns. The competent warfighter should understand that the factors include:

- humanitarian concerns based on moral precepts;
- the concept of reciprocity in behavior;
- the desire for reparations;
- the desire to limit the scope and duration of the conflict and to facilitate the restoration of peace;
- the effective use of military resources; and
- the necessity for securing homefront support.

5.11 Lesson Two—Soldiers Must Be Trained in the Law of War

The second lesson from My Lai needs little introduction—to be effective the law of war must be constantly taught to soldiers. To a large degree the United States military has long held an outstanding reputation for adherence to the law of war because of its commitment to training.[82] Unfortunately, there have been periods where training has not been properly emphasized, providing fertile ground for violations of the law of war. If nothing else, the massacre at My Lai served as the "catalyst for a complete review of Army training in the law of war."[83]

The United States Army has proponency for the law of war for all branches of the military. This means that the army is responsible for developing and publishing the written doctrine. The current methodology for teaching the law of war attempts to tailor the training to the particular unit.

Since Special Operations Forces are the primary tool used on the ground in the War on Terror it is efficacious to review the current level of training that these forces receive in the law of war. In short, Special Operations Forces not only receive constant classroom instruction on the law of war but also have difficult law of war questions dealing with special operations built into their training missions which are constantly practiced.[84] The much-reported event in the Gulf War in which an Army Special Forces team had to choose between killing an Iraqi girl or being discovered by enemy forces was actually a well-rehearsed scenario resulting in a correct application of a very difficult law-of-war issue.[85] The girl was spared.

The red thread that runs throughout the issue of training the law of war is the role of the military lawyer or judge advocate. In this regard, the Army has dramatically expanded its use of military attorneys to ensure that its forces comply with all aspects of the law of war.[86] All combat forces have an operational law[87] attorney assigned at the Division level. Likewise, all Army Special Forces groups have a specialized military attorney assigned. The function of this judge advocate is not only to ensure compliance with and adherence to the law of war but to examine the full range of international and domestic laws that affect specifically "legal issues associated with the planning for and deployment of United States forces overseas in both peacetime and combat environments."[88] This is a major change from the role of the judge advocate in Vietnam—a role primarily delegated to the administration of criminal law, well behind the front lines of combat.

Currently, the function of the judge advocate in the field can be divided into two elements—he has both preventive and active roles. In the preventive role, the judge advocate advises commanders on potential issues dealing with rules of engagement, targeting enemy military objectives, and all other relevant aspects of the law of war. In addition, the judge advocate is deeply involved in providing instruction and training to soldiers within his particular command.

In the active role, the judge advocate is involved in the investigation of allegations of war crimes. The requirement to investigate is either carried out directly by the legal officer or is closely monitored by the judge advocate. Finally, the judge advocate will be called upon to either prosecute or defend those charged with violations.

5.12 Lesson Three—Preventing Violations of the Law of War in the War on Terror

As noted, the importance of professional conduct on the battlefield extends to both the strategic, political, and social realms. In turn, the primary responsibility for inculcating professional conduct falls directly on the officer corps. Nowhere is the need for training in the law of war more critical than in the proper development of the military's officer corps. Thus, no officer should be given the responsibility of leadership without two essential factors: (1) technical proficiency in the profession of arms; and (2) the highest ethical and moral courage. Under the ancient Roman adage that no man can control others until he can first control himself, officers must be thoroughly prepared in both of these areas. Combat command should only be offered to officers who have been thoroughly scrutinized and put through extensive field training exercises designed to test their reaction under combat pressures.

There can be no question that the primary cause of My Lai was the lack of disciplined control (i.e., the lack of any real leadership). Such leadership is absolutely essential in preventing war crimes. The associated tensions set out by the Peers Report were not the real problem at My Lai—tensions of combat will always be present in one form or another. The real problem was in the effective control of those tensions. Control of warfighting pressures rest not only with the individual soldier but directly with his commanding officer. Sadly, many of the officers in Charlie Company not only allowed the illegal manifestations of battlefield stress to be exhibited by their troops, but through their orders and example they initiated and actively participated in the atrocities. There can be little doubt that proper officer leadership could have prevented the murders at My Lai. Consequently, the primary responsibility for these crimes is on their heads. The function of leadership is to hold up the professional torch at all times, at all costs.

Great armies are neither created, nor sustained, by accident. To a large degree, great armies are maintained by officers who understand, and then are able to apply, the lessons of military history. In this respect, no officer truly can be called a professional without a firm commitment to the moral and ethical rules regulating combat. Quite naturally, this objective requires constant training, as well as a comprehensive understanding of one's moral roots. Consequently, the military of the United States constantly must reaffirm its commitment to the positive values of military proficiency and ethical integrity.

For instruction, inspiration, and inculcation, American officers can find no better role model than General Robert E. Lee. While some may forget, ignore, or purposefully deny the role that Lee has had in shaping our modern military, to those who are objective, his impact never can be obscured. To those who rediscover him through the pages of history, he still has much to impart. That the American military establishment proudly has maintained its reputation not only for sound military tactics, but also for an unmatched sense of humanity, is well known.[89] One of the men most responsible for all of this—General Lee—is not as well advertised. Perhaps the passage of time has concealed his name. On the other hand, Lee's fame may have been reduced by an unfortunate legacy, marred in the minds of many Americans who still lack an understanding of his motive for joining his State of Virginia when it left the Union.

In spite of the fact that its greatest champion often is overlooked, Lee's tactics and civility have become ingrained into the character of the United States military establishment. Although these qualities certainly existed before the emergence of Lee the general, his genius and humanity have epitomized and translated them into the very fabric of subsequent American military doctrines. For this reason, any analysis of the United States military—either in terms of tactics or comportment with the law of war—that ignores the tremendous contributions of General Lee never can be more than a fraction of the truth. More closely than any other officer in this nation's history, Lee has proved to be the most qualified to project the American standard of behavior in these areas.

For example, although some Southerners criticized Lee for not authorizing lawful reprisals[90] to deter Union violations of the law of war, General Lee firmly believed that reprisals were not the answer. Responding to a letter from the Confederate Secretary of War regarding possible Confederate responses to Union atrocities, Lee reiterated his position in the summer of 1864:

> As I have said before, if the guilty parties could be taken, either the officer who commands, or the soldier who executes such atrocities, I should not hesitate to advise the infliction of the extreme punishment they deserve, but I cannot think it right or politic, to make the innocent . . . suffer for the guilty.[91]

With Americans fighting Americans, Lee knew that the long-term effects of engaging in reprisals would not be profitable for the nation or the South. He was undoubtedly correct; Lee's strict adherence to the rules regulating warfare, coupled with his firm policy prohibiting reprisals, contributed greatly to the healing process after the War.

One of the driving forces that created the legend of Lee, the ultimate gentleman, was his unmatched sense of humanity. "Lee was the soldier-gentleman of tradition, generous, forgiving, silent in the face of failure . . . a hero of mythology."[92] No matter how great the temptation for legitimate reprisals, a concept well recognized in international law, R. E. Lee would not stoop to the level of his enemies. This is one of the reasons he has been called the "Christian General,"[93] as reflected in his address to the troops as they marched into Pennsylvania during the Gettysburg campaign of 1863:

> It must be remembered that we make war only on armed men, and that we cannot take vengeance for the wrongs our people have suffered without lowering ourselves in the eyes of . . . Him to whom vengeance belong-eth." Instructing his officers to arrest and punish all soldiers who committed any offense on the person or private property of civilians, he reminded them that "the duties exacted of us by civilization and Christianity are not less obligatory in the country of the enemy than in our own.

Perhaps the most telling tribute to Lee came from his former enemies. When General Lee died in 1870, newspapers throughout the North universally praised his military genius and morality.[94] The *New York Herald* said: "In him the military genius of America was developed to a greater extent than ever before. In him all that was pure and lofty in mind and purpose found lodgment. He came nearer the ideal of a soldier and Christian general than any man we can think of."[95]

Unfortunately, even the best lessons of history quickly fade unless they are inculcated. Future My Lais cannot be prevented unless the answers to the "why" of My Lai are repeated over and over; until they are ingrained into every warfighter in uniform. Just as Americans must never forget their rallying cries of honor and nobility—"Remember the Alamo"[96]—they must be forced to deal with their nightmares—"My Lai." On the other hand, it is precisely because of its horror and repulsiveness that My Lai is uniquely suited to serve as the primary vehicle to address the entire issue of adherence to the law of war as well as the necessity for effective leadership in the modern era.

The final caveat in the War on Terror is that the American military cannot afford to take these lessons lightly. Given the fact that knowledge acquired beyond basic trial and error methodologies requires varying degrees of academic effort, it is not surprising that over time, both individually and collectively, many lessons of history will be forgotten and thus, repeated.[97] This fact is particularly devastating when viewed in the context of man's efforts to reduce the continuing pattern of human warfare. Accordingly, not only must the lessons of My Lai be remembered—they must be inculcated.

Endnotes

1. Leo Tolstoy, *War and Peace* 45 (New York: The Modern Library, 1983).

2. See, generally, Dietrich Schindler, ed., and Jiri Toman, *The Laws of Armed Conflicts* (Norwell, MA: Kluwer Academic, 1988).

3. See Department of Army Pam 27-161-2, *International Law* Vol. 11, at 35 (23 Oct. 1962).

4. The 1949 Geneva Conventions cover four categories: (1) Geneva Convention of August 12, 1949, for the Amelioration of the Condition of the Wounded and Sick in Armed Forces in the Field, 6 U.S.T. 3114, T.I.A.S. No. 3362, 75 U.N.T.S. 31; (2) Geneva Convention of August 12, 1949 for the Amelioration of the Condition of the Wounded, Sick, and Shipwrecked Members of Armed Forces at Sea, 6 U.S.T. 3217, T.I.A.S. No. 3363, 75 U.N.T.S. 85; (3) Geneva Convention of August 12, 1949, Relative to the Treatment of Prisoners of War 6 U.S.T. 3316, T.I.A.S. No. 3364, 75 U.N.T.S. 135; and (4) Geneva Convention of August 12, 1949, Relative to the Protections of Civilian Persons in Time of War, 6 U.S.T. 3316, T.I.A.S. No. 3365, 75 U.N.T.S. 287.

5. FM 27-10, at para. 2.

6. FM 27-10.

7. FM 27-10, at para. 509.

8. FM 27-10 at para. 506(a). See also supra Chapter 2, note 34, at 870–91, *Law Among Nations* 870-91 (Princeton. NJ: Princeton University press, 1972).

Chapter 5: Necessity and Rationale for the Law of War . . . 127

9. See, e.g., *The Vietnam Debate* (John Norton Moore, ed., 1990); John Norton Moore, *Law and the Indo-China War* (1972). There exists an entire series of myths concerning the Vietnam War dealing with such issues as the lawfulness of the United States intervention, the nature and purpose of the Communist Party in North Vietnam, and the reasons for the failure of the United States to carry the war into North Vietnam to win a military victory.

10. See Rummel, supra Chapter 3, note 14.

11. Id.

12. Id. at 48–52.

13. Id. at 46.

14. Lt. Gen. W. R. Peers, *The My Lai Inquiry* (1979) [hereinafter Peers Report]. The Secretary of the Army and the Chief of Staff, United States Army, issued a joint directive for Lt. Gen. William R. Peers to explore the original Army investigations of what occurred on March 16, 1968 in Son My Village, Quang Ngai Province, Republic of Vietnam. The overall investigation is known as the Peers Report. Specifically, General Peers was tasked to determine:
   1. The adequacy of such investigations or inquiries and subsequent reviews and reports within the chain of command; and
   2. Whether any suppression or withholding of information by persons involved in the incident had taken place.

   See also Joseph Goldstien et al., *The My Lai Massacre and Its Cover-Up: Beyond the Reach of Law?* 29 (1976) [hereinafter *My Lai Massacre*].

15. For an excellent discussion of the initial breaking of the story see William Wilson, "I Prayed to God That This Thing Was Fiction . . . ", *American Heritage*, Feb. 1990 [hereinafter Wilson], at 44.

16. Id. The troops making up the task force were from the 1st Battalion, 20th Infantry, 11th Light Infantry Brigade.

17. Peers Report, supra note 14, at 47. Total enemy strength in Quang Ngai Province in the spring of 1968 was thought to be between 10,000–14,000 men.

18. Id. The Son My area had been the scene of numerous incidents where many Americans had been killed or wounded by booby traps and snipers during the past few months. Charlie Company had lost two dead and thirteen wounded in a minefield on February 25, 1968. On March 14, 1968, a popular sergeant had been killed and three other soldiers wounded by a booby trap. In total,

Charlie Company had lost twenty soldiers killed or wounded in the Son My area.

19. Id. at 103. Of enemy combatants the Peers Report found the following: "The evidence indicates that only three or four were confirmed as Viet Cong, although there were undoubtedly several unarmed Viet Cong men, women and children among them and many more active supporters and sympathizers . . . ."

20. Although the official count of the dead was 175, this figure was certainly low. The dead may have reached almost 400. Id. at 1, 314. But see George Esper, "Twenty Years Later, My Lai Remains a Symbol of Shame," *Los Angeles Times*, 13 March 1988, at 2A; Rummel, supra note 10, at 32. Rummel puts the figure at 347. The current communist regime in Vietnam has erected a plaque in My Lai with the names of 540 men, women and children listed as dying in the massacre.

21. See Peers Report, supra note 14, at 277. The report from the Son My Village Chief dated March 22, 1968 listed as destroyed 90 percent of the animals and houses.

22. See *My Lai Massacre*, supra note 14, at 343. The Peers Report made specific findings in reference to one platoon leader, Lieutenant Steven K. Brooks: "Although he knew that a number of his men habitually raped Vietnamese women in villages during operations, on 16 March 1968, he observed, did not prevent, and failed to report several rapes by members of his platoon while in My Lai . . . on 16 March."

23. Id. at 493. It is probable that the single casualty was a self-inflicted gun shot wound by one of the members of Company C who was seeking to avoid participation in the operation.

24. Wilson, supra note 15, at 49. One of the soldiers who had refused to participate was Sergeant Michael Bernhardt. Sergeant Bernhardt did not, however, attempt to halt his fellow soldiers from the killings. He stated, "It was point blank murder, and I was standing there watching it."

25. Id. at 50.

26. Id.

27. Id. at 46.

Chapter 5: Necessity and Rationale for the Law of War . . .   129

28. The letter read in part:

> It was late in April, 1968 that I first heard of "Pinkville" [My Lai] . . . . It was in the end of June, 1968 when I ran into Sargent [sic] Larry La Croix at the USO in Chu Lai. La Croix had been in 2nd Lt. Kally's [sic] platoon on the day Task Force Barker swept through "Pinkville." What he told me verified the stories of the others, but he also had something new to add. He had been a witness to Kally's gunning down of at least three separate groups of villagers. "It was terrible. They were slaughtering the villagers like so many sheep." Kally's men were dragging people out of bunkers and hootches and putting them together in a group. The people in the group were men, women and children of all ages. As soon as he felt that the group was big enough, Kally ordered an M-60 (machine gun) set up and the people killed. La Croix said he bore witness to this procedure at least three times . . . . This account of Sargent La Croix confirmed the rumors that Gruver, Terry and Doherty had previously told me about Lieutenant Kally . . . . I have considered sending this to newspapers, magazines, and broadcasting companies, but I somehow feel that investigation and action by the Congress of the United States is the appropriate procedure . . . .

29. Peers Report, supra note 14, at 7. See also *My Lai Massacre*, supra note 20, at 274–75. The Army knew that the Communists had reported the alleged killing of civilians at My Lai but the reports were largely ignored as in keeping with the common communist technique of outrageous propaganda. One notice that was captured in late March 1968 was entitled "Concerning Crimes Committed by US Imperialists and Their Lackeys Who Killed More Than 500 Civilians at Tinh Khe Village (Son My), Son Tinh District." It stated:

> Xam Lang (Thuan Yen) Subhamlet of Tu Cung Hamlet and Xom Go Subhamlet of Co Luy were pounded by artillery for hours. After shelling, nine helicopters landed troops who besieged the two small hamlets, killing and destroying. They formed themselves into three groups: one group was in charge of killing civilians, one group burned huts, and the third group destroyed vegetation and trees and killed animals. Wherever they went, civilians were killed, houses and vegetation were destroyed and cows, buffalo, chickens, and ducks were also killed. They even killed old people and children: pregnant women were raped and killed. This was by far the most barbaric killing in human history.

30. See Peers Report, supra note 14.

31. Two other key officers involved in the massacre, Lieutenant Steven Brooks and Lieutenant Colonel Frank Barker, had been killed in Vietnam before the formal investigation into My Lai had begun. The Peers Report found that Lieutenant Brooks had "directed and supervised the men of his platoon in the systematic killing of at least 60–70 noncombatants in the subhamlets of My Lai and Binh Tay." The Peers Report found that Colonel Barker had been involved in the cover-up of the massacre. See *My Lai Massacre*, supra at 343. The officers charged with murder were Captain Ernest L. Medina, Captain Eugene M. Kotouc, 1st Lieutenant William L. Calley, Jr., and 1st Lieutenant Thomas K. Willingham. See Peers Report, supra at 227.

32. The enlisted men charged with murder were Sergeant Kenneth L. Hodges, Sergeant Charles E. Hutton, Sergeant David Mitchell, Sergeant Escquiel Torres, Specialist 4 William F. Doherty, Specialist 4 Robert W. T'Souvas, Corporal Kenneth Schiel, Private Max Hutson, and Private Gerald A. Smith. See Peers Report, at 227.

33. These consisted of Major General Samuel W. Koster, Brigadier General George H. Young, Colonel Oran K. Henderson, Colonel Nels A. Parson, Lieutenant Colonel Robert B. Luper, Major Charles C. Calhoun, Major David C. Gavin, Major Robert W. McKnight, Major Frederic W. Watke, 1st Lieutenant Kenneth W. Boatman, and 1st Lieutenant Dennis H. Johnson. See Peers Report, at 221–222.

34. *United States v. Calley*, 22 U.S.C.M.A. 534, 48 C.M.R. 19 (1973).

35. William Calley, Jr., actually only served a total of three years under house arrest at Fort Benning, Georgia and nine months at the confinement facility at Fort Leavenworth, Kansas. Calley was released from confinement at Fort Leavenworth when his sentence was overturned by a Federal District Judge in Georgia. When the Fifth Circuit Court of Appeals reinstated the conviction, Calley was not returned to confinement, he was paroled by the Secretary of the Army. He works today in his father-in-law's jewelry store in Columbus, Georgia.

36. Peers Report, supra note 14, at 229.

37. See *United States v. Calley*, 46 C.M.R. 1131 (A.C.M.R.) aff'd. 22 C.M.A. 534, 48 C.M.R. 19 (1973). But see Interview with Lindsay Dorrier, in Charlottesville, VA. (12 Mar. 1992). A former classmate of Calley, Mr. Dorrier recalls that the Officer Candidate School did provide adequate law of war training to the students. Indeed, all those going through Officer Candidate School received training in the four Geneva Conventions.

Chapter 5: Necessity and Rationale for the Law of War... 131

38. Peers Report, supra note 14, at 230.

39. See *My Lai Massacre*, supra note 20, at 220. Four of the cards were entitled "The Enemy in Your Hands," "Nine Rules," "Code of Conduct," and "Geneva Conventions."

40. Military Assistance Command Vietnam (MACV) Directive 20-4 (20 Apr. 1965) required the immediate reporting of any alleged violation of the law of war to the next higher military authority as well as directly to MACV Headquarters located in Saigon.

41. See FM 27-10 at 179.

42. Peers Report, supra note 14, at 230.

43. While one may possess a propensity for criminal behavior, all behavior is directly controlled by the individual's volition. In turn, the act of choosing to commit a crime is often related to crude cost benefit analysis. Obviously, crime is more likely to occur in an environment where the likelihood of punishment is minimal. For an excellent discussion on how the criminal mind functions, see Dr. Stanton E. Samenow, Jr., *Inside the Criminal Mind* (New York: New York Times Books, 1984).

> Criminals cause crime—not bad neighborhoods, inadequate parents, television, schools, drugs, or unemployment. Crime resides in the minds of human beings and is not caused by social conditions. Once we as a society recognize this simple fact, we shall take measures radically different from current ones. To be sure, we shall continue to remedy intolerable social conditions for this is worthwhile in and of itself. But we shall not expect criminals to change because of such efforts.

44. In World War II Americans called the German "Krauts" and the Japanese were called "Nips." In the Gulf War some American troops referred to the Iraqis as "rag heads."

45. Peers Report, supra note 14, at 230.

46. Rummel, supra note 10, at 24.

47. *My Lai Massacre*, supra note 20, at 199.

48. Id. at 198–99.

49. Id.

50. Peers Report, supra note 14, at 234. The suggestion that members of Task Force Barker were high on marijuana or alcohol were found to be without substance and not a significant factor in the operation.

51. Id. at 235.

52. Id.

53. Id. at 235.

54. Id. Many of the combat officer positions were rotated after only six months in the field.

55. Peers Report, supra note 14, at 236. The term "search and destroy" is a term no longer used in the military. During Vietnam it was defined as a "military operation conducted for the purpose of seeking out and destroying enemy forces, installations, resources, and base areas." See *My Lai Massacre*, at 389.

56. Peers Report, supra note 14, at 237.

57. My Lai was not the only command directed atrocity in Vietnam. A few less extensive killings did take place where superiors ordered subordinates to kill civilians. See, e.g., Gary D. Solis, *Marines and Military Law in Vietnam: Trial by Fire* (1989) [hereinafter *Marines and Military Law*] at 176. Lance Corporal Michael S. Krichten (Vietnam, 1970):

> [Lance Corporal] Herrod gave the order to kill . . . the people, and I told him not to do it . . . . Then he says, "Well, I have orders to do this by the company commander, and I want it done," and he said it again, "I want these people killed!" And I turned to PFC Boyd, and I said to PFC Boyd, "Is he crazy, or what?" And Boyd said, "I don't know, he must be" . . . And then everybody started opening up on the people.

58. Peers Report, supra note 14, at 232.

59. Wilson, supra note 15, at 44. Another witness, Private First Class Dennis Conti, related at the trial of Lieutenant Calley that he and Meadlo were told to "take care of the people." But when Lieutenant Calley returned he was upset that the civilians had not been killed. Lieutenant Calley then stated, "I mean kill them."

60. Id. at para. 509.

61. Id.

62. Id.

63. Porter B. Williamson, *Patton's Principles: A Handbook for Managers Who Mean It* at 35 (Tucson, AZ: Management & Systems Consultants, Inc., 1979).

64. See Lawrence Taylor, *A Trial of Generals* at 165–67 (South Bend, IN: Icarus Press, 1981).

65. Wilson, supra note 15, at 50.

66. Id.

67. Id. Remarks of rifleman Roy L. A. Wood.

68. *Art of War*, supra Chapter 1, note 17, at 9.

69. See Kevin M. Generous, *Vietnam, The Secret War* (Twickenham, England: Hamlyn, 1985). The term "revolutionary war" refers to a strategy characterized by disinformation and guerilla tactics.

70. Thomas J. Begines, "The American Military and the Western Idea," *Military Review*, March 1992, at 39, 42.

71. See Louis Henkin, et al., *Might v. Right* 126 (New York: Council on Foreign Relations, 1991) at 126. The Iraqi conduct during the Gulf War made a mockery of almost every precept in international law. In fact, throughout the entire Gulf War, Saddam Hussein made no attempt to even conceal his open and flagrant violations of the law of war, the United Nations Charter, or any other applicable international norm. As one Pentagon official noted, "It was as if Saddam Hussein awoke each morning and asked, 'What international law shall I violate today?'"

72. *Deuteronomy* 20:10–20. But see *Deuteronomy* 21:17–18. Some mandates were given for the Hebrews to kill all of the citizens of a few selected cultures. This practice was the exception and was related to halting the spread of systematic human sacrifice and phallic cult practices associated with those cultures.

73. Alexander the Great (356–323 B.C.) conquered an enormous empire which extended from India to Europe and Asia Minor to North Africa. Alexander is recognized as the finest strategist, tactician and military commander in the

ancient world. See Ernest Dupuy and Trevor N. Dupuy, *The Encyclopedia of Military History,* (New York: Harper & Row, 1977) at 47–54.

74. Id.

75. See Thomas Robertson, "The War in Words," *Civil War Times Illustrated,* Oct. 1979, at 20. "Although the havoc wreaked by Sherman's hordes contributed to the Confederate defeat, this contribution was so indirect and ambiguous that it did not justify militarily, much less morally, the human misery that accompanied and followed it;" Jeffrey F. Addicott, "Operation Desert Storm: R. E. Lee or W. T. Sherman?" 136 *Military Law Review* 115 (1992).

76. See, e.g., Russel F. Weigley, *History of the United States Army* (Bloomington, IN: Indiana University Press, 1984), at 301.

77. See William V. O'Brien, *The Conduct of Just and Limited War* (New York: Praeger, 1981), at 37–70.

78. Karl von Clausewitz, *On War,* at 4 (J. Graham trans. 1918).

79. H. Wayne Elliott, "Theory and Practice: Some Suggestions for the Law of War Trainer," *Army Lawyer*, July 1983, at 1 [hereinafter Theory and Practice].

80. Id.

81. See *Marines and Military Law,* supra note 57, at vii. The vast majority of military personnel in Vietnam served with honor. In the Marines, "[o]f the 448,000 Marines that served in Vietnam, only a small percentage came into contact with the military justice system. By far the greater number served honorably and never committed illegal or improper acts."

82. But see Fredrick A. Graf, "Knowing the Law," *Proceedings*, June 1988, at 58. If the U.S. record is measured against the rules and not against its adversaries the record has "been far from perfect."

83. Theory and Practice, supra note 79, at 9.

84. See Gary L. Walsh, "Role of the Judge Advocate in Special Operations," *The Army Lawyer*, Aug. 1989, at 6–8.

85. Douglas Waller, "Secret Warriors," *Newsweek*, 17 June 1991, at 20. Each Special Forces Group has a military attorney assigned as the Group Judge Advo-

Chapter 5: Necessity and Rationale for the Law of War . . . 135

cate. Part of the function of this officer is to deal with operational law issues associated with special operations.

86. See, e.g., James A. Burger, "International Law—The Role of the Legal Advisor, and Law of War Instruction," *The Army Lawyer*, Sept. 1978, at 22; William H. Parks, "The Law of War Advisor," 31 *JAG J.* 1 (1980).

87. See David E. Graham, "Operational Law (OPLAW)—A Concept Comes of Age," *The Army Lawyer*, July 1987, at 9.

88. One major effort to better prepare operational law attorneys was the establishment of the Center for Law and Military Operations (CLAMO) by Secretary of the Army, John O. Marsh Jr., in December of 1988. CLAMO is located at the Judge Advocate General's School in Charlottesville, Virginia. The goal of the Center is to examine both current and potential legal issues attendant to military operations through: the use of professional exchanges such as symposia, consultations, and advice; writing, reviewing, editing, commenting on, and publishing, as appropriate, reports, treatises, articles, or other written materials; and ensuring access to a well stocked joint service OPLAW library. In short, the Center serves as a source for, guide to, and clearinghouse of information about operational law and national security law. See Jeffrey F. Addicott, "Operational Law Note: Proceedings of the First Center for Law and Military Operations Symposium," 18–20 Apr. 1990, *The Army Lawyer*, Dec. 1990, at 47–57.

89. See David K. Hall et al., *Force Without War* (Washington, DC: Brookings Institution, 1979) at 9. No nation has been as active as the United States in adherence to the rules of warfare, as well as the peacetime use of its forces "in providing disaster assistance and similar supportive activities."

90. When one party to the conflict violates an established rule of law, the injured party has the right to respond with a use of force that otherwise would be unlawful. Reprisals are not designed to punish the offending party, but to persuade it to cease and desist the illegal conduct. Under current rules, several criteria—some required by domestic policy—must be met before the United States may resort to reprisals. At the time of the Civil War, the injured party first would have to provide a warning to the wrongdoing belligerent. If the wrongdoer refused to comply, then the injured belligerent could employ a response proportionate to the initial illegal act. See FM 27-10, para. 497.

91. 30 *Southern Historical Society Papers* 94 (1902).

92. Id. at 1.

93. See, e.g., Paul C. Nagel, *The Lees of Virginia* (New York: Oxford University Press, 1990) at 301. Lee's view on Christian salvation was devoid of any form of human merit or morality although by the measure of any society, his own moral standards were impeccable. Grace oriented, he wrote, "I can only say that I am a poor sinner, trusting in Christ alone for salvation."

94. Lee died in Lexington, Virginia, where he served as the president of Washington College from 1865 to 1870.

95. See J. William Jones, *Life and Letters of General Robert Edward Lee* (1906) at 482. The *Cincinnati Enquirer* said, "He was the great general of the Rebellion. It was his strategy and superior military knowledge which kept the banner of the South afloat for so long . . . ." The Philadelphia Age called him "a great master of defensive warfare . . . probably not [to be] ranked inferior to any general known in history."

96. See Lon Tinkle, *13 Days to Glory: The Siege of the Alamo* (New York: McGraw-Hill, 1958). For thirteen days in March of 1836, 187 Americans fought off a Mexican Army that outnumbered them by 30 to 1. The battle took place in the Alamo at San Antonio, Texas. Although all of the Americans could have escaped they choose to fulfill their duty, even knowing it meant certain death—all died in combat (killing 1,600 Mexicans in the process) to buy time for the birth of the Texas Republic. The subsequent battle cry of "Remember the Alamo" was used by General Sam Houston in the defeat of the same Mexican forces later that year.

97. Many military writers have lamented the fact that basic historical lessons related to combat are not emphasized, even at our military academies. See, e.g., Jeffrey Record, "Our Academies Don't Teach The History of War," *Harper's Magazine*, Apr. 1980, at 26; Jay Luvaas, "Military History: Is it Still Practicable?" *Parameters*, Mar. 1982, at 2; Colonel T. N. Dupuy, "Practical Value Largely Unappreciated, History and Modern Battle," *Army*, Nov. 1982, at 18.

Chapter 6

A New Paradigm for War and Terrorism Avoidance

Before we bring all the U.S. troops and all the coalition troops out of here . . . we must set conditions that prevent a reintroducing of the sorts of people that caused us to be standing where you and I are standing right now.[1]

—General Tommy Franks

Synopsis
6.1 The Causes of Aggression and Terrorism
6.2 The New Paradigm for War and Terrorism Avoidance
6.3 Defining Democratic Values and Democracy
6.4 Origins of Human Rights
6.5 The Corpus of Human Rights Law
6.6 United Nations Efforts to Promote Human Rights
6.7 Non-Governmental Organizations Devoted to Human Rights
6.8 Regional Organizations to Promote Human Rights
6.9 Traditional Efforts of the United States in Promoting Human Rights
Endnotes

Apart from the fact that the United States emerged from the Cold War as the sole remaining superpower, a promising by-product of the disintegration of the communist dictatorship was the addition of dozens of nascent democracies into the community of nations. At the time, little thought was given to the long-term effect of this phenomenon. Nevertheless, some recognized very quickly that the world was more secure not only because an evil system of government had been swept into the dust bind of history, but because it was replaced by governments that earnestly wanted to embark on the road of democracy. Strongly advocating the need for the world community to foster the development of these new and struggling democracies, the director of the Center for International Studies at New York University School of Law noted: "The world will certainly miss the boat if it does not use the end of the cold war to create a global system for the new millennium, one which preserves peace, fosters economic growth, and prevents the deterioration of the human physical and environmental condition."[2] In essence, a handful of scholars recognized the efficacy of a very simple truth in both war and terrorism avoidance. As previously noted, this truth was best summed up in the words of Anthony Lake: "[D]emocracies tend not to wage war on each other and they tend not to support terrorism—in fact, they don't. They are more trustworthy in diplomacy and they do a better job of respecting the environment and human rights of their people."

Now, just over a decade later, a new window of opportunity is opening for a similar shift towards democracy. This time the winds of freedom are poised to fan across the Arab world. Separated from all the horror, misery, and tragedy of war associated with the United States led campaign against terrorist aggression, there is comfort in the fact that America and the international community of civilized nations may be able to further advance an often ignored paradigm for reducing the likelihood of terrorism and war, at least at the international level.

Although it is true that the Islamic and Arab community of nations are plagued with non-democratic governments, it is erroneous to label that corner of the globe as a monolithic conglomerate of countries that embrace the radical Nazi-like totalitarianism of Iraq, Iran, Libya, Syria, and the virtual state of the al-Qa'eda. In addition, it is equally erroneous to assume that the vast majority of people who live under the tyranny of these dictatorships do so with any degree of loyalty or enthusiasm. Basic denials of human rights are not a matter of "cultural heritage." Given the choice between freedom and dictatorial rule, rational humans will always choose freedom. This basic truth was demonstrated with the fall of the Taliban regime. Even without a viable frame of reference for what democracy really entails, the common people of Afghanistan enthusiastically welcomed the promise of freedom. Over 1.8 million Aghans have returned since the fall of the Taliban, the largest movement in thirty years. The window of opportunity, then, centers in the hope that as dictatorships fall in the War on Terror they will be replaced with some form of liberal democracy. This certainly must be the ultimate goal in Afghanistan. This is the hope in the rest of the region as the War on Terror intensifies.

The international community, especially the well-established democracies led by the United States, has a critical role to perform in the promotion of democratic values and human rights. The task of promoting genuine democratic standards of behavior into whatever new governments take hold will not be a simple undertaking. In far too many instances, forces of intolerance—ethnic, nationalistic, racial, and religious—will certainly permeate both the new governments and the societies from which they are formed. For instance, the new government in Afghanistan may desire the concepts associated with democracy but a general pattern of ethnic and sectarian fragmentation has introduced an escalating and often uncontrollable level of disorder and violence. Thus, if America and the international community does not find a realistic way to promote and foster at least the most fundamental categories of democratic values and human rights, the flames of terrorism and aggressive war will burn bright once again. Totalitarianism always stands hungrily at the door of freedom.

6.1 The Causes of Aggression and Terrorism

The most troubling aspect of all in addressing terrorism and war avoidance begins with the question of what causes people, or more precisely, governments, to commit gross violations of human rights and unlawful violence? Clearly, this is a critical issue as it is directly related to the attendant matter of how to best halt terrorism and aggression. Thus, the question becomes whether there is a way to rid the planet of these scourges apart from the use of armed force?

In reviewing the human experience of the last six thousand years, one could list a host of factors related to the use of aggression by a country against both its own people and its neighbors to include such things as religious conflict, ethnic strife, territorial disputes, population pressures, and competition for limited resources. While all of these external factors may be catalysts for aggression, any discussion that fails to examine the basic nature of man can never capture more than a part of the real truth. Theologians such as R. B. Thieme, Jr., often stress that the root of the matter centers on the makeup of man: "In our beings are all the seeds of great conflicts."[2] Holocaust victim Anne Frank also amplified this point in her diary:

> I don't believe that the big men, the politicians and the capitalists alone, are guilty of war. Oh no, the little man is just as guilty, otherwise the peoples of the world would have risen in revolt long ago. There's in

people simply an urge to destroy, an urge to kill, to murder and rage, and until all mankind, without exception, undergoes a great change, wars will be waged, everything that has been built up, cultivated, and grown will be destroyed and disfigured, after which mankind will have to begin all over again.[4]

Moreover, nations are made up of people. The troubles of the world are not beamed onto earth from some hostile alien force. Since violations of the rule of law in terms of aggression and terrorism are generally associated with corresponding human lusts for power and approbation, one must put the responsibility for violations not only on the external factors created by man, but on the darker angles of mankind himself. Although numerous excuses are always voiced by the perpetrator, violations are ultimately a reflection of the problems that rest inside each individual, who, according to the basic tenets of every major religion, is morally flawed. Thus, the question of what causes a person to commit a *malum in se* crime can be asked collectively of a government that engages in a consistent pattern of aggression and human rights violations.

On the individual level, observations about the sinister side of some societies strongly reinforces the Judeo-Christian doctrine of the total depravity of man. However, the view that there will always be aggressive warfare and terrorism in the world, like crime in society, is only partially correct. Crime on the national level and aggressive violence on the international level can be controlled. The concept of the total depravity of man voiced by Anne Frank applies primarily to theological questions (e.g., the mechanics of salvation).[5] The concept does not mean that mankind is in a state of total helplessness and wickedness *vis-à-vis* other people. On the contrary, operating under the principles of freedom and self-determination, civilized peoples have come together to form national entities so that they might produce the by-products of privacy, justice and economic prosperity.

Under such a model, nation-states have prospered and flourished, but only to the extent that they have recognized the collateral need to protect those rights on interior and exterior lines. On interior lines, states must recognize the legitimate functions of a police and judicial system to punish criminal behavior; on exterior lines, nation-states must recognize the need for a strong military establishment to protect the nation from the aggressive behavior of dictatorships and the supporters of terrorism.

Objectively, much of what we know about the nature of governments created by man comes from the record of their histories; records written in streams of blood. For example, to observe that various governments have engaged in horrendous acts of aggression against their own people and others simply describes their behavior, but only partially explains it. In fact, no one has ever satisfactorily explained why certain societies—ancient Assyria, Soviet Russia, Nazi Germany, North Vietnam, Communist China, or Iraq—turned into aggressive war machines that committed murderous human rights violations against their own people.

What has been established, are the characteristics of those nations that have a high propensity for engaging in aggressive war, terrorism, and human rights abuses. National Security law expert and ABA Director of the Center for National Security Law, Professor John Norton Moore, argues that totalitarian regimes like the Taliban and Iraq are considerably more likely to resort to aggressive violence than democracies. Professor Moore terms this phenomenon the "radical regime" syndrome.

> A radical totalitarian regime . . . seems to blend together a mixture of a failing centrally planned economy, severe limitations on economic freedom, a one party political system, an absence of an independent judiciary, a police state with minimal human rights and political freedoms at home, a denial of the right to emigrate, heavy involvement of the military in political leadership, a large percentage of the GNP devoted to the military sector, a high percentage of the population in the military, leaders strongly motivated by an ideology of true beliefs including willingness to use force, aggressively anti-Western and antidemocratic in behavior, and selective support for wars of national liberation, terrorism, and disinformation against Western or democratic interests.[6]

Tyrants seek the destruction of freedom loving peoples. Some, like the Taliban and Iranian regimes, cloak themselves in radicalized versions of Islam, others, like Iraq and Syria have no driving religious affiliation. All of these regimes are linked, however, by a common bond of hate, power lust, and aggression to gain, maintain, and extend power. Human rights, the rule of law, and civilian control are alien concepts to totalitarian governments because the freedom inherent in these concepts cannot coexist with tyranny.

6.2 The New Paradigm for War and Terrorism Avoidance

Recognizing a nexus between the nation that mistreats its own citizens and the nation that fosters aggression against its neighbors, "[b]oth the preamble and Article 1 of the United Nations Charter make crystal clear that the drafters were under the impression that the unleashing of aggressive war occurred at the hands of those States in which the denial of the value . . . of the individual human being . . . was most evident."[7] Furthermore, with the outstanding research of eminent scholars such as Professor R. J. Rummel, it is now possible to demonstrate numerically the validity of the proposition that totalitarian regimes are the chief abusers of human rights:

> War is not the most deadly form of violence. Indeed, I have found that while about 37,000,000 people have been killed in battle by all foreign and domestic wars in our century, government democide [genocide and mass murder] have killed over 148,074,000 million more. Plus, I am still counting. Over 85 percent of these people were killed by totalitarian governments.[8]

So, the new paradigm for war and terrorism avoidance is a very simplistic model: If democracies make better neighbors, *a fortiori*, it is certainly in the best interests of the United States to do all it can to foster democratic values and human rights in the emerging nations and to thereby enlarge respect for the rule of law in international relations. In the words of Professor B. Russett, "[D]emocracies have almost never fought each other . . . By this reasoning, the more democracies there are in the world, the fewer potential adversaries we and other democracies will have and the wider the zone of peace."[9]

All can understand the simplicity of Russett's argument. In fact, Professor Moore firmly believes this simple fact represents a "new and more accurate paradigm about war, peace, and democide."[10] It replaces the old thinking of peace through appeasement and rubricates the only hope for reducing the threat of weapons of mass murder, terrorism and human

Chapter 6: A New Paradigm for War and Terrorism Avoidance 143

rights abuse. Appeasement leads to more aggression. This view is further amplified by a recent RAND study:

> The failure of regimes to provide for peaceful political change and the phenomenon of economies unable to keep pace with population growth and demands for more evenly distributed benefits can provide fertile ground for extremism and political violence affecting U.S. interests. For this reason, the United States has a stake in promoting political and economic reform as a means of reducing the potential for terrorism, some of which, as in Latin America, the Middle East, and the Gulf, may be directed at us.[11]

Unfortunately, the paradigm seems to be extremely difficult to propagate. In part, this is because democratic ideals are not spread through the use of force—of fire and sword—so that windows of opportunity for change generally only appear in the aftermath of the defeat of a totalitarian regime. This occurred in the Axis powers of Germany, Italy, and Japan following World War II and then again with the end of the Cold War in the former territories of the Soviet Union. In addition, the paradigm is difficult to advance because people in democracies are often lulled into complacency and apathy about the conditions of fellow humans on the planet. They forget the truth that democracies are far better systems of government than any other. To borrow a phrase from the British novelist Rebecca West, "The trouble with man is twofold; he cannot learn those truths that are too complicated and he forgets those truths that are too simple." The realization that democracies do not engage in terrorism or aggressive war is clearly a "simple truth" that must be reinforced at every turn.

In the War on Terror, the United States needs to accelerate efforts to encourage the full development of any fledgling democracy under the truism that democracies do not wage war or allow terrorism to flourish. If the RAND study is correct, this strategy will go far in reducing the root causes of terrorism.

The primary criterion for winning the War on Terror, then, must concentrate on a realistic examination and application of this simple, yet powerful, formula, a formula related directly to the enhancement of United States' interests as it addresses the long-term goal of curtailing of the aggressive use of force. In fact, the truism about the behavior of democracies is predicated upon United States' interests; in no way does it pit American domestic interests against issues of international concern. In the context of either peace or deterrence, they are one and the same.

If one accepts the paradigm as valid three issues immediately arise. First, what precisely are these values associated with democracy? Second, are these values merely a Western ethnocentric assertion of power over other non-democratic nations? Third, what is the best way to promote these values?

6.3 Defining Democratic Values and Democracy

In 1788, Massachusetts adopted a state bill of rights which proclaimed: "A frequent recurrence to fundamental principles is absolutely necessary to preserve the blessings of liberty and to maintain a free government." These fundamental principles generally refer to all of those basic rights associated with democratic forms of governments and is best encapsulated in the Constitution's Bill of Rights approved by Congress in 1789 and ratified in 1791.

Before America stood up as a democracy, early Western scholars such as John Locke, David Hume, Baron de Montesquieu, and Jean-Jacques Rousseau wrote extensively on the subject of "civic humanism" or "natural rights" and the proper function of government in relation to the citizen. These scholars agreed with the premise that individuals came together to form national entities so that the individual could, within the framework of a state, better protect and advance his inherent rights to life, liberty, and property.

Contrary to the practice of the majority of the countries of their day, these men pointed out that the government was formed to be the guardian of basic human freedoms, not the usurper. For instance, in his *Second Treatise of Government*, John Locke wrote: "The legislative or supreme authority cannot assume to itself a power to rule by extemporary, arbitrary decrees, but is bound to dispense justice, and to decide the rights of the subject by promulgated, standing laws, and known authorized judges."[12]

The writings of these early scholars had a tremendous impact on the American rebels of 1776. Faced with the task of articulating a moral justification for their armed secession against the colonial rule of Great Britain, Thomas Jefferson and others were obliged to carefully translate Locke's natural rights into legal and enforceable rights. Apart from dealing with the continued evil of human servitude, the American drafters were largely successful. In their Declaration of Independence to the British Crown, they declared that the individual, simply by virtue of his God-given being, possessed the "right to life, liberty, and the pursuit of happiness." The Declaration of Independence's powerful opening showed that the framers were not inventing out of whole cloth the ideas and ideals they embraced. The men who penned the Constitution and the Declaration of Independence were drawing on the wisdom of the ages to bring together a proper balance between freedom and authority. Freedom without authority is anarchy and authority without freedom is tyranny. In the Declaration of Independence they proclaimed:

> We hold these truths to be self-evident, that all men are created equal, that they are endowed by their Creator with certain inalienable rights that among these are Life, Liberty, and the pursuit of Happiness. That to secure these rights, Governments are instituted among Men, deriving their just powers from the consent of the governed.

In two sentences, the framers laid out a fantastic manifesto that recognized the dignity of man exercising his God-given rights through a democratic government formed to protect the fundamental rights of its citizens. For the Americans, these rights were rooted in Divine providence which made them inalienable and morally justified *ab initio*. As Benjamin Franklin remarked at the Constitutional Convention in 1787, "I have lived, Sir, a long time, and the longer I live, the more convincing proofs I see of this truth: that God governs the affairs of men."

With their freedom purchased through six long years of bloodshed on the battlefield, the colonial Americans produced one of the most phenomenal documents in the history of mankind—the Constitution of the United States of America. The Constitution established a democratic government operating under principles which forever united the terms freedom and democracy. In the minds of many, the terms are synonymous. When one speaks of the desirability of promoting democratic values, however, this does not necessarily imply the adoption of a direct democracy as the ideal form of government.

The United States of America was created as a representative democracy (i.e., a republic); it is not a true direct democracy in the fashion of the ancient Greek city-states. The founding fathers were extremely careful in their choice of government. They rejected the concept of a pure democracy where all citizens have an equal and direct voice in government and chose instead a representative democracy. The framers restricted the franchise of participants and established three separate independent branches of government, with checks and balances to ensure that the authority of the central government was truly limited. *Webster's Third New International Dictionary* defines a representative democracy as "a form of government in which the supreme power is vested in the people and exercised by them indirectly through a system of representation and delegated authority in which the people choose their officials and representatives at periodically held free elections . . . ."

In weighing the usefulness of a direct democracy against a representative democracy, it is interesting to note the words of historian Alexander Fraser Tytler, who wrote about the decline and fall of the Athenian Republic. He concluded:

> A [direct] democracy cannot exist as a permanent form of government. It can only exist until the voters discover that they can vote themselves money from the public treasury. From that moment on, the majority always votes for the candidates promising the most benefits from the public treasury with a result that a democracy always collapses over loose fiscal policy always followed by dictatorship.[13]

If democratic principles do not necessarily mesh with direct democracy as the best form of government, they certainly do equate to what Daniel Webster envisioned as "a state of society characterized by tolerance toward minorities, freedom of expression, and respect for the essential dignity and worth of the human individual with equal opportunity for each to develop freely to his fullest capacity in a cooperative community." It is certainly possible that a government that is honest, accountable, predictable, and efficient can conform to democratic principles and protect human rights; although the modern era has demonstrated repeatedly that a representative democracy is best suited to produce democratic principles and is, therefore, the government of choice in reference to the paradigm for war and terrorism avoidance.

Still, governmental authority in a state may be vested in one person, a small group, a large group, or the entire body. Measured in the light of human rights and democratic principles, none of these systems are necessarily per se worse than any other; it is just that representative democracies have institutional safeguards (such as checks and balances on power) that can guarantee fundamental freedoms over the long term.

For instance, the framers instituted three basic types of activities for the government. First, a system of checks and balances was established to ensure that the government fulfilled its obligation to protect the life, freedom, privacy, and property of law-abiding citizens. Second, laws were instituted to better regulate commercial and social disputes between individuals. And third, the government was asked to set up certain physical infrastructures to provide essential services that were beyond individual capabilities, such as providing for basic primary education, law enforcement, and a military establishment.

The factor that divides good government from bad government is in the degree to which the government allows the functioning of democratic principles under the framework of the law. Clearly, a ruling system that provides its citizens with freedom of expression, peaceful assembly, a free market economy, and some degree of participation in government rests on democratic principles. Thus, a monarchy, an aristocracy, or a representative democracy that rules for the common good of the citizen under democratic principles can each be positive manifestations of government. Other forms of government such as a tyranny or an oligarchy wield authority based solely on the self-interest of the ruling elite and refuse to embrace freedom.

In addressing the issue of writing democratic constitutions for the emerging democracies of Europe, Professor A. E. Dick Howard of the University of Virginia School of Law, commented on this friction concerning what government is all about.

> The Bill of Rights of the United States Constitution declares what government may not do; it is what Justice Hugo Black once called a list of "thou shalt nots." The document reflects the view that the function of a bill of rights is to limit government's powers. Central and East European drafters have enlarged this meaning of "rights." A legacy of the twentieth-century notion of positive government, an age of entitlements, is

bills of rights that declare affirmative rights. Such bills include, of course, the traditional negative rights, but they also spell out claims upon government, such as the right to an education, the right to a job, or the benefits of care in one's old age.[14]

Forced equality through social engineering is the policy and propaganda of the totalitarian system. As Professor Howard has discovered, many of the emerging democracies out of the former U.S.S.R. have still not shaken this old thinking. The true function of good government emphasizes freedom and self-determination which will always lead to varying degrees of social inequality. Faced with Lord Acton's often quoted truism that "power tends to corrupt, and absolute power corrupts absolutely," the government that adheres to principles of freedom is much preferred.

In the modern era the terms democratic principles and fundamental freedoms have been joined by the concept of human rights. The report of the June 1993 World Conference on Human Rights held in Vienna and attended by 171 states, defined the relationship between democracy, fundamental freedoms and human rights as follows:

> Democracy, development, and respect for human rights and fundamental freedoms are interdependent and mutually reinforcing. Democracy is based on the freely expressed will of the people to determine their own political, economic, social and cultural systems and their full participation in all aspects of their lives .... The international community should support the strengthening and promoting of democracy, development and respect for human rights and fundamental freedoms in the entire world.[15]

Indeed, since some wrongly criticize the concept of democracy as a Western value it may be more appropriate to speak to the world politic in terms of the normative concept of human rights. Human rights evokes a more inclusive standard which can apply to all the peoples and nations of the world. As a practical matter, of course, there is no difference between democratic values and human rights.

6.4 Origins of Human Rights

When the framers of the Constitution wrote about the Law of Nations they were addressing those principles of international law that governed state-to-state contacts. The individual, at most, was viewed only as an object in the process. As recently as fifty years ago, the leading treatise on international law reflected the absence of legal recognition to the issue of international human rights. Lassa Oppenheim wrote: "[A]part from obligations undertaken by treaty, a State is entitled to treat both its own nationals and stateless persons at discretion and that the manner in which it treats them is not a matter with which International Law, as a rule, concerns itself."[16]

While general humanitarian concerns for individuals have always been around in the marketplace of world ideas, it has only been since the close of the Second World War that legal norms in the context of human rights have emerged. Before this period, humanitarian concerns such as eradicating the evil of slavery were handled to a large degree by each individual state. Nevertheless, as each of the Western powers eradicated the institution, the abolition of slavery gradually became a principle of customary international law. Thus, fueled by the formation of the United Nations in 1945, an entire system of human rights legal principles, some by treaty and some by custom, slowly emerged.

In the last half of the twentieth century, no concept has done more to advance positive change in the social and political spheres of human experience than human rights. In the quest for bettering the quality of human life, human rights have had a major impact in shaping world opinion and events. In this context, human rights have increasingly served as the basis for reaching consensus on defining the fundamental pillars upon which all "just" governments should be anchored. As the preamble to the Universal Declaration of Human Rights asserts, human rights serve "as a common standard of achievement for all peoples and all nations."

In the modern era, human rights have emerged as a significant moral and legal force in modern domestic and international relations. In its most comprehensive meaning, human rights encompasses all those principles and concerns associated with ensuring respect for the inherent dignity of the individual human being. In this sense alone can individuals ever be called equal, since each human being, regardless of his abilities or handicaps, possesses the same right of respect for his person and property. The problem, of course, is in the extent to which individual governments are willing to define, recognize, and then enforce the inherent human rights each citizen possesses.

Because mankind is organized into national entities or states, human rights have their primary meaning as they relate to the relationship of the individual and the national entity. In contrast to the situation of only a few generations ago, when the sovereignty of the state was the fundamental principle upon which international law was based, the rapid development of international human rights norms and standards now requires the sovereignty of the state to be weighed and measured against what might be called the sovereignty of the individual.

Despite the phenomenal inroads that human rights have made in the world arena, the goal of universal acceptance and adherence has not been achieved; the path continues to be strewn with adversity. Although the term human rights rolls off the tongue with great ease, one of the most frustrating issues associated with the study of human rights is the fact that there is no standard definition of the term human rights. The legal definition of rights usually refers to claims recognized and enforced by law, but human rights can encompass a far broader category of issues, many not deemed to be legally binding in the context of either domestic or international law. Thus, without a clear definition, the range of issues human rights should encompass continues to be debated.

Juxtaposed to the strict definitional problem, another obstacle in reaching a universal consensus on defining human rights rests in the polarization of the term. Without question, the term human rights has numerous connotations, making it extremely popular over the entire political and social spectrum to describe, with equal vigor, almost any and every aspect of the human condition. Furthermore, because the term is freely used by groups with diametrically opposed agendas and ideologies—often without honest assessment or examination—human rights are often treated as a disposable tool to achieve a political end. The result is that the unwary or casual observer is left with a term that is saddled with wide-ranging ambiguities as to its meaning and goals.

For example, during the Cold War both the Soviet Union and the United States routinely accused one another of human rights abuses. The United States would accuse the Soviets of violating human rights, pointing to the systematic denial of all categories of human freedom related to person and property as a function of the totalitarian regime. In turn, the Soviets would vehemently charge the United States and other capitalist countries with "headline grabbing" human rights abuses (in order to divert attention from their own abuses and to further ongoing machinations to advance communist ideology throughout the globe.)

Of course, in the debate of which system of government commits the worst violations of human rights, one point is generally clear, totalitarian governments are hypocritical in their professed support for human rights, democracies are not. Although individual acts of human rights abuse can occur under any form of government, there is a vast difference between totalitarian regimes and democratic governments. Totalitarian regimes are guilty of institutional denials of human rights, routinely carried out as the *modus vivendi* of government.

In contrast, human rights violations in democracies are generally caused by individuals operating under their own authority and outside of normal institutional procedures. Accordingly, democracies are far more likely to care about human rights and to investigate and punish those public officials guilty of human rights violations.

Another mark of the phenomenal degree of support for human rights in democracies is that human rights are accepted as vitally important considerations across the entire political spectrum. For instance, in the United States, all major political platforms, be they conservative or liberal, recognize and endorse the need for the promotion of the most fundamental categories of human rights both in America and throughout the globe. Liberals and conservatives may disagree on the degree or method of promotion, but both advocate the pursuit of human rights as the primary vehicle for the advancement of peace and stability.

As a consequence of the support given to human rights by the democracies, the world community by treaty and custom formed essentially since the close of World War II, has arrived at a general consensus on certain basic human rights which all mankind should enjoy. Because this basic category of international human rights is universally recognized, they are commonly referred to as "international human rights." In the realm of international law, international human rights can be generally defined as that body of universally recognized inalienable rights that every individual is entitled to and that every government must guarantee.[17]

At least in the sphere of this consensus, international law no longer recognizes the unrestricted right of the state to deal with its citizens or aliens in any manner it so desires. International human rights law transcends international borders. The often-heard quip of England's King

George when asked for help during France's reign of terror no long applies—"If a country chooses to go mad within its own borders, it may do so."

Without question, the linchpin of international human rights law advocates one of the most fundamental functions of the national entity—to protect the human rights of the individual. In this sense, respect for international human rights is the *sine qua non* of civilized society and failure of the state to afford such protection can lead to a wide range of sanctions—political, economic and even judicial.

Apart from the desire to halt external aggression, the U.N. Charter was also designed to address fundamental issues related to international human rights. If the desire for curtailing aggressive war was the justification for restricting some aspects of the external exercise of a state's sovereignty, the drafters intended human rights to be the justification for examining a state's internal ability to generally treat its citizens in any manner it wished.

Although the references to human rights in the U.N. Charter are set out in extremely general terms, they nonetheless clearly set the tone for all future treaties and covenants related to human rights. For example, the preamble to the U.N. Charter states that the peoples of the United Nations have determined to "reaffirm faith in fundamental human rights, in the dignity and worth of the human person [and] in the equal rights of men and women . . . ." This is followed by language in Article 1 (3) which, under the purpose of the U.N., calls for member nations to promote and encourage "respect for human rights and for fundamental freedoms for all without distinction as to race, sex, language, or religion . . . ."

With the creation of the United Nations, work quickly began on a series of international agreements and instruments designed to accomplish the two major themes in the Charter—restricting war and promoting human rights. Many of the efforts resulted in widespread and immediate acceptance of various international agreements throughout the nations of the world to include the 1949 Geneva Conventions.[18] While the Geneva Conventions do not deal with restricting warfare, *jus ad bellum*, they are deeply concerned with *jus in bello*.[19]

It was at this time that human rights moved from a "vision in the minds of some men, of an ideal aspiration towards universal values of law,"[20] to the reality of a world that began to acknowledge the existence and validity of international human rights. Next to the U.N. Charter, the primary document that frames the basic principles, as well as the future aspirations, for an international legal corpus for human rights is the U.N. Universal Declaration of Human Rights.[21] The Universal Declaration was passed unanimously (eight abstentions) by the General Assembly in 1948, just three years after the creation of the United Nations.

Unlike the U.N. Charter, the U.N. Universal Declaration of Human Rights is not as yet regarded as legally binding among the nations of the world. The Universal Declaration is a declaration of the international body relating to moral and political issues of governments. Although it is not legally binding, the Universal Declaration has gained considerable authority as a legal guide to all member states and serves as a foundation for future expansion of international human rights law.

Another problem with the Universal Declaration is that it possesses no machinery for enforcing any of the human rights that it lists. The Universal Declaration has, however, inspired two major covenants which contain more detailed assertions of fixed categories of human rights. Approved by the General Assembly in 1966, these are the International Covenant on Civil and Political Rights[22] and the International Covenant on Economic, Social, and Cultural Rights.[23] Both of these covenants continue to receive growing acceptance from many nations of the world community.[24]

Other treaties that relate to human rights speak to a whole series of specific concerns such as the International Convention on the Elimination of All Forms of Racial Discrimination,[25] the Convention on the Elimination of All Forms of Discrimination Against Women,[26] and the Convention on the Prevention and Punishment of the Crime of Genocide.[27]

Obviously, the evolution of the international corpus for human rights law is still ongoing. As with all aspects of international law, international human rights law develops as states become bound by treaty or by custom. Even absent consent via treaty nations can still be obligated. Again, when a norm or standard has reached widespread acceptance in the international community, it is said to have passed into the realm of customary international law. For example, in respect to the U.N. Charter, even those few nations who are not members of the United Nations are bound by the provisions of the Charter under the concept of customary international law.

6.5 The Corpus of Human Rights Law

What then is the current corpus of human rights and how much of it falls into the category of recognized international human rights law? Many scholars view human rights as chronologically evolving in "generations." For the purposes of this study, it is particularly helpful to divide human rights into three generations.

The first generation of human rights deals basically with the individual's right to be secure in the most sacred asset of all—his person. All nations are bound by treaty and custom to observe these basic protections which are clearly included as the most fundamental of international human rights.

Specifically, a state violates international human rights law if, as a matter of state policy, it practices, encourages, or condones seven types of actions that have gained universal recognition. Codified in the Restatement (Third) of the Foreign Relations Law of the United States (1987), Section 702, Customary International Law of Human Rights, those actions consist of:

1. genocide;
2. slavery or slave trade;
3. the murder or causing the disappearance of individuals;
4. torture or other cruel, inhuman, or degrading treatment or punishment;
5. prolonged arbitrary detention;
6. systematic racial discrimination; and
7. a consistent pattern of gross violations of internationally recognized human rights.

Any nation who violates these first generation human rights is deemed to have committed a "gross violation of international human rights."

The second generation of human rights is related to political and civil claims. In short, the individual has the right to be "free from the State in his civil and political endeavors."[28] Second category rights are set forth in the International Covenant on Civil and Political Rights and include the broader civil and political freedoms of religion, movement, peaceful assembly, association, expression, privacy, family rights, fair and public trial, and participation in government—all sacred principles related directly to democratic principles of freedom. Unfortunately, while many countries have adopted these rights, nations who do not enter into international agreements to follow these rights are not obligated to do so. In other words, second generation rights are not yet customary international law.

Second generation human rights are fundamental to the complete development of the individual, for without the basic guarantees of freedom which these rights speak to, the full potential of the individual will never be realized. For those who mistakenly equate human rights with social equality, however, second-generation rights are a paradox, as each individual is free to enjoy the consequences of his own decisions without government interference, good or bad. Furthermore, second generation human rights directly parallel the fundamental freedoms that are never offered under totalitarianism. A government committed to second generation human rights is tantamount to a democracy.

In contrast to the second generation of human rights, there is no great or growing international movement toward agreeing on the status of the third generation of human rights. Third generation rights are different from first and second generation rights because they move from restricting governmental behavior toward the individual, to mandating that the government perform numerous social and welfare actions for the individual. Third-generation rights include such issues as working conditions, social security, education, health care, resource development, food, the environment, humanitarian assistance and peace.

Finally, while good government can certainly be measured by how closely it protects and provides for first- and second-generation human rights, it is not at all clear that the promotion of the third category of human rights is beneficial to society as a whole, especially over the long term. Apart from very basic obligations for any government to provide for the general welfare, many would argue that the obligation of the state is not to provide third-generation human rights such as food, shelter, or employment to its citizens, but to protect the individual's freedom in the lawful pursuit of these things. Under this reasoning, the primary function of the state is to protect, not to give.

6.6 United Nations Efforts to Promote Human Rights

Thomas Paine once wrote: "Had we a place to stand upon, we might raise the world." If a program's success is ultimately measured by how effectively its goals are achieved, it is clear that the world community, embodied especially in the United Nations, has so far failed to develop any viable program to assist in institutionalizing the observance of first and second generation human rights in many of its member states. In short, the United Nations has not materialized as Paine's place upon which to stand.

To be sure, the United Nations has been extremely effective in codifying a body of binding international law so that basic human rights are clearly defined. Nevertheless, restricted by the sovereignty of its members, this tremendous contribution to the advancement of human rights has not been followed by a viable mechanism to ensure compliance of human rights standards within the community of nations. The United Nations thus far has proven to be more suited to building consensus among states about the nature of human rights than to enforcing observance of these rights by individual countries. If the new paradigm for war and terrorism avoidance is to flourish, gaining individual state commitment to at least first-generation human rights must be the foundational basis of a workable and realistic plan of action.

One of the major challenges of the War on Terror will be what steps the United Nations can take to encourage member countries, particularly the Islamic and Arab nations, to follow human rights standards. The question, of course, is whether the United Nations has both the will and ability to offer the type of long-term assistance that is needed. The answer seems to be no.

Although a key purpose of the United Nations is to promote and encourage respect for human rights, the human rights provisions that actually guide the U.N. are set out in extremely general terms. Nowhere in the Charter is the term human rights defined; this work is left to later conventions and declarations. Article 1, paragraph 3, of the U.N. Charter lists as the purposes of the organization: "To achieve international cooperation in solving international problems of an economic, social, cultural, or humanitarian character, and in promoting and encouraging respect for human rights and fundamental freedoms for all without distinction as to race, sex, language, or religion." Article 55 of the U.N. Charter provides:

> With a view to the creation of conditions of stability and well-being which are necessary for peaceful and friendly relations among nations based on respect for the principle of equal rights and self-determination of peoples, the United Nations shall promote . . . universal respect for,

and observance of, human rights and fundamental freedoms for all without distinction as to race, sex, language, or religion

In turn, Article 56 states that "[a]ll members pledge themselves to take joint and separate action in cooperation with the Organization for the achievement of purposes set forth in Article 55." The burden for enforcement and compliance is clearly placed on the individual states.

Under the U.N. Charter, the U.N. General Assembly does have a defined role with respect to the promotion of human rights. Article 13 of the U.N. Charter provides that the General Assembly "shall initiate studies and make recommendations for the purpose of . . . assisting in the realization of human rights and fundamental freedoms for all without distinction as to race, sex, language, or religion." Within the framework of this mandate, the General Assembly's role has been to adopt numerous declarations or conventions concentrating on human rights matters.

Since the adoption of the Charter, the General Assembly has expended considerable effort to codify principles of human rights that nations should follow to guarantee the prosperity and well being of their citizens. These principles now form an important part of international law. Although codification has been a major contribution, so no nation can seriously contend that first generation human rights are not binding universal international law, mechanisms to curb the actual violations of these codified principles have been difficult to establish. In fact, the United Nations currently relies chiefly on what some have termed the "mobilization of shame"—the embarrassment of being under investigation, or even condemned, by the United Nations—as the primary means of motivating governments to comply with internationally recognized standards of human rights in the treatment of their citizens. Obviously, public condemnation means very little to totalitarian regimes. Paradoxically, it is democracies such as the United States, who have far superior records in respecting human rights, that are often singled out for their criticism. The world body of the United Nations often looks at the speck of sand and ignores the boulder in the eye of dictatorships.

During the Cold War, the United Nations seemed to restrict its active concerns to resolving disputes between sovereign states and not to dealing with human rights abuses committed within the borders of sovereign states. Even in the process of resolving international disputes, U.N. forces had to be invited to play such a role by both parties to a conflict. While the term is not used in the U.N. Charter, the phrase "peacekeeping" was coined to describe this process.

With the end of the Cold War, the United Nations has attempted to enlarge its active concern to "peace-building," a concept inexorably linked to human rights concerns. Peace-building involves "action to identify and support structures which will tend to strengthen and solidify peace in order to avoid a relapse into conflict."[29] In this context, the United Nations has been involved in numerous peace-building operations designed to help alleviate the suffering of a particular state through promoting human rights, democratization, and economic development.

As with the United Nation's attempt to shift from peacekeeping to peace-building, the War on Terror demands strong new approaches to promote the observance of human rights in such emerging nations as the new Afghanistan. Hopefully, those approaches will come from one of the human rights organizations that operate under the United Nations' umbrella.

Always reluctant to employ or authorize the more forceful categories of sanctions such as the use of military force or embargoes, the United Nations traditionally draws on a series of weak sanctions based on embarrassing the government that has engaged in human rights violations. To better track human rights violators, the United Nations relies on several commissions and committees that derive their authority from key international human rights instruments or from the U.N. Charter itself. Chief among these organizations are the Commission on Human Rights, the Human Rights Committee, the Center for Human Rights, and the U.N. High Commissioner for Human Rights.

Because many of the instruments that established these organizations are not binding or, if binding, drafted in terms that are ambiguous with respect to the responsibilities of individual member states, it is sometimes difficult to evaluate the specific obligations of individual U.N. member states. Also, each United Nations committee or commission generally has the task of reporting, commenting and studying only a specific category of human rights. As a result, these organizations have proven adept in developing human rights principles in specific areas of concern, but have been of little use in working toward the enforcement of these principles in practice.

The proponent for most actions taken by the General Assembly is the Economic and Social Council (ECOSOC). Under the terms of the U.N. Charter, the ECOSOC may:

1. make recommendations for the purpose of promoting respect for, and observance of, human rights and fundamental freedoms for all;
2. prepare draft conventions for submission to the General Assembly, with respect to matters falling within its competence; and
3. call . . . international conferences on matters falling within its competence.[30]

The ECOSOC may also ask member states to fully report on their own compliance with human rights obligations.[31] The ECOSOC meets several times annually and matters related to human rights issues typically are handled by the ECOSOC's Second (Social) Committee. Under the U.N. Charter, the ECOSOC has the right to establish commissions for, *inter alia*, the promotion of human rights.[32] Pursuant to this authority, the ECOSOC has formed two major commissions: the Commission on Human Rights (also known as the Human Rights Commission) and the Commission on the Status of Women. Of these two, the Commission on Human Rights has played the more significant role in the development and promotion of international human rights principles.

The ECOSOC established the Commission on Human Rights on February 16, 1946. The Human Rights Commission's role in the process of advancing human rights includes the following:

> Draft an international bill of rights; draft international declarations or conventions on civil liberties, the status of women, freedom of information and similar matters; protect minorities; prevent discrimination on grounds of race, sex, language, or religion; handle any other matter concerning human rights and . . . assist the [ECOSOC] in coordination of activities concerning human rights in the United Nations System.

The crowning achievements of the Human Rights Commission includes the drafting of the Universal Declaration of Human Rights, the International Covenant on Economic, Social and Cultural Rights, and the

International Covenant on Civil and Political Rights. Taken together, these instruments comprise what has commonly become known as the International Bill of Human Rights.

In addition to functioning as a vehicle to codify and promote human rights, the Human Rights Commission also monitors and identifies human rights violations. Since its enforcement powers are limited, however, the Human Rights Commission relies primarily on persuasion and dialogue to curb human rights violations.

The Human Rights Commission generally operates through the appointment of a special rapporteur or special envoy who acts as a fact-finder, investigating general human rights issues or a particular country's human rights record. The Human Rights Commission also recommends measures for state compliance and will act in an advisory function to governments that request such assistance. At other times, the special rapporteur will assist a particular government on specific human rights issues. The Human Rights Commission has also established several working groups which tackle such projects as drafting new international instruments.

Another organization under the United Nations umbrella is the Human Rights Committee. The Human Rights Committee serves as the chief administrator of the International Covenant on Civil and Political Rights. Established in 1977, the Human Rights Committee is responsible for studying, commenting and transmitting reports from United Nations member states to the Secretary General on the progress of implementing the obligations assumed by the member states under the International Covenant on Civil and Political Rights. Those obligations include:

1. ensuring to all individuals the rights enunciated in the covenant;
2. enacting legislation to give effect to those rights; and
3. guaranteeing to individuals remedies that can be exercised if those rights are violated.

The Human Rights Committee generally receives periodic reports from member nations in response to a series of questions and issues that the Committee wishes that nation to address. In compliance with Article 40 of the Covenant on Political and Civil Rights, the committee then passes a report on to the General Assembly. For example, in response to a

Human Rights Committee request, a nation will usually send a delegation of public officials to Geneva with extensive written remarks on concerns raised by the Committee. The Committee will consider the written remarks and the oral input by the host nation delegation before issuing their report.

The Optional Protocol to the International Covenant on Civil and Political Rights[33] contains provision for the final implementation mechanism. In this regard, the Committee may consider individual complaints alleging human rights violations by state parties. Although the Committee may reach a decision on the merits and forward that decision to the state and individual concerned, it may not issue judgments. It is a paper tiger.

The Center for Human Rights falls under the auspices of the U.N. Secretariat. Its function is to assist all of the aforementioned committees and commissions in the promotion and protection of human rights. Once again, an examination of the responsibilities of the Center for Human Rights reveals that it has few real enforcement mechanisms. It may:

1. research and stud[y] on human rights at the request of organs concerned;
2. follow up and prepare reports on the implementation of human rights;
3. administer the program of advisory services and technical assistance on human rights;
4. coordinate liaison with non-governmental organizations, external institutions and the media on human rights; and
5. collect and disseminate information, and prepare publications.

Finally, the latest human rights initiative taken by the United Nations was the 1994 creation of a U.N. High Commissioner for Human Rights. This appointment has proven to be less than productive in the real world.

6.7 Non-Governmental Organizations Devoted to Human Rights

Non-governmental organizations (NGOs) serve an important function as watch dogs for human rights issues. The most widely recognized human rights NGO is Amnesty International. It is a worldwide movement that represents the main stream of NGOs and is premised on the "conviction that governments must not deny individuals their basic human rights." For its continuing efforts to promote worldwide observance of the Universal Declaration of Human Rights, Amnesty International was awarded the 1977 Nobel Peace Prize.

The three primary goals of Amnesty International are to work for:

1. the release of prisoners of conscience—men, women and children imprisoned for their beliefs, color, sex, ethnic origin, language or religion, provided they have neither used nor advocated violence;
2. fair and prompt trials for all political prisoners; and
3. an end to torture and executions in all cases.

With the exception of Amnesty International's opposition to the long recognized right of a state to exercise the death penalty, all of its goals are clearly consistent with the common body of first generation international human rights.

One powerful NGO that has attempted to actually implement human rights promotion programs in individual states is the International Committee of the Red Cross (ICRC). Beginning in 1976, the ICRC has sponsored scores of human rights symposia for numerous developing countries. From the establishment of the International Institute of Humanitarian Law in San Remo, Italy, to specific training programs for various militaries worldwide, the ICRC has taken the NGO lead in trying to promote institutional change. While other NGOs have sponsored human rights conferences, absolutely no organization has made as much progress as the ICRC in getting governments to at least address the issue of institutional change in the conduct of armed forces *vis-à-vis* human rights and the law of war. Unfortunately, because the ICRC constantly strives for neutrality, it can have difficulty establishing the necessary rapport with the host nation military to carry out significant training programs.

6.8 Regional Organizations to Promote Human Rights

In accordance with the provisions of the U.N. Charter regarding regional organizations, there are several major regional organizations that have been formed to better represent the desires of sovereign nations in the same geographic location. Like the United Nations approach in dealing with and enforcing compliance with human rights, all of the regional approaches rely simply on categorizing human rights abuses and little else.

Chapter 6: A New Paradigm for War and Terrorism Avoidance   163

For example, the Charter of the Organization of American States (OAS),[34] which is the largest regional organization in the Americas (consisting of 32 members states), includes the same generalist human rights language that is found in the U.N. Charter. Article 3(j) holds that OAS member states will "proclaim the fundamental rights of the individual without distinction as to race, nationality, creed, or sex." Article 16 states that in exercising the right to freely develop its cultural, political, and economic life, the member states agree to "respect the rights of the individual and the principal of universal morality."

Similar to the United Nations approach to further define human rights by means of the Universal Declaration on Human Rights, the OAS passed the American Declaration of the Rights and Duties of Man (American Declaration)[35] to provide a clear indication of what was meant by human rights. Indeed, when the OAS created the Inter-American Commission on Human Rights, it specified that the human rights listed in the American Declaration were the ones to be used by the Commission in evaluating evidence and issuing reports. The American Declaration includes in its list of human rights: the right to life, liberty, and security of person (Article 1); the protection from abusive attacks on honor, reputation, and family (Article 5); the inviolability of the home and correspondence (Articles 9 and 10); and due process of laws (Articles 18, 25, and 26).

As noted, the OAS has not created an enforcement mechanism. The OAS has passed the American Convention on Human Rights in 1978 which requires all members to respect "the rights and freedoms recognized herein and to ensure to all persons subject to their jurisdiction the free and full exercise of those rights and freedoms." To promote compliance, Articles 34 through 73 of the American Convention on Human Rights established the Inter-American Commission on Human Rights and the Inter-American Court on Human Rights. The Inter-American Commission on Human Rights is authorized to receive individual or state complaints alleging violations of human rights. After ensuring that all domestic remedies have been exhausted, the Commission can conduct investigations, make reports, and release information.

The Inter-American Court on Human Rights, located in San Jose, Costa Rica, is authorized to hear human rights cases, but only from parties who voluntarily submit to the jurisdiction of the court. If the parties do submit to the courts' jurisdiction, they pledge obedience to the judicial findings which may include reparations.

6.9 Traditional Efforts of the United States in Promoting Human Rights

If the U.N., NGOs, and regional organizations have been less than effective in developing a serious methodology to promote the institutionalization of first- and second-generation human rights in new democracies, the United States government has only been slightly more effective. Recognizing that promoting human rights is in its best interest, as well as a responsibility to the world community, the United States relies on two means to achieve this end—through foreign assistance funding and through political pressure.

Political pressure is difficult to gauge in its success and varies according to each situation. In terms of politics, for example, the United States has signaled that it will not subordinate perceived security interests in Asia to the desire to promote human rights; the consequences for regional stability could be jeopardized if China is the recipient of an intensified human rights crusade. Under both the Clinton and Bush administrations, even linking China's trade benefits to its human rights record has been viewed as counterproductive—China might become resentful and retaliate in ways that would be destabilizing for the region, such as not cooperating in the Security Council or making irresponsible arms sales.

The traditional mechanism for encouraging countries to develop acceptable human rights records rests with the policy of denying foreign assistance aid or security assistance to countries who are human rights abusers. Security assistance is generally defined as the complete body of statutory programs and authorities under which the United States provides defense articles, military training, and other defense related services to foreign governments and international organizations for the purpose of enhancing American national policies and objectives. Without question, the security assistance program is a principal element of American foreign policy.

The main objective of security assistance is to enhance American strategic objectives, not only from a regional perspective, but also in key countries within the region. Thus, the basic elements of security assistance involves assisting allies and friendly nations in meeting security threats; securing route access, over flight and base rights essential to rapid deployment of United States forces; promoting force commonalities; and improving or maintaining access to critical raw materials.

It is well known that there are also domestic benefits associated with the security assistance program. Not only does the production of defense items provide domestic employment, it generates capital investment and improves the nation's industrial defense mobilization base.

Although the Department of State is responsible for the operation of the security assistance program, it is the National Security Council (NSC) that establishes the overall strategic planning and goals of the program. From the military aspect of security assistance, the Defense Security Assistance Agency (DSAA) is the primary Department of Defense (DOD) office.

Each United States military Unified Command (collectively they have responsibility for all major regions in the world where American forces are stationed) is required to develop a security assistance program for their region which will assist in achieving assigned strategic goals and missions. After developing a security assistance program, the Commander of each Unified (and Specified) Command (CINC) forwards his security assistance proposal to the Joint Chiefs of Staff (JCS) in Washington where they are evaluated and passed to the NSC for final incorporation into the overall United States strategic plan.

The subordinate component commands of Unified Commands are responsible for the actual implementation of security assistance programs within individual countries in the region. Furthermore, in the countries that are major recipients of security assistance, a Security Assistance Organization (SAO) operates on the ground as part of the Country Team to the American Ambassador in the country. The SAO includes all DOD elements located in the foreign country with assigned responsibilities for carrying out the various security assistance programs for that country. Because of their position, SAOs are afforded a great deal of deference by both the host nation and other Americans working in the host country.

Chief among the legislative authorities for security assistance is the Foreign Assistance Act (FAA) of 1961 (as amended).[36] This act authorizes five basic types of programs as follows:

1. The Foreign Military Financing Program (FMFP).[37] Under this program, defense articles are transferred to friendly nations either through grants, loans, or sales. Defense articles include such things as weapons, munitions, aircraft, vessels, and military equipment.
2. International military education and training (IMET).[38] This program allows the United States military to provide training to foreign military students, primarily in the United States. A primary goal of IMET is to expose the foreign military students to the benefits of a free and democratic society based on the rule of law. Key in this process is the demonstration to the foreign soldiers of how a military is properly subordinated to civilian control. Not only are channels of communication opened between United States and foreign nationals, but it is hoped that the personal contacts made as a result of the training will encourage the promotion of democratic values and human rights in the future.
3. Antiterrorism assistance.[39] A relatively new program, the antiterrorism program attempts to assist those democratic nations that are plagued by terrorist organizations.
4. Economic support fund.[40] This program provides direct grant monies to the recipient nation in an effort to assist in economic recovery or development.
5. Peacekeeping operations.[41] This provision authorizes assistance in the form of personnel and equipment to friendly countries and international organizations for peacekeeping operations.

The second major piece of security assistance legislation is the Arms Export Control Act (AECA).[42] The AECA directly ties in with the applicable provisions of the FAA and provides for the sale of defense articles and services to other countries. The definition of what constitutes a defense article remains the same as under the FAA. A defense service includes any service, test, inspection, repair, training, publication, or other assistance, or defense information used for the purpose of making military sales.

A key element in the AECA defense service definition is "training." As defined in the act:

Training includes formal or informal instruction of foreign students in the United States or overseas by officers or employees of the United States, contract technicians, or contractors (including instruction at civilian institutions), or by correspondence courses, technical, educational, or information publications and media of all kinds, training aid, orientation, training exercise, and military advice to foreign military units and forces.

Depending on the type of training mission, American training teams fall into one of three general types: (1) mobile training teams; (2) technical assistance teams; or (3) technical assistance field teams. A letter of offer and acceptance of the training is executed in all cases. Besides the standard issues related to providing the service, this letter also spells out the status which the DOD team members will have while performing training duties in the foreign country. The status is usually the same privileges and immunities accorded to the administrative and technical staff at the American embassy in that country.

As stated, the Department of State is the executive branch agency charged with the operation of security assistance. Congress, however, through its power over the authorization and appropriation of funds, has actually become the key policy player in the process. In fact, much to the chagrin of executive branch, Congress views security assistance as a prime opportunity to influence and even establish foreign policy.

Congress exercises its authority in two ways, through the budget process and through the legislative process. Under the budget process, Congress does not simply allocate a fixed sum of money to the Department of State to allow them to operate the security assistance program through DSAA. Exercising their "power of the purse" Congress engages in micromanagement by earmarking specific dollar amounts to specific countries.

From the earmarking of about half of the security assistance budget in the 1980s, Congress now earmarks about 90 percent of all security assistance monies. In addition, not content with earmarking monies to individual recipient states, Congress increasingly directs through functional accounts exactly how the earmarked money for a particular country will be spent. This Congressional practice has taken almost all of the flexibility away from the State Department and hence, the security assistance administrators.

In an effort to further increase its management role, Congress now establishes "mission accounts." For example, under the IMET funding for fiscal year 1994, Congress set up specific mission accounts in which money could be spent for particular countries. These accounts were: Middle East Peace; Promotion of Democracy and Human Rights; Counter-narcotics; Regional Stability and Defense Cooperation; and Promote Professional Military Relationships. All IMET money had to be spent in one of these mission accounts or returned to the general treasury.

The second manner in which Congress has inserted itself in the process rests in myriad legislative prohibitions on providing security assistance. Apart from numerous country specific restrictions, a sampling of the general prohibitions reveals just how complex the administration of security assistance program has become:

1. The prohibition against American personnel performing defense services of a combatant nature. Set out at 21(c)(1) of the AECA, 22, "Personnel performing defense services sold under this act may not perform any duties of a combatant nature, including any duties related to training and advising that may engage United States personnel in combat activities outside the United States in connection with the performance of those defense services." Thus, if American military personnel find themselves in any situation where hostilities occur, or are imminent, they must cease training and withdraw from the area. This has occurred on many occasions in the past, particularly in situations where Army Special Forces are training host nation soldiers in unstable countries.
2. The prohibition against American forces training police forces, found at Section 660 of the FAA, provides that foreign assistance funds cannot be used to "provide training, advice, or financial support to police, prisons, or other law enforcement forces of a foreign government or for any program of internal intelligence or surveillance on behalf of a foreign government." This section has been amended to allow such training to longtime democracies with no standing armed forces and which do not violate human rights. Costa Rica, for example, has no military.
3. The Kennedy Amendment, at 502B of the FAA, requires that all federal assistance be cut off to any country that "engages in a con-

sistent pattern of gross violations of internationally recognized human rights."
4. The Hickenlooper Amendment, at 620(e)(1) of the FAA, deals with halting aid to any nation that engages in the expropriation of American property.
5. The Symington–Glenn Amendments at 669 and 670 of the FAA, deals with issues associated with the transfer of and receipt of nuclear materials. The intent is to keep nuclear arms from spreading to other countries.
6. The Brooke Amendment at 620(q) of the FAA, mandates the complete termination of foreign assistance (to include United States military assistance) to any country more than twelve months in arrears on payment of debts accrued.

As disruptive as these restrictions appear on the ability of the Executive Branch to conduct foreign affairs, the Congress has given the President special authorities in both the FAA and AECA that allow him to override almost all Congressional restrictions. Because the entire process of planning, budgeting, and delivering security assistance requires substantial lead-time, the President is given this special authority to deal with exigent circumstances. This authority is exercised only as an exception to the rule, generally requires written notification and is limited by dollar ceilings.

Through a series of federal statutes and directives, the United States government is required to consider human rights in conducting foreign relations with other countries. Countries that engage in a consistent pattern of gross violations of human rights are generally restricted from American foreign aid—military and economic. Obviously, this advantage is significant only in those areas that receive foreign aid from the United States.

In regard to the major legislative authority through which foreign assistance is rendered, the Kennedy Amendment and Harkin Amendment leave no doubt that the promotion of human rights is a key objective of American foreign policy. Indeed, Section 502B(a)(3) of the Kennedy Amendment directs the President to administer security assistance in a manner which promotes human rights and avoids "identification of the United States . . . with governments which deny to their people internationally recognized human rights and fundamental freedoms . . . ."

Section 502B(a)(1) establishes as "a principal goal of the foreign policy of the United States . . . to promote the increased observance of internationally recognized human rights by all countries." Section 502B(a)(2) prohibits security assistance to countries which "engage in a consistent pattern of gross violations of internationally recognized human rights."

As with most pieces of legislation, there is a limited exception clause in the Kennedy Amendment. Section 502B(e) allows the president to waive the restrictions imposed if he finds that "extraordinary circumstances exist warranting provision of such assistance," or if the president finds "that the human rights record in that country has significantly improved."

Similarly, Section 116(e) authorizes and encourages the President to identify and conduct "programs and activities which will encourage or promote increased adherence to civil rights, as set forth in the Universal Declaration of Human Rights . . . ." The Harkin Amendment also has an exception clause which prohibits economic assistance to "the government of any country which engages in a consistent pattern of gross violations of internationally recognized human rights . . . unless such assistance will directly benefit the needy people of such country."

Gross violations of internationally recognized human rights are defined under both Sections 502B(d)(1) and 116(a) as the types of violations falling under the first generation of international human rights. The language describes gross violations as:

> [A] consistent pattern of gross violations of internationally recognized human rights, including torture or cruel, inhuman, or degrading treatment or punishment, prolonged detention without charges, causing the disappearance of persons by the abduction and clandestine detention of those persons, or other flagrant denial of the right to life, liberty, and the security of person.

Finally, both Sections 5O2B and 116 require the State Department to submit to Congress an annual status report on human rights for all countries receiving economic or security assistance. The process of collecting information for the report is conducted by the Assistant Secretary of State for Human Rights and Humanitarian Affairs. Information is gathered chiefly from the applicable American embassy and various respected human rights NGOs.

There exist numerous other legislative provisions that deal with the issue of providing assistance to nations that exhibit an unwillingness to abide by first generation human rights. For example, Section 701 of the International Financial Institutions Act[43] requires the United States to do everything in its power to influence international financial institutions to prevent the grant of economic aid to countries whose governments engage in "a consistent pattern of gross violations of internationally recognized human rights." Because the United States exercises tremendous influence in organizations like the World Bank and International Finance Corporation over loans and grants to specific countries, it is able to act as an overseer for human rights issues.

Congress also enacts country-specific legislation which attempts to link American assistance to a particular country to that country's compliance with specific human rights standards. This conditional funding may be triggered by an unacceptable country report issued by the State Department. These violations mirror those found in Common Article 3 of the Geneva Conventions:

1. violence to life and person, in particular, murder of all kinds, mutilation, cruel treatment, and torture;
2. taking hostages;
3. outrages upon personal dignity, in particular, humiliating and degrading treatment;
4. the passing of sentences and carrying out of executions without previous judgment pronounced by a regularly constituted court affording all the judicial guarantees which are recognized as indispensable by civilized peoples.

In terms of promoting peace and advancing human rights, the Middle East remains the most difficult area of the world for the United States to influence. A continuing pattern of violence and bloodshed accurately defines the character of the region, a pattern which was brought home to Americans by the heinous attacks by al-Qa'eda operatives on the United States, on September 11, 2001.

Until the War on Terror, the policy of the United States toward the Middle East was rooted primarily on maintaining stability in this oil-rich region, with human rights concerns taking a back seat to financial concerns. To accomplish this, the United States still spends about two billion dollars each year in military and economic assistance on the two major powers in the region—Israel and Egypt.

Unfortunately, Islamic radicalism is seeking to fill the ideological power vacuum in the region left by the decline of communism and could easily engulf other Arab countries in the same manner as it did with Iran, Afghanistan and the Sudan. Islamic radicalism, which is diametrically opposed to most all of the normative values of human rights, is offered as the only alternative to the moderate, yet non-democratic Muslim and Arab leaders who are unwilling to address the economic and social disparities of their people. It is this strained radicalism which prompted the terrorist attacks upon the United States and began the War on Terror.

In the context of advancing human rights issues in the region, only Israel can be considered as a stable democratic environment. Egypt by constitution is a socialist democratic republic in which the Islamic Sharia is the principal source of legislation. Unfortunately, Egypt has shown little willingness to improve its record. Tragically, the majority of countries considered by the State Department of the United States as sponsors of terrorism are located in the Middle East (e.g., Libya, Iraq, Iran, Syria, Algeria, Sudan and Afghanistan).

Endnotes

1. Cesar G. Soriano, "U.S. General: 'Long Way to Go' in Afghanistan," *USA Today*, Aug. 26, 2002 at A6.

2. Thomas M. Franck, "United Nations Based Prospects for a New Global Order." 22 *N.Y.U.J. Int'l L. & Pol.*, 601 (1990).

3. R. B. Thieme, Jr., lecture given at Houston, Texas, July 18, 1999.

4. *The Dictionary of War Quotations*, Justin Wintle, ed. (London: Hodder and Stroughton, 1989) at 341.

5. The doctrine asserts in part that because of human sin, mankind is in a state of total helplessness when compared to the absolute perfect character of God.

Thus, mankind cannot achieve a relationship with God based on human works, only by the grace mechanics provided by God. For an excellent discussion of the grace mechanics of salvation, see Robert B. Thieme, Jr., *The Integrity of God* (Houston, TX: R. B. Thieme, 1979).

6. *National Security Law*, supra Chapter 1 note 4, at 77.

7. Richard B. Lillich and Frank C. Newman, *International Human Rights,* (Boston, MA: Little, Brown and Co., 1991) at 776–77.

8. *Rummell*, supra Chapter 3, note 14, at 12.

9. B. Russett, *Grasping the Democratic Peace: Principles for a Post-Cold War World,* (Princeton, NJ: Princeton University Press, 1993) at 4.

10. John Norton Moore, "Enhanced Effectiveness in United Nations Peacekeeping, Collective Security, and War Avoidance," at 12 (unpublished manuscript, 1997).

11. Ian O. Lesser, Bruce Hoffman, John Arquilla, David Ronfeldt and Michele Zanini, *Countering the New Terrorism,* (Santa Monica, CA: RAND, 1999) at 128.

12. *Great Books of the Western World*, Robert Maynard Hutchins, ed. (Chicago: W. Benton, 1952) at 57.

13. Mr. Tytler, who lived from 1748 to 1813, also went on to develop a fascinating general trend in the rise and fall of nations. He wrote: "The average age of the world's greatest civilizations has been 200 years. These nations have progressed through the following sequence:
   From bondage to spiritual faith;
   From spiritual faith to courage;
   From courage to liberty;
   From liberty to abundance;
   From abundance to selfishness;
   From selfishness to complacency;
   From complacency to apathy;
   From apathy to dependency;
   From dependency back to bondage."

14. A. E. Dick Howard, *Constitution Making in Eastern Europe,* (Washington, DC: Woodrow Wilson Center Press, 1993) at 16.

15. U.N. Document A/CONF.157/24 at 19 (Part I) (Oct. 13, 1993).

16. Lassa Oppenheim, *International Law: A Treatise*, (London: Hersch Lauterpacht, 1955) at 649–641.

17. See John T. Humphrey, *No Distant Millennium: The International Law of Human Rights,* (Paris: UNESCO, 1989) at 20. "Human rights are those rights without which there can be no human dignity."

18. The 1949 Geneva Conventions cover four categories: (1) Geneva Convention of August 12, 1949, for the Amelioration of the Condition of the Wounded and Sick in Armed Forces in the Field, 6 U.S.T. 3114, T.I.A.S. No. 3362, 75 U.N.T.S. 31; (2) Geneva Convention of August 12, 1949 for the Amelioration of the Condition of the Wounded, Sick, and Shipwrecked Members of Armed Forces at Sea, 6 U.S.T. 3217, T.I.A.S. No. 3363, 75 U.N.T.S. 85; (3) Geneva Convention of August 12, 1949, Relative to the Treatment of Prisoners of War 6 U.S.T. 3316, T.I.A.S. No. 3364, 75 U.N.T.S. 135; and (4) Geneva Convention of August 12, 1949, Relative to the Protections of Civilian Persons in Time of War, 6 U.S.T. 3316, T.I.A.S. No. 3365, 75 U.N.T.S. 287.

19. See William V. O'Brien, *The Conduct of Just and Limited War,* (New York: Praeger Press, 1981) at 37–70.

20. *Lloyd's Introduction to Jurisprudence*, supra Chapter 2 note 18, at 1060.

21. U.N.G.A. Res. 217A (III), 3(1) U.N. GAOR Res. 71, U.N. Doc A/810 (1948). See Centre for Human Rights, United Nations, European Workshop on the Universal Declaration of Human Rights: Past–Present–Future, U.N. Doc. GE. 89-15100 (1989).

22. International Covenant on Civil and Political Rights, Dec. 16, 1966, G.A. res. 2200A(XX), 21 U.N. GAOR Supp. (No. 16) at 52, U.N. Doc. A/6316 (1966), 999 U.N.T.S. 171, entered into force Mar. 23, 1976. See also Optional Protocol to the Covenant on Civil and Political Rights, Dec. 16, 1966, G.A. res 2200A (XXI), 21 U.N. GAOR Supp. (No. 16) at 59, U.N. Doc. A/6316 (1966), 999 U.N.T.S. 302, entered into force Mar. 23, 1976.

23. International Covenant on Economic, Social and Cultural Rights, Dec. 16, 1966, G.A. res 2200A (XXI), 21 U.N. GAOR, Supp. (no. 16) at 49, U.N. Doc. A/6316 (1967), 993 U.N.T.S. 3, entered into force Jan. 3, 1976.

24. As of December 1993, the International Covenant on Civil and Political Rights has been signed and ratified by 123 state parties; the International Covenant on Economic, Social, and Cultural Rights has been signed and ratified by 125 state parties. U.N. Document ST/HR/4/Rev. 9, (Dec. 1993) Human Rights International Instruments Chart of Ratification, as at Dec. 1993.

Chapter 6: A New Paradigm for War and Terrorism Avoidance   175

25. Mar. 7, 1966, 660 U.N.T.S. 195.

26. U.N.G.A. Res. 34/180 (XXXIV), 34 U.N. GAOR, Supp. (no. 46)193, U.N. Doc. A/34/46 (1979).

27. 78 U.N.T.S. 277, Mar. 7, 1966.

28. Centre for Human Rights, United Nations, Fact Sheet No. 16, The Committee on Economic, Social and Cultural Rights (1991).

29. Id.

30. U.N. Charter art. 62.

31. U.N. Charter art. 64(1).

32. U.N. Charter art. 68.

33. Optional Protocol to the Covenant on Civil and Political Rights, 16 Dec. 1966, G.A. res. 2200A (XXI), 21 U.N. GAOR Supp. (No. 16) at 59, U.N. Doc. A/6316 (1966), 999 U.N.T.S. 302.

34. Charter of the Organization of American States, 13 Dec. 1951, 2 UST 2394; TIAS 2361; 119 UNTS 3.

35. American Declaration of the Rights and Duties of Man, 2 May 1948, OEA/Ser.L./V/II.71, at 17 (1988).

36. 22 U.S.C. 2301–2349aa-6

37. 22 U.S.C. 2311.

38. 22 U.S.C. 2347.

39. 22 U.S.C. 2349aa.

40. 22 U.S.C. 2346.

41. 22 U.S.C. 2348.

42. 22 U.S.C. 2751–2796c.

43. 22 U.S.C. 262(d).

Chapter 7

Leading the Way— Pax Americana or the Rule of Law?

Let he who desires peace, prepare for war.
—Flavius Vegetius Renatus (first century A.D.)

Synopsis
7.1 Collective Security
7.2 Peace, Freedom and Appeasement—Lessons from the Gulf War of 1991
7.3 Stay with the Rule of Law

The fact that the United States saved Western Europe and the free world in two World Wars by the use of its magnificent military establishment, coupled with its even greater industrial complex, does not imply that the ongoing military campaigns in the War on Terror will set the stage for a pax Americana. Much like President Roosevelt's attempt to color the participation of the United States in World War II with a far greater purpose than national self-interest,[1] President George W. Bush's concern for world peace is primarily centered on protecting the United States. To his great credit, President Bush has chosen the rule of law as his rallying point and has not fallen into the trap of embracing issues and matters that appeal to utopian ideals beyond the scope of the War on Terror. Some believe this error was made by his father, President George H. Bush, in his desire to advance an idea known as the New World Order in the context of the Gulf War.

7.1 Collective Security

Collective security has always required a dominant leader with a sufficient military establishment. Devoid of any military arm of its own, the United Nations cannot deal with, for example, Saddam Hussein and his

177

continued violations of international law. In the twentieth century, that has always meant the United States. This is true in every case in which international collective security has functioned. The lesson of the War on Terror and is the same as that of the Gulf War and the Korean War; the United Nations does not have the capacity to guarantee the security of its members absent the direct participation of the United States.

In the real world, the question will be the same as it has always been. Will the people of the United States continue to possess the resolve to assist in the struggle to halt major acts of aggression in the future? As demonstrated in the War on Terror, it is probable that a majority of Americans will continue to possess such resolve. Apart from matters of self-interest, the United States of America does have a continuing responsibility to the world to enforce the rule of law. Judged by any positive standard, be it in the field of human rights, self-determination, economic opportunity, or privacy related to property and person, the United States stands out as the pearl of all that is possible for any given nation to achieve. Furthermore, America, like great nations before it, has related all of these positive values to a strong heritage of law. The framers of the nation established certain democratic values, and subsequent generations have generally exhibited the discipline and courage to maintain those values.

America's most fundamental value does not reside in her military might or industrial complex. Those pillars merely provide support for the United States' most precious commodity—freedom as related to the rule of law. Although the United States military most certainly deterred the aggressiveness of the Soviet Empire from 1945 to 1991, it was the beacon of American freedom that ultimately dispelled the darkness of communism. To the world, then, the United States offers a pattern of prosperity and freedom under the rule of law. This is the message that the United States must continue to send to the world.

The world is still a very dangerous place; and, as never before, it is time for forward thinking in the long term as the nation prosecutes the War on Terror. Coming out of the Cold War just a decade ago, millions of people in Central Asia and Eastern Europe still have little frame of reference for a nation or, for that matter, a world that is ruled by law.[2] Indeed, the governments of the Middle East lag far behind in fulfilling the requirements of first and second generation human rights.

Under the leadership of President George W. Bush, the United States has so far successfully validated the logic and necessity for following the rule of law. Undeniably, the legitimate interest of the United States in halting international terrorism in the era of weapons of mass destruction has benefited the entire civilized world. For freedom loving peoples everywhere, the victory in Afghanistan against the evil of terrorism ensured that the cost of maintaining freedom was paid by another generation of patriotic Americans. To a large degree, this sacrifice not only enforces the rule of law, but undoubtedly serves as a deterrent to other tyrants and terrorists.

7.2 Peace, Freedom and Appeasement—Lessons from the Gulf War of 1991

It is a fundamental principle that all free states have a common interest in maintaining peace. Peace, like security, however, is a precious commodity rarely attained without great sacrifice. In addition, peace is far more than the absence of war; it is an elusive intangible which only takes on meaning when related to freedom. Although the goal of abolishing war, like eradicating crime, is certainly commendable, given the basic nature of man, neither goal is totally feasible. As long as there are demagogues like Sennacherib, Hitler, Stalin or Saddam Hussein, nation-states must have strong military establishments to protect themselves. Under this truism, the symbol of freedom for Americans is not a cracked liberty bell in Philadelphia, but the military uniform of its soldiers.

Accepting the premise that human beings are morally flawed creatures, it stands to reason that the best that mankind can ever hope to achieve is to control aggression. Like criminals, aggressive nations can only be deterred through the proper functioning of two principles: (1) the threat of lawful force; or (2) the application of lawful force. To the extent that the function of these two principles fail, wars will certainly continue to exist. Paradoxically, those groups who resist this truism, demonstrated by irrational demands for peace through the continued restriction of all categories of force, blissfully lay the groundwork for the next war.

If peace at any price, with compromise as the only means to achieve it, is the major concern of a national entity, then the destruction of that nation will be the inevitable consequence. Freedom, not peace, must always be the issue for free nations; when nations are no longer willing to pay the price of freedom, then they, too, will lose their freedom. As Woodrow

Wilson so wisely reflected in May of 1917, "It is not an army that we must train for war; it is a nation."[3]

Tragically, every democratic nation has within it the very seeds which will eventually destroy it, for the choice between freedom or peace must be made by each successive generation. With freedom, war is inevitable, periodically. By choosing peace without maintaining the power to enforce the peace, however, war will come more often and with a greater probability of resulting in the annihilation of the nation. Just as crime increases when society gets sentimental about the criminal[4] and forgets about the victim, so to will the probability of war increase as the nation emphasizes peace instead of freedom.

Ultimately, the cost of achieving freedom can only be understood by those who have paid the price. Indeed, there is no permanent guarantee that the United States will continue to function as a national entity beyond a strong military-industrial complex coupled with the people who have the will to fight if necessary.

For this reason, it is dangerous rhetoric to confuse the distinction between the need for the legitimate use of force and unlawful aggression. Despite disclaimers that the concept of "world peace" should not be related to restricting the use of force or promoting unilateral disarmament, the connotation is otherwise. No anti-war movement has ever been premised on maintaining a strong and viable military, and no proponent of the use of lawful violence can ever hope to be immune from the wishful thinking of those who demand the dismantling of the very forces that sustain and protect the freedom of the nation—the military establishment.

On the other hand, the concept of the rule of law does not necessarily carry with it the connotation that man is ever capable of achieving the panacea of world peace. For the rule of law, it is enough if aggressive war can be controlled. As one expert in international law noted during the Gulf War, "At the root of United States policy in the Gulf war was the principle of upholding the Rule of Law. Article 2(4) of the U.N. Charter outlaws armed international aggression, and the massive Iraqi invasion of Kuwait was a direct challenge to that principle."[5]

In short, how does one react to those nations or groups who either contemplate the use of unlawful force or who actually engage in such unlawful force? To date, the U.N. Charter is undeniably the foremost tool in dealing with and deterring aggression; it is an integral component of the rule of law. The classic McDougal and Feliciano, *Law and Minimum Public Order*, states:

> The most difficult problem which today confronts world public order is that of characterizing and preventing unlawful violence. The history is familiar how over the centuries—through bellum justum, the Covenant of the League of Nations, the Pact of Paris, the judgments at Nuremberg and Tokyo, and the U.N. Charter—the public order of the world community has at long last come to a prohibition of certain coercion as a method of international change and to a distinction between permissible and nonpermissible coercion.[6]

Although history has proven time and again that the curtailment of aggression can only come through the threat of force, or the application of force, the authority for those responses must be firmly rooted in law. Despite this truism, the necessity for and legality of Article 51 is, nonetheless, constantly under attack by those groups who intentionally blur the difference between lawful and unlawful uses of force. In their search for the panacea of brotherhood, various peace groups refuse to acknowledge any distinction regarding the use of force. Left unchallenged, this attitude will only encourage aggression, not forestall it.

President George W. Bush has done an admirable job in the continuing task of articulating to the world the distinction between the unlawful use of force by an aggressor and the lawful use of force under the rule of law by civilized nations. In fact, those who advocate ending war by destroying the forests of bayonets[7] (i.e., unilateral disarmament) hinder the validity of the rule of law to that extent.

Historically, the desire of numerous organizations to curtail or eliminate the use of force as a national option, regardless of the justification for the employment of that force, is always present in any debate on how to best answer aggression. While these voices are helpful if kept in proper perspective, appeasement is nothing new. The Biblical prophet Jeremiah heard the same voices almost 2,500 years ago as peace activists in the Southern Kingdom of Judah proposed how to deal with the aggression of Chaldean militarism. Jeremiah analyzed the peace at any cost advocates as follows: "They allege to solve the problems of my people, [they cry] "Peace, peace when there is no peace."[8]

Similarly, the voices in the War on Terror who call for peace at any price say nothing new—the same voices occurred in the Gulf War of 1991, although far more loudly. Calling for peace in the Gulf War at any price, some paid little regard for even the most clearly worded rules and norms associated with the rule of law as it applies to the lawful use of force. This phenomenon extended all the way from the highest levels of the United Nations to, as to be expected, an assortment of politically active anti-war groups.

At the top echelon, this phenomenon was brought out rather dramatically on November 8, 1990, when none other than the Secretary General of the United Nations, Perez de Cuellar, opined that because no nation had taken military action against Iraq since the occupation of Kuwait in August 1990, "that the passage of three months time had terminated the right of individual states to use force against Iraq under the 'collective self-defense' provisions of Article 51."[9] Not only did de Cuellar's statement exhibit a gross misunderstanding of the U.N. Charter, it did nothing but encourage the continued aggression of the Iraqi military.

Certainly, de Cuellar knew that Article 51 did not create the right of self-defense, that such a right was an inherent right which Article 51 simply acknowledged and reinforced. Furthermore, Iraq's aggression did not end on August 2, 1990, but was a continuing offense, since none of the Security Council resolutions had succeeded in "maintaining international peace and security."

The policy implications of the Secretary General's position reveals its total absurdity; a rule that requires nations to respond immediately to an armed attack or else forfeit their rights to take defensive action effectively nullifies the principles embodied in Article 2(3) and 2(4) of the U.N. Charter. By making a mockery of this critical rule of law, de Cuellar sent two disastrous signals: one to Saddam Hussein and one to the community of nations. First, the Secretary General's total misreading of Article 51 only encouraged Iraq's continuing occupation of Kuwait and was completely counterproductive to the international movement to force Iraq out of Kuwait short of armed force. Second, the requirement that nations act immediately in self-defense is the antithesis of what the United Nation encourages, i.e., the peaceful settlement of disputes through diplomacy and every other peaceful channel for resolution of conflict. Finally, the longer the hesitation in the use of legitimate force, "give peace a chance," the more probable that the same peace activists will view the coalition forces as the aggressor!

The more common variety of anti-war groups also hoped that the end of the Cold War would be the catalyst for their simplistic notions concerning the abolition of war. Advocating peace, but having no concept of what the concept must necessarily entail—the willingness to fight for peace—numerous anti-war activists demanded appeasement. Paradoxically, the loud demands for peace during the six month Iraqi occupation of Kuwait probably ensured that the threat of force as a deterrence would most surely fail, leaving no alternative but the use of lawful violence.

As Saddam Hussein held firm in Kuwait, with no signs of withdrawal, various religious groups also voiced dismay over those who contemplated the exercise of lawful armed force against Iraq under Article 51. For example, both the Vatican daily newspaper, *Losservatore Romano*, and the official publication of the Jesuit order, *La Civilta Cattolica*, spoke out against using force to expel Iraq from Kuwait.[10] *La Civilta Cattolica* wrote on November 17, 1990: "The [coming] war in the Gulf will be a moral shame and a political disaster."[11]

In his traditional Christmas message, Pope John Paul II gave the following heartfelt warning to those who contemplated the use of force to expel Saddam Hussein: "May leaders be convinced that war is an adventure with no return. By reasoning, patience and dialogue with respect for the inalienable rights of people and nations, it is possible to identify and travel the paths of understanding and peace."[12] In the final analysis, the Pope's sincere desire for "[n]o more war, war never again,"[13] is a beautiful ideal but, unfortunately, can sometimes prove counterproductive in the maintenance of world peace. Often, such signals encourage aggression if no room is left for the use of lawful force to halt aggression *ab initio* or to challenge aggression once it has become entrenched. In fact, one commentator observed that of the thirty-eight times that the Pope spoke out against the Gulf War, that "[t]here was not an echo of a hint of a suggestion that the United States and its allies (including Italy) were in a battle against a tyrant who had just invaded and [sic] occupied and brutally destroyed a small neighbor . . . ."[14]

Some religious leaders, emotionally obsessed by the fact that large numbers of soldiers were going to be killed in war, irrationally concluded that all war in the modern era was immoral, regardless of the motivation.

Fueled by reports that some Iraqi soldiers had been buried alive in their defensive positions by American tanks,[15] a religious publicist, Guy Munger, concluded that "any discussion of whether Desert Storm was a just war seem[s] to border on the insane. Indeed, practical application of the theory may have ended with the crossbow."[16] According to Munger, "modern war is always immoral." Of course, the argument is totally fallacious for two reasons. First, long before the crossbow, battle casualties could easily mount into the hundreds of thousands. For example, during the Second Punic War (219–202 B.C.), the Carthaginian forces under Hannibal killed in combat over 60,000 Roman soldiers in a single day.[17] And second, Munger fails to understand the real world consequences associated with a refusal to defend oneself.

Claiming to be a spokesperson for morality and justice, the wife of Martin Luther King, Jr., Coretta King, attempted to derail the United States-led military coalition to eject Saddam Hussein from Kuwait. She referred to the American actions as a "low [point] since the death of Dr. King."[18] Speaking on January 11, 1991, Mrs. King called on a new anti-war movement to be launched on January 15, 1991, the date of the United Nations' deadline for Iraq to withdraw from Kuwait or face the use of force.[19] "And so I am urging everyone who believes in Martin Luther King, Jr.'s dream of peace to use this holiday to launch a new anti-war movement that will not rest until a peaceful resolution of the conflict in the Persian Gulf is secured."[20]

Failing to elaborate on how this peace movement could force a brutal dictator to relinquish his death grip on Kuwait, Mrs. King called the American participation in the Gulf War "wrong and immoral."[21] Like the other peace activists who refuse to consider the application of force under any circumstances, Mrs. King's call for "peace-loving people everywhere to accelerate their efforts to stop it" did nothing except encourage the ruthlessness of the Iraqi occupation.[22]

Similarly, the president of the Southern Christian Leadership Conference, Reverend Joseph Lowery, objected to the United States military action on moral grounds saying, "Let us call upon the nations to spend our resources on medical supplies, not military supplies; to make tractors, not tanks; to beat missiles into morsels of bread to feed the hungry; to build housing, not foxholes."[23] Again, if history has demonstrated anything, it has demonstrated that utopian rhetoric about turning "swords into plowshares" is not helpful in deterring people and nations who exhibit aggressive tendencies.

Obviously, man is always confronted with aggression; a world without conflict is not something that is in the here and now. Those who wish to enter a new world order in which "swords are turned in plowshares," need to recall the comments of Haynes Johnson of the *Washington Post*, this "is not the millennium; the new world order has not arrived."[24] Unfortunately, the sincere but unrealistic belief that war can be curtailed by third-party dispute settlement processes or by massive disarming processes was not buried in the lessons of the Gulf War of 1991.

7.3 Stay with the Rule of Law

To a large degree, history is defined by the workings of spheres of power which are commonly categorized into eras. Within these eras, the trends of history are replete with great wars whose goal was to end all wars. While the natural tendency of mankind is to promote and to nourish the resulting periods of peace between wars, history gives no encouragement to the notion that war will be no more or that peace will be more than a mere handful of years. The collective memory of the world has traditionally proved to be very short.

With the liberation of Kuwait in 1991, President George H. Bush became the primary proponent of an ambiguous phrase which he called the "New World Order." President George H. Bush attempted to advance this phrase as an international rallying cry for the future of the world. The New World Order was to herald a new era in international affairs, an era of collective security sponsored and reinforced by the United Nations. Expectations for the fulfillment of this goal were understandably high and recalled the old Roman proverb, "For he who desires to become rich also wishes that desire to be soon accomplished." In reality, however, the natural desire to create some form of a New World Order quickly met with failure. Even more disturbing, the promotion of the term New World Order by President Bush served only to minimize or cast doubt on the viability of the rule of law. President George W. Bush must be careful not to repeat this mistake as the War on Terror progresses. Catchy utopian phrases are counterproductive to the critical mission of promoting the rule of law and democratic behavior.

To the serious student of history, the concept New World Order is neither new in its origin, nor, as the concept might imply universal in its interpretation; it has existed in many forms. From the *pax Romana* of ancient Rome[25] to the *novus ordo seclorum* printed on the reverse side of the one-dollar bill, the concept of the New World Order has been used by public figures to represent a variety of agendas associated, of course, with a vision for how the world should be ruled.

In the past century, both the Germans under Adolph Hitler and the British under Winston Churchill used the concept to describe their respective notions about the world's future. Although both were seeking to rally public opinion to support a particular objective, they were diametrically opposed in their meaning and application of the concept. Hitler envisioned *Die neue Ordnung* (the New Order)[26] as a world ruled by the master German race, while Churchill wielded it as a sword of international force against Nazi expansionism.

Addressing the League of Nations in 1936, Churchill warned of Hitler's continued pattern of aggression and announced that the "fateful moment [had] arrived for choice between the New Age and the Old." For Churchill, the new age for the world was squarely based on establishing a defensive alliance to defeat the Nazi's quest of conquering Europe and the world.

Adolph Hitler employed the concept in its most aggressive connotation and irrationally believed that he had a sacred mission to establish a New Order through terror, violence and warfare. The Axis powers set out the parameters of their New Order for the world by signing a joint agreement in Berlin in January of 1942. Linking their New Order to economic prosperity, the Germans envisioned the world divided into four *Grossraumwirtschaften* (great economics), each led by an authoritarian leader under the ultimate control of Germany. Once the Axis forces had won World War II, "a conclave was to be held in Vienna to legalize Nazi Germany's hegemony within the New Order."[27] Hitler's New Order would initially be made up of German dominated Europe, Africa and the Near East, but ultimately it would encompass the entire world.

In the end, Hitler's "New Order for the World" collapsed in a bloody inferno while "Churchill's New Age for the World" silently slipped into the bookshelves of history after it helped to inspire the formation of the

United Nations. Although the concepts were similar, the meanings were not.

The New World Order witnessed its latest reincarnation during the Iraqi invasion of Kuwait in August of 1990. In an unprecedented use of the United Nations, [28] President George H. Bush used the concept of the New World Order as the focal point for gathering world opinion against the Iraqi occupation of Kuwait.[29] In an effort to consolidate support for the possible use of military force against Iraq, President Bush not only followed Churchill's example against Hitler, but simultaneously offered this old term to describe American foreign policy in the post-Cold War era.

Just a month after the invasion, President Bush proclaimed that the New World Order "would be a world where the rule of law supplants the rule of the jungle. A world in which nations recognize the shared responsibility for freedom and justice. A world where the strong respect the rights of the weak."[30] As the months passed and Iraq became more entrenched in Kuwait, the Bush administration increased the usage of the concept. In a statement delivered on December 5, 1990, before the Senate Foreign Relations Committee, Secretary of State James Baker said: "Historically, we must stand with the people of Kuwait so that the annexation of Kuwait does not become the first reality that mars our vision of the new world order."[31]

Without a doubt, America's vision of the New World Order was to be firmly rooted in the new founded efficacy of the United Nations to function as the primary legal instrument for maintaining peace in the world, the assumption being that Gorbachev's Russia would no longer use its veto power to hinder the effectiveness of the Security Council. By the close of the Gulf War, the tenets of the New World Order were set: "Peaceful settlements of disputes, solidarity against aggression, reduced and controlled arsenals and just treatment of all peoples."[32]

Unfortunately, from the viewpoint of epistemology, the concept of New World Order was not very successful for the administration of President George H. Bush. First, although the New World Order was undeniably catchy, the concept was not really a simple phrase to understand. In reality, the New World Order stood for a whole regime of policies, ranging all the way from universal human rights issues to the peaceful settlement of international disputes. Apart from a handful of scholars devoted to the study of those topics, the hope that a wider audience would understand the concept, without fully grasping the categories behind it, was the primary failure of its proponents.

Second, because President George H. Bush chose as his rallying cry a phrase that, throughout the past hundred years, has been used to stand for various propositions, he should have necessarily exerted an even greater amount of time and effort to achieve a minimum amount of association to his meaning. In other words, if a concept is to gain acceptance, the rate of forgetting must not exceed the rate of learning. This, too, was never accomplished, reflected in part by a remarkable lack of attention given to the phrase by the public media.

In his September 1991 address to the United Nations, President Bush specifically stressed the concept New World Order several times,[33] even deliberately choosing the theme of the New World Order to close out his final remarks to the world body. Seeking to establish a straightforward definition, the President dramatically spelled out the elements of the New World Order.

> [The] new world order [is] an order in which no nation must surrender one iota of its own sovereignty; an order characterized by the rule of law rather than the resort to force; the cooperative settlement of disputes, rather than anarchy and bloodshed; and an unstinting belief in human rights.[34]

Unfortunately, this definition was not really the same given at the close of the Gulf War; then it was "peaceful settlements of disputes, solidarity against aggression, reduced and controlled arsenals and just treatment of all people."[35] In addition, despite a conscious effort by President Bush to fully sponsor the phrase, the domestic media concentrated on the President's condemnation of Iraqi interference with United Nations inspection teams and the ill-conceived "Zionism is racism" General Assembly resolution.[36] Predictably, the news reports that followed Bush's speech failed to mention the New World Order even once.[37] While one might criticize the news media for exhibiting a total failure to publicize the concept, judged by the standards of keeping it simple and promoting repetition, the blame also rested with the Bush administration.

As to simplicity, President George H. Bush erred by expanding his initial meaning of the New World Order, which most associated with the

Chapter 7: Leading the Way—Pax Americana . . .   189

enforcement of the international rule of law against the raw aggression of Iraq, to a definition which equated the New World Order to various categories of international principles—each requiring a sophisticated level of comprehension. By lumping other concepts ranging from nuclear disarmament to human rights with the concept of the New World Order, the vast majority of the public had no idea what the New World Order "really" entailed. At the time, Harvard's Joseph S. Nye, Jr., remarked: "No one really knows what it means."[38]

Most of the world can quickly grasp the idea of halting an aggressor who has broken the law (e.g., Iraq broke the most critical provision of the rule of law, the prohibition of aggression, in its use of force against Kuwait). But, when one adds, for example, the concept of creating norms for international human rights to the concept of the New World Order, the audience is lost. A brief survey of the concept of humanitarian law reveals that it is, at best, an evolving idea; and not an idea that is very well understood.

As to repetition, when the public was told that President George H. Bush was going to issue a major address to the nation on sweeping nuclear arms initiatives, many "New World Order watchers" anticipated that the concept would be woven throughout the speech.[39] Set for September 27, 1991, the address would follow soon after the United Nations address, which provided President Bush with the perfect opportunity to promote the concept, but this time at the domestic level. Indeed, in President Bush's September 1990 address to the United Nations, he had already set the precedent and employed the concept of the New World Order to urge a worldwide ban on chemical weapons and to continue the efforts to stop the proliferation of nuclear and biological weapons. At that time, President Bush said: "It is in our hands to leave these dark machines [nuclear, chemical and biological weapons] behind, in the dark ages where they belong . . . to cap a historic movement toward a new world order, and a long era of peace."[40]

When the 1991 address to the nation was made, President Bush did not invoke the concept New World Order even once. President Bush concentrated on an entirely new concept called "the new age."[41] Pointing out that not only had the Cold War ended, but the Soviet Union was undergoing drastic change, President Bush preferred to justify his proposals for disarmament as in keeping with the new age. Once against the press exhibited no interest in reporting unfamiliar terminology; the new age was unmentioned.

In summation, after a full year-and-a-half of being in the market place of ideas, the New World Order was still unfamiliar to the American public. Consequently, the general domestic understanding of what the New World Order really meant remained inexorably clouded. Of course, if the American public could not understand the New World Order, it was certain the rest of the world was at an even greater disadvantage. This was especially true for emerging democracies. For example, having a vague frame of reference for the notion of a state ruled by law, the vast territories of the old Soviet Empire had only just begun to awaken from a seventy-year nightmare of the most vicious brutality. Although, the republics had renounced the twisted and flawed premise upon which the Communist party had rested for seven decades, there was tremendous confusion. Indeed, even with the dawn of the twenty-first century it will be sometime before the former communist states will be able to implement many of the components associated with democratic values. It is difficult enough for them to grasp the concept of being ruled by law and not by force.

The first application of the New World Order was against Iraq in 1991, but was only partially successful. The Gulf War drove Saddam Hussein out of Kuwait, but also drove him to ruthlessly turn his military on his own people. In addition, the failure of the international community to press for international war crimes trials for Saddam Hussein and his henchmen dealt a major blow to the most central ideal of the New World Order. It is now the dawn of 2003, and Saddam Hussein is still actively engaged in a totalitarian dictatorship of the most brutal sort.

The second application of the New World Order envisioned the formation of a joint defense force, composed of Arabs and Americans, to deter future aggression in the Middle East. This application of the New World Order never materialized. The Damascus Declaration, hammered out just days after the war ended, called for Syrian and Egyptian participation in the Arab security force. As quickly as the Declaration was adopted, however, the age old problems of distrust and animosity emerged—the Declaration died less than a month after its birth. Similarly, the New World Order visions of a new Kuwait based on more democratic principles and self-reliance have not been fulfilled. Outside of some limited Israeli-Arab peace talks, the region has essentially returned to its pre-war status. Except for a new found respect for the military power of the United States, "[c]enturies-old attitudes have not changed, new alliances have not jelled, and the historic suspicion of Western influence has receded only slightly."[42]

As the failures of the New World Order mounted, the phrase lost any power it may have had and quickly faded into history as a small footnote. On the other hand, breaches of the rule of law do not necessarily weaken the utility of the term rule of law; failures only reinforce the continued need for deterrence and enforcement of the rule of law. Simply put, the New World Order proved to be the jargon of politicians. The rule of law is the tool of nations.

The hope that the victory in the Gulf War set the pattern of some sort of a New World Order in which the United Nations would guarantee the security of its members through collective security was sophomoric. The response to the al-Qa'eda and their supporters in the War on Terror was the exact same response taken against the aggression of Saddam Hussein a decade ago—the application of the rule of law in the context of the lessons learned in Munich.

Despite the missed opportunity to promote the concept, the rule of law, not the New World Order, emerged from the dust of the Gulf War. As in former times, the New World Order quickly faded into history where it will silently await its next master to call it forward; the shallowness of the concept sealed its own fate.

Catchy phrases such as the New World Order have nothing positive to offer those who seek to foster, strengthen and advance the rule of law. If the United States is serious about promoting the rule of law as the basis for its war on terror, then it must stand as the chief champion of the rule of law as the basis for the War on Terror. The challenge must be to abandon all such new age and new world[43] phrases and to concentrate fully on the never ending business of promoting the rule of law in word as well as deed. In the never ending struggle to move the credibility of the concept forward, the United States must exhibit a faithful sponsorship of the rule of law in every international forum available.

Many of the most fundamental values, particularly those dealing with the illegality of aggressive war, have been translated into well-rooted rules of law at the cost of untold blood and fortune. Hope remains that many more democratic values will be added to that book, and that the attendant sacrifices will not have been in vain. Although there is no need to speak of the United States as the world's policeman, there is a need for the United States to fully sponsor the rule of law, which remains the best hope to those nations that wish to exist in a sphere of freedom. As the United States fights the War on Terror, it must continuously place emphasis on the rule of law and avoid the use of any descriptive phrase that casts doubt on the supreme function of the rule of law.

Endnotes

1. As part of his "New Deal," and just before America's participation in World War II, President Roosevelt issued his famous four freedom speech, reflecting values long recognized as legitimate aspirations for all mankind: freedom of speech, freedom of worship, freedom from want, and freedom from fear.

2. Anthony Carty and Gennady Danilenko, "Perestroika and International Law," *Current Anglo-Soviet Approaches to International Law*, 1 (1990).

3. *War Quotations*, supra Chapter 2 note 31, at 315. President Wilson made this remark in an address on May 12, 1917.

4. *Inside the Criminal Mind*, supra Chapter 5 note 43, at 6.

5. Robert F. Turner, "The Gulf War—and Its Fallout," *Freedom Rev.*, May–June 1991, at 17, 19.

6. *Law and Minimum World Public Order*, supra Chapter 2 note 24, at 59–60.

7. See Frank Przetacznik, "The Catholic Concept of Peace as a Basic Collective Human Right," 39 *Revue De Broit Militaire Et De Droit De La Guerre*, 523, 559 (1990).

8, *Jeremiah* 6:14.

9, Robert F. Turner, "Councils of Caution Undercut Peace in the Gulf," *Christian Science Monitor*, 3 Dec. 990, at 19.

10. Furio Colombo, "Vatican: The Pope's War Record," *New Republic*, Apr. 8, 1991, at 12.

Chapter 7: Leading the Way—Pax Americana . . .   193

11. Id.

12. Clyde Haberman, "Pope, In Christmas Message, Warns on a Gulf War," *New York Times*, 26 Dec. 1990, at A19 (quoting Pope John Paul II).

13. Peter Steinfels, "War in the Gulf: Religious Leaders; Cardinal Says Iraqi's Acts Prove Bush Right," *New York Times*, Jan. 26, 1991, at A9 (quoting Pope John Paul II).

14. Furio Colombo, "Vatican: The Pope's War Record," *New Republic*, 8 Apr. 1991, at 12. The article compiled some of the Pope's statements about the use of force by the United States and its allies. On January 10, 1991: "This war is an adventure with no return." On January 16: "International law cannot be seen as a protection for hegemonic interests." On January 21: "The intoxication of war has prevailed over the courage of peace." On January 26: "This war is a threat to humanity." On February 4: "This war is a virus of death."

15. Barton Gellman, "Reaction to Tactic They Invented Baffles 1st Division Members," *Washington Post*, Sept. 13, 1991, at A21.

16. Guy Munger, "Lessons From the Desert Death Plow," *NC Catholic*, Sept. 22, 1991, at 4.

17. R. Ernest Dupuy and Trevor N. Dupuy, *The Encyclopedia of Military History*, (New York: Harper & Row, 1986), at 65–66.

18. Ronald Smothers, "Thousands Recall Quest for Equality," *New York Times*, Jan. 22, 1991, at A18 [hereinafter Thousands Recall Quest].

19. Richard Walker, "Martin Luther King's Widow Urges New Anti-War Movement," *Reuter Library Rep.*, Jan. 11, 1991.

20. Id. (quoting Coretta King).

21. Lynne Duke, "Coretta Scott King Deplores Decision," *Washington Post*, Jan. 17, 1991, at A30 (quoting Rev. Joseph Lowery).

22. Id.

23. *Thousands Recall Quest*, supra note 18, at A18.

24. Haynes Johnson, "Renewed Perils to Peace," *Washington Post*, Sept. 27, 1991, at A2.

25. Edward Gibbons, *The History of the Decline and Fall of the Roman Empire*, Vol. I, 85–86 (1914). Literally, the "peace of Rome. *Pax Romana* refers to the peace and prosperity in the known world, i.e., the Mediterranean, brought about by Roman rule from 27 B.C. to 180 A.D. Gibbon, widely recognized as the foremost modern scholar on the Roman empire, places the high point of *pax Romana* at 96–180 A.D., the period of the Antonine Caesars:

> If a man were called to fix the period in the history of the world during which the condition of the human race was most happy and prosperous, he would without hesitation, name that which elapsed from the death of Domitian [A.D. 96] to the accession of Commodus [A.D. 180]. The vast extent of the Roman Empire was governed by absolute power, under the guidance of virtue and wisdom. The armies were restrained by the firm but gentle hand of four successive emperors, whose characters and authority commanded in voluntary respect. The forms of the civil administration were carefully preserved by Nerva, Trajan, Hadrian, and the Antonines [Pius], who delighted in the image of liberty, and were pleased with considering themselves as the accountable ministers of the law.

26. See Norman Rich, *Hitler's War Aims*, (New York: Norton, 1973).

27. See Robert F. Burke, "A World in Chains: The New World Order of the Axis Powers," *Command*, Nov./Dec. 1991, at 64.

28. Before the Gulf War, the only parallel to the Security Council's authorization for the use of force was in the Korean War. On July 7, 1950, responding to North Korea's aggression into South Korea, the Security Council authorized the creation of a unified command under the authority of the United States. The resolution was passed, however, only due to the temporary absence of the Soviet Union. See Bruce Russett and James S. Sutterlin, "The U.N. in a New World Order," 70, *Foreign Affairs*, 69, 73.

29. The United Nations Security Council immediately condemned the Iraqi invasion of Kuwait, calling on Iraq to withdraw. See S.C. Res. 660 (Aug. 2, 1990), reprinted in I.L.M. 1325 (1990). After a series of subsequent Security Council resolutions authorizing the use of force, on November 29, 1990, the Security Council invoked its authority under Chapter VII of the U.N. Charter and passed a use of force resolution. See S.C. Res. 678 (Nov. 29, 1990), reprinted in I.L.M. 1565 (1990). Resolution 678 reads in relevant part:

> The Security Council

> ...
> 2. Authorizes member states cooperating with the government of Kuwait, unless Iraq on or before January 15, 1991 fully implements . . . the foregoing Resolutions, to use all necessary means to uphold and implement the Security Council Resolution 660 and all subsequent relevant Resolutions and to restore international peace and security in the area.

30. President George H. Bush, the Persian Gulf Crisis and the Federal Budget Deficit, Address Before a Joint Session of Congress (Sept. 11, 1990), in *Weekly Compilation of Presidential Documents*, Sept. 17, 1990, at 1359.

31. James A. Baer, "America's Strategy in the Persian Gulf Crisis, Address Before the Senate Foreign Relations Committee" (Dec. 5, 1990), U.S. Dept. of State Dispatch, Dec. 10, 1990, at 307, 309.

32. President George H. Bush, Remarks at Maxwell Air Force Base War College in Montgomery, Alabama (Apr. 13, 1991), in 27:16 Weekly Compilation of Presidential Documents 431 (Apr. 22, 1991); After the War; Bush Stands Firm on Military Policy in Iraqi Civil War, *New York Times*, Apr. 14, 1991, at A1.

33. President George Bush, The United Nations in a New Era, Address Before the U.N. General Assembly (Sept. 23, 1991), in 2:39 U.S. Dept. of St. Dispatch, Sept. 30, 1991, at 718–21.

34. Id at 720.

35. See infra note 43.

36. See "U.N., Iraq near Showdown; Bush Calls for Firmness," *Washington Post*, Sept. 24, 1991 at A1; "What's News," *Wall Street Journal*, Sept. 24, 1991, at A1. Both articles concentrated on the President's remarks concerning Iraqi hindrance of U.N. weapons inspectors. See also Fouad Ajami, "Where the Warrior Comes to Rest," *U.S. News and World Report*, Oct. 7, 1991, at 10.

37. Id.

38. Carla Anne Robbins, "Is There a New World Order?" *U.S. News and World Report*, Mar. 11, 1991, at 50 (quoting Joseph S. Nye, Jr.).

39. "President Orders Sweeping Reductions in Strategic and Tactical Nuclear Arms," *Washington Post*, Sept. 28, 1991, at A1.

40. William Safire, "The New New World Order," *New York Times*, Feb. 17, 1991, at 14 (quoting President George H. Bush).

41. President Bush's unilateral reductions in strategic and tactical weapons were unprecedented. They include the following: (1) the withdrawal of all short range nuclear weapons from Europe, to include nuclear artillery; (2) the elimination of all nuclear missiles from all U.S. Navy surface ships and attack submarines, to include nuclear-tipped cruise missiles; (3) the disarming of and taking off of all U.S. bombers on an active alert status; and (4) the entering into negotiations for the elimination of all missiles carrying multiple, independently targeted warheads.

42. Michael Kramer, "Kuwait: Back to the Past," *Time,* Aug. 5, 1991, at 32.

43. "We Stand . . . Before a New World of Hope and Possibility for Our Children," *Washington Post*, Dec. 26, 1991, at A35 (President Bush's televised speech on the breakup of the Soviet Union).

Chapter 8

The Role of the Military and Army Special Forces in Promoting Human Rights

Yours is the profession of arms, the will to win, the sure knowledge that in war there is no substitute for victory, that if you lose, the nation will be destroyed, that the very obsession of your public service must be duty, honor, country.

—General Douglas MacArthur

Synopsis
8.1 The United States Global Strategic View
8.2 New Non-Traditional Roles—Human Rights as a Force Multiplier
8.3 The Role of Special Forces

History has shown that one of the most vital components of any democratic society is its military establishment. True democracy cannot exist without a military establishment dedicated to the principles associated with civilian control of the military and respect for fundamental human rights. While such principles are taken for granted in societies resting on stable democratic traditions, this is not the case in the militaries of totalitarian states. The antithesis of a democratic military, the military under the totalitarian system wields tremendous power over the internal affairs of the state; in many cases they are the government.

For better or worse, the United States has entered a period of profound change in the use of military capabilities to meet the new circumstances of the War on Terror. Not only has the use of overt military force as a tool of national security reemerged, but the War on Terror has led to a rethinking of military roles and missions with a search for "force multipliers." The term force multipliers applies in many ways, but in the War on Terror there are two significant force multipliers. First, the American strategy of using local indigenous fighters to help displace totalitarian regimes is a tremendous force multiplier in the short term. Coupled with a small cadre of United States Special Operations Forces, President George W. Bush has correctly used these local forces in conjunction with America's strongest military suit—its fantastic air and sea power.

The military campaign in Afghanistan was easily won and the new government easily established because the war was seen less as an American invasion than as American help for the freedom-loving people to retake their own country. If the War on Terror reaches Iraq, the central element of any use of force must involve the use of local democratic opposition forces.

The other force multiplier speaks to the long-term goal of developing and institutionalizing a democratic ethos in the new militaries of the liberated lands. One of the greatest force multipliers imaginable would be to develop a methodology to encourage the growth of democracies throughout the community of nations. Since, for all practical purposes, democracies do not engage in aggressive warfare or terrorism, it is only logical for the United States to find ways to encourage the solidification of the new democracies that have emerged in the post-Cold War era and might emerge in the wake of the War on Terror.

The use of the United States military to promote democracy and human rights values to newly liberated countries will take on a much added significance in the War on Terror. In particular, the new Afghan government looks to American soldiers to assist them in establishing both order in the land and a law based Afghan military whose policies, rules, and practices are rooted in human rights. For now, many of these efforts are being conducted by American Special Operations Forces.

Although the term human rights and democratic values does not immediately bring to mind images of Special Forces soldiers in action, the decade of the '90s actually witnessed, for example, the use of "Green Berets" in missions that clearly reflect America's desire to inculcate human rights values within the militaries of our friends and allies. Special Forces soldiers have proved themselves to be a premier vehicle in this regard and are now heavily engaged in Afghanistan in this same effort. Given the new paradigm of democracy building, promoting human rights is clearly a priority mission for which Special Forces are uniquely qualified.

8.1 The United States Global Strategic View

Although the War on Terror has seen a dramatic shift to homeland security as the primary mission of the United States military, the overall strategy since the end of the Cold War has been one of active engagement or deterrence through power projection. At least in theory, active engagement also has a positive aim of promoting democracy, regional stability, and economic prosperity. However, in the context of conducting "operations other than war," the orientation has shifted from containing the menace posed by an expansionist Soviet Union to responding to regional conflicts throughout the world.

Since regional conflicts may vary and are far less monolithic than the old Soviet threat, ad hoc coalitions have replaced formal alliances. This was seen in the Gulf War as well as in the ongoing War on Terror. To support the active engagement theory, force generation has also changed from forward deployment to forward presence—no longer are large numbers of United States forces permanently stationed in foreign countries to ensure the peace. The new strategy in the War on Terror envisions a force projection of small contingents of American forces deployed on the foreign soil of our allies, such as Yemen and the Philippines, to assist in tracking down remaining al-Qa'eda forces and other like-minded terrorist groups.

Another purpose of these small scale deployments of American fighters is to deter aggression simply by being present in the region. Ultimately, deterrence remains a key component of strategic policy in the War on Terror, with the United States able and ready to use full scale force to punish aggression should the challenge arise.

Undoubtedly, the projection of its forces in this engagement strategy requires a strong leadership role by the United States. In the post-Cold War era, the cement of anti-communism that held democratic alliances together is no longer valid and many allies and friends no longer have the same degree of need for United States protection. Consequently, America is required to walk a thinner line between leadership and arrogant dominance, as selected coalitions are temporarily built to deal with the threat of terrorism. Furthermore, to be successful under the collective engagement strategy, American leadership must be exercised in conjunction with the interests of the people of the host nation. Indeed, the strongest coalition partners in defeating a totalitarian terrorist regime are the people enslaved in their own country.

Still, in the face of drastic military reductions in United States military forces since the 1990s, the elite ground forces available for these unique missions are being stretched to the breaking point. Demanding that the military do more with less, causes many to express skepticism about maintaining the required effectiveness to fight and win a war with the ever elusive remnants of al-Qa'eda and the renegade states who seek access to weapons of mass murder.

One fact stands certain. The United States cannot continue the War on Terror or take a strong leadership role in promoting democracy in liberated lands with an emasculated military. There is no historical basis to validate the proposition that a nation can successfully increase its influence in the world while simultaneously reducing its armed forces. In the context of deterring future aggression and winning the War on Terror this proposition is extremely disturbing. If history has proven anything, it is that the machinations of aggressor nations bent on expansion are not stopped by negotiation or peace overtures. In dealing with aggressor nations, the avenues of unilateral military reduction, negotiation, or appeasement do not lead to the path of peace—all are false concepts. The shared revulsion against war and terrorism that all free people possess will have no good effect unless it is coupled with an enforcement mechanism.

8.2 New Non-Traditional Roles—Human Rights as a Force Multiplier

Rubricated by the disintegration of the USSR in 1991, the world has changed drastically and with breathtaking speed. Just twelve years ago, the free world was focused on containing a heavily armed and expansionist Soviet Empire. Suddenly, primarily through internal aspirations for greater human rights (first and second generation), the Soviet Union and its ideology of repression were gone, and the attendant winds of freedom have blown to peoples and nations throughout the world. While these winds did not much impact the Middle East, other formerly repressed peoples of the world have expressed aspirations leading to hurried attempts to establish democratic governments and free market economies, the principal coins of the realm of human rights.

The Cold War period was the classic example of the traditional use of military force to deter aggression—combat soldiers trained and prepared to go to war at any moment. The American armed forces were war-fighters, pure and simple.

As the Soviet Union began to implode, the free world realized that it was not only the military might of the United States that defeated communism—it was the ideals represented by the United States. It was what Americans have always represented to the world—respect for human rights and freedom. It can be argued that the United States military fixed the Soviets in place, but freedom ultimately caused Soviet communism to disintegrate.

Unfortunately, the United States entered the post-Cold War era with only a vague and ill defined understanding that fostering democracies was vital to American national security interests. Nevertheless, in the War on Terror, the export of human rights values is a powerful weapon against those renegade nations and peoples who still seek to wage war and terrorism. Without question, democratic values and promoting human rights are needed force multipliers in the War on Terror, primarily because the new-styled terrorists cannot be deterred by the threat of force.

The promise of a new era where the world strives to be free from the constant evils of war, terrorism and human rights abuse demands that the United States military expand its traditional role of war-fighter and actively enter into new, nontraditional roles. Indeed, beginning in the 1980s, the United States military has in limited areas responded by assisting in such things as drug reduction, disaster relief, humanitarian assistance, peace operations, and nation building.

In the War on Terror, the United States military has a much-needed role to play in two key force multipliers—humanitarian assistance and nation building. In fact, the concern for human rights in general mirrors the overall United States national security policy of peacetime engagement by maintaining contacts with allies and friendly governments for the purpose of imparting values and ideals associated with democratic principles. These forces must also be brought to bear on terrorist regimes.

One of the force multipliers in the War on Terror is the use of the United States military for humanitarian peacemaking missions or peace operations. The term peace operation is now defined in United States military doctrine. The United States military definition is drafted in broad terms to capture the full range of possible activities associated with maintaining or restoring peace. According to the United States Army's Center for Strategy and Force Evaluation, the term "peace operation" is defined as:

> The umbrella term encompassing observers and monitors, traditional peacekeeping, preventive deployment, internal conflict resolution, security assistance to a civil authority, protection and delivery of humanitarian relief, guaranteeing and denial of movement, imposing sanctions, peace enforcement, high intensity operations, and any other military, paramilitary or non-military action taken in support of a diplomatic peacemaking process.[1]

In assessing the efficacy of a peace operation, from both a legal and a practical perspective, it is preferable to engage the backing and support of the United Nations as well as the financial assistance of fellow states. Not only do deepening fiscal concerns at home mitigate against the United States becoming the policeman for the world, common sense dictates that if the world is to move forward, all peace loving nations must join together in the effort. For these reasons, it is critical that other nations also share the burden and responsibility of future peace operations.

The other nontraditional role of the United States military is in the realm of nation building. This is what is happening in Afghanistan and will happen in Iraq following the departure of Saddam Hussein. The United States military defines nation building as "assisting a host nation in its efforts to restructure, reinforce, or rebuild its formal and informal institutions."[2] Starting in the 1960s, the United States military has been involved in providing nation assistance through the Foreign Assistance Act of 1961 and other Congressional authority to friends and allies throughout the world.

In the War on Terror, many of these activities will be centered on helping new nations develop the military capability to defend themselves from internal and external aggression. The United States military is currently utilizing special Congressional authority to undertake activities designed to improve the standard of living for the inhabitants of Afghanistan. As a result of this specific authority, United States military forces are engaged in numerous humanitarian and civic action (HCA) projects such as road building, medical care, well drilling, and other minor construction projects.

The hope for conducting these humanitarian efforts is that by raising the standard of living for the local population, the causes of internal unrest that are associated with conflict can be curtailed before they start. This concept has reaped tremendous benefits in fledgling democracies as far apart as Honduras and Thailand.

Of course, the most immediate concern in fostering the new Afghan government is the formation of a military establishment that respects human rights and adheres to democratic principles. The new military of Afghanistan has little frame of reference for a nation or, for that matter, a military establishment that is ruled by law and guided by human rights concerns. This new military will undoubtedly be absolutely essential in protecting the fledgling nation as it finds its path on the road to democracy. Ironically, although totalitarian based militaries were the chief violators of international human rights in the old nondemocratic Taliban system, the new military force of Afghanistan must establish itself as the single most influential institution during the transition period to democracy.

Because the chief violators of human rights in the old Taliban system were the military, it is absolutely essential that the new military arm of the Afghan government be fully exposed to the basic norms and standards of behavior commonly held by militaries in a democratic society. At a minimum, they must be apolitical, respectful of human rights, personally accountable, and responsive to the civilian leadership in a democratic process.

The hallmark of a successful democracy is the military's acceptance of human rights concerns. In a democracy the military cannot be an abuser of human rights; it must respect human rights and be held accountable to civilian authority under a rule of law for the way it carries out its missions. The military must understand that soldiers are not just people who have technical and fighting skills, but citizens who understand their role as a member of an organization with rights and responsibilities in a constitutional democracy.

Obviously, this goal can only be achieved through a systemic program designed to institutionalize these concepts. In past efforts with other emerging democracies since the fall of the Soviet Union, the United States relied on a variety of military security assistance programs to try to instill human rights values compatible with democratic principles in the host nation military. Since the United States effort was geared only at exposing the individual foreign soldier to human rights ideals, institutional reform within the host nation military never occurred. Essentially, the promotion of human rights and democracy were indirect benefits at best rather than explicit goals.

By their very nature, the promotion of human rights and democratization of the new Afghan government involves matters that cannot be assigned to the jurisdiction of any single department of the United States government. However, the promotion of human rights and democratic principles in the military of any new democracy is best left to the United States military.

The primary concern for the Afghan government rests with how, over the long term, the host nation military can be encouraged to accept a reduced and more professional role appropriate to a democracy. Ideally, this concern exceeds the minimally accepted standards for human rights and extends to the fullest possible range of meaningful human rights. These rights include freedom of religion, freedom of association, freedom of speech, and all of those principles indicative of a truly democratic society.

One of the major obstacles in imparting concepts relating to human rights and democratic principles is the fact that Afghanistan is faced with the social and economic turmoil traditionally associated with lesser developed countries—from economic chaos to actual armed insurgency by bands of terrorists and bandits. Thus, the effectiveness of any program of assistance must be measured against the realities associated with the specific problems facing Afghanistan.

A successful strategy to achieve these democratization goals must be based on three clearly focused themes directed to the host nation military (and appropriate civilian government officials):[3]

1. instilling a greater respect for internationally recognized standards for human rights;
2. fostering greater respect for and an understanding of the principle of civilian control of the military; and
3. improving military justice systems and procedures to comport with internationally recognized standards of human rights.

More than any other single endeavor one might imagine, the institutionalization of human rights values has the potential to directly reduce the threat of aggressive warfare. To be sure, true democracy cannot exist without a military establishment dedicated to the principles associated with a healthy respect for human rights. In his book on warfare in the twenty-first century, *Race to the Swift*, Richard Simpkin encapsulates this concept by noting that the militaries of democratic governments "rest on the rule of law, [of which human rights is the core] and must so rest."[4] While such values may be taken for granted in societies resting on stable democratic traditions, this is clearly not the case in Afghanistan or other nondemocratic states wishing to abandon totalitarian rule.

It is a simple fact that those militaries who truly abide by human rights will support and not threaten democratic development. In turn, healthy democracies are less likely to resort to aggressive warfare to settle international disputes.

8.3 The Role of Special Forces

The goal of creating a law based Afghan military has, to be sure, many challenges. Apart from the issue of funding such a force, they must be properly trained. Nevertheless, the training aspect is not as difficult as it may sound due to the fact that in large part, militaries of many emerging democracies have always looked to the American military in general, and the Army Special Forces in particular, as a model to assist them in defining how human rights concerns should properly function in their respective military establishments and how the military itself should fit into a more democratic form of government.

The genesis of modern Special Forces is most closely identified with President Kennedy who first officially authorized the wearing of the distinctive green beret for Army Special Forces. Although the entire force structure virtually disappeared with the end of the Vietnam era, revitalization of Special Forces occurred in the 1980s, culminating with the 1987 Congressional creation of a separate unified command—the United States Special Operations Command. This command has direct responsibility for every type of special operational force in the Navy, Army, Air Force and Marines. Congress further helped structure the types of forces and named specific mission activities: direct action, strategic reconnaissance, unconventional warfare, foreign internal defense, counterterrorism, civil affairs, psychological operations, humanitarian assistance, theater search and rescue, and other activities. Army Special Forces are one component of Special Operations Forces. They are elite professionals, trained to operate in any type of environment. Because they know the language, culture, and environment the soldiers foster an atmosphere of unity with the indigenous people.

The public mystique of the Green Beret as the ultimate jungle fighter capable of single-handedly defeating entire enemy battalions clearly belies the real importance of these specialized and highly skilled soldiers.[5] While they certainly have significant wartime missions, Special Forces are most effective when executing their dual peacetime roles of prevention and deterrence. Paradoxically, when executing their peacetime role, it is in part because of, not in spite of, the aura of invincibility that they enjoy public support and successes far in excess of what their limited numbers would imply. Currently, the Army has five active-duty, brigade-size Special Forces groups, each group operationally directed toward a particular segment of the world. In the War on Terror, prevention and deterrence roles are proving just as important as the fighting mission.

The preventive Special Forces role covers a full range of activities in the Third World whose principle purpose is to prevent escalation of conflict. This is done by training indigenous people to defend themselves and, to a lesser degree, engaging in limited humanitarian missions in the more remote parts of the country. This civic action includes providing medical and veterinary aid, conducting various public services, and other activities aimed at improving living conditions. The primary mission in the prevention role is training. It was during the Vietnam era that Special Forces earned the coveted reputation of being premier trainers of indigenous forces in military skills. Thousands of tribesmen and local Vietnamese were successfully organized into effective self-defense forces. Then, as now, the secret to their achievements was hard training, common sense, and empathy. These professionals were required not only to be experts in their technical skills, but also they had to be proficient in the host language, totally familiar with the culture, and able to literally live in the same, often-times primitive, environments.[6] To accomplish these tasks, these men undergo extensive, intensive, and expensive training.

Carrying on this tradition, Special Forces continue to teach host nation forces fundamental military skills, as well as more advanced tactics in desert, jungle and urban warfare. The training activities are directly aimed at assisting the host nation through long-term, in-depth courses and instruction. Accordingly, the mission to train and help organize indigenous local forces remains the cornerstone of modern Special Forces. The efforts crystallize as the host nation is better prepared to deal with overt manifestations of conflict through strengthened military capabilities.

When used in their preventive capacity, Special Forces are inherently successful in establishing an excellent rapport with the local population. This, quite naturally, helps defeat terrorism at its roots. One Special Forces medic conducting missions in Honduras described the typical attitude of the locals: "[I]t is also a morale boost for them [Hondurans]; if we're out in the field with them, sweat with them, eat their food and drink their beer, then, by God, they appreciate what we're doing and what we're going through."[7]

The other critical role of Special Forces is that of deterrence, a role that is particularly important in a crisis situation. In this role, the Special Forces are used to "wave the flag"—to be nothing less than concrete evidence that America is strongly committed to the host nation. A good illustration of this function occurred in 1987. Soldiers from the 1st Special Forces Group were sent to Thailand at the request of that government to demonstrate American support. At the time, the Thais were fighting North Vietnamese forces seeking to exert control over Cambodian resistance fighters. In keeping with the deterrent function, the Special Forces were directed to perform numerous well-publicized mass parachute jumps and exercises with their Thai counterparts along the Cambodian border. More recently this role of deterrence assigned to Special Forces has been illustrated by numerous events in Afghanistan. Special Forces operatives assigned to a bodyguard detail for Afghan President Karzi thwarted an assassination attempt on Karzi.[8] These Special Forces soldiers killed the would-be assailant, while sustaining a casualty to an American soldier.

Show of force functions are relatively well-suited to the Special Forces, due again in part to the universal reputation as America's elite fighters. In 1987 the *Soviet Military Review* described them as being "professional killers . . . with . . . a brutal hatred of the Communist countries."[9] Such puffing aside, these soldiers never fail to make an impression; no matter the story line, headlines always start with the same two words: "Green Berets."

Now, in the War on Terror, Special Forces are the preferred weapon of choice when it comes to ground operations with local counterparts and just as critical, in the task of promoting democratic values. Host nation forces who join the fight against terrorism instinctively turn to United States Army Special Forces for the following reasons.

First, Army Special Forces are uniquely positioned to influence the attitudes and, in some cases, even the structure and function of the host nation military. Why? Because they go where no other element of the United States military can. As noted by Major General Kenneth R. Bowra, the former commanding general of the Army's Special Forces (1996–1998), "Other than Special Forces, there is no element of the United States military forces that is capable of instilling human rights into the militaries of emerging democracies."

Special forces soldiers perform hundreds of missions each year in support of the war fighting combatant commands and other government agencies. These operations span the entire spectrum of conflict, to include direct action, foreign internal defense, special reconnaissance, unconventional warfare, security assistance training, humanitarian assistance, counter-narcotics, de-mining, and combating terrorism. Simply put, when it comes to operating with host nation forces, Green Berets are everywhere, doing everything. The deployment figures tell the tale. In FY 2001, for instance, United States Army Special Forces soldiers were deployed on over 2,500 missions to over 200 countries throughout the world.

Second, since Special Forces soldiers are extensively trained in the language, culture, religion, and politics of the countries in which they operate, they are best able to foster genuine military-to-military relationships. This fact applies to individual host nations, as well as to the geographic region as a whole. Thus, based on cultural nuances only they can appreciate, Special Forces can tailor each particular mission in order to make the maximum impression on their military counterparts regarding the importance of human rights concerns.

Third, more than any other arm of the United States military, Special Forces exemplify to foreign militaries the success story of how a professional military force can maintain a superb operational record while functioning in accordance with human rights concerns. Almost without exception, foreign soldiers are deeply impressed with how human rights and military efficiency can go hand-in-hand. Foreign forces know that, for the Green Berets, concern for human rights has always been the *sine que non* for United States military operations.

Indeed, the promotion of international human rights and democratic behavior has long been critical themes of the United States Army's Special Forces, regardless of the mission that they happen to be performing. President Kennedy routinely praised this unique quality, and no one who has followed the success story of Army Special Forces soldiers in Operations Provide Comfort (Iraq/Turkey), Restore Hope (Somalia), Just Cause (Panama), Desert Storm (Middle East), Uphold Democracy (Haiti), IFOR (Bosnia), and Enduring Freedom (Afghanistan) can doubt their value in this regard.

In short, Army Special Forces soldiers are universally recognized and respected as efficient, professional, and humanitarian. The former United States Army Special Operations Commander, Lieutenant General (ret.) James T. Scott, stressed this truism during a speech given in the summer of 1996: "I can tell you that Special Forces soldiers will . . . continue to serve as the conscience and the example of lesser developed nations regarding human rights."

The motto of Special Forces, *De Oppresso Liber*, reflects a profound concern for the inherent dignity of those who are denied international human rights. Crossing all cultural and societal boundaries, this mentality makes Special Forces soldiers an ideal model as they train host nation forces and assist in alleviating many of the conditions that breed human rights abuses. By word and deed, Special Forces promote the message that the hallmark of a professional military serving the interests of a democratic nation is its commitment to human rights. This message is not lost on the host nation.

The four basic themes taught and stressed to the developing Afghan military are:

1. human rights abuses are never tolerated by a democratic populace;
2. such violations do not shorten a conflict, be it internal or external in nature, but usually have the opposite effect;
3. the soldiers guilty of human rights violations must be punished, or similar abuses will certainly follow; and
4. in order to maintain discipline and esprit de corps, the chain of command must constantly train soldiers to respect internationally recognized human rights and the law of war.

Shortly after assuming command of the Army Special Forces Command at Fort Bragg, North Carolina, Major General Bowra took affirmative action to ensure that all Special Forces soldiers thoroughly understood their rights and responsibilities regarding human rights *vis-à-vis* any host nation military. A first ever Special Forces Human Rights Policy Memorandum[10] was issued by General Bowra, directing that all Special Forces soldiers who deploy overseas must:

1. be trained in the full range of human rights issues, both generally and as they may apply to the host nation to which they are deploying; and
2. report through the chain of command all gross violations of human rights they may encounter while overseas.

The four-page policy memorandum also requires commanders, whenever practicable, to integrate human rights training as a part of the training provided to the host nation military. In addition, senior commanders must review all exercise and deployment "after action reports" to evaluate the impact that human rights training initiatives have had on host nation military forces and then make recommendations for improvements to higher headquarters.

Special Forces soldiers and their commanders have many resources available to them to promote human rights. The most important resource, other than a soldier's solid moral compass, is the group judge advocate (GJA) assigned to each of the Special Forces groups. Each GJA is thoroughly trained in human rights law and has compiled an extensive collection of information dealing with human rights issues related to the group's area of responsibility.[11] Apart from providing the mandatory pre-deployment legal briefings to all soldiers deploying to foreign soil, these specialized military attorneys stay abreast of current doctrine in the form of international agreements, human rights doctrine, and political and social changes in the region concerned. They are currently on the ground in Afghanistan taking a proactive view and performing crucial implementation missions with the local Afghan leaders as a new Afghan military stands up.

Endnotes

1. The U.S. Army's Center for Strategy and Force Evaluation, *Peacekeeping Operations* 5 (Sept. 1993).

2. *The Management of Security Assistance,* The Defense Institute of Security Assistance Management 3 (12th ed., 1992).

3. See the Foreign Assistance Act of 1961, as amended, 22 U.S.C. 2347, which provides the authority for security assistance under the International Military Education and Training (IMET) program. These goals are taken from Title II of the Foreign Operations, Export Financing, and Related Programs Appropriations Act, 1991, Public Law 101-513; 104 Stat. 1997.

4. Richard Simpkin, *Race to the Swift: Thoughts on Twenty-First Century Warfare* (Washington, DC: Pergamon Press, 1985), at 320.

5. See, generally, H. Halberstadt, *Green Berets: Unconventional Warriors* (Novato, CA: Presidio Press, 1988) [hereinafter *Green Berets: Unconventional Warriors*].

6. See *Low-Intensity Warfare,* Michael T. Klare and Peter Kornbluh, eds. (New York: Pantheon Books, 1988).

7. *Green Berets: Unconventional Warriors*, supra note 5, at 50.

8. John F. Burns, "Traces of Terror: Kandahar and Kabul; Afghan President Escapes Bullets; 25 Killed by Bomb," *New York Times*, Sept. 6, 2002, at A1.

9. "Privileged Killers," *Soviet Military Review*, Jan. 1987, at 4.

10. USASFC (A) Policy Memorandum, dated August 13, 1996, "Special Forces Human Rights Policy." Issued by MG Kenneth Bowra, CG, USASFC (A).

11. See USASFC (A) *Human Rights Handbook* (on file with the OSJA, USASFC (A), Fort Bragg, NC).

Chapter 9

America Must Stay the Course

> *We reject the condescending view that freedom will not grow in the soil of the Middle East—or that Muslims somehow do not share in the desire to be free.*[1]
>
> —Condolrezza Rice

Since the events of September 11, 2001, the world has entered into a period fraught with uncertainty and yet, strangely, there shines a renewed hope to enlarge the peace and advance human rights. Although it is true that the chief characteristic of the War on Terror is the fact that the United States stands alone as the worlds only remaining superpower, this is not the central hope of the era. The central hope rests in the great promise of a world more fully based on governments who adhere to human rights and democratic values.

Unlike other historical eras, the War on Terror offers a chance to advance human rights and democracy in areas of the world heretofore untouched. Contrary to the voices of totalitarian despots, such as Saddam Hussein, there is an intense global interest in securing the blessings of peace, prosperity and human rights that the West has so long enjoyed. The positive aspect of the War on Terror is that it will create one of those rare moments in history where a window of opportunity opens for the world to make serious and lasting strides toward the ever elusive goals of controlling aggressive warfare and terrorism, and at the same time improving respect for human rights.

If the international community led by the United States does not find ways to realistically promote and foster at least the most fundamental categories of human rights, the terrorism exemplified by the attacks on America is sure to be only a taste of things to come. Global terrorism will only meet its end because of the efforts of America, but battlefield victories alone will not bring a peace that can extend beyond a handful of years. Long-term periods of peace and stability require an attendant advance in institutionalizing the blessings of human rights.

Assisting in the incorporation of human rights values into the institutional framework of, for example, a new Afghan government is not merely an end worthy unto itself, but in the quest for war avoidance and promoting the full range of human rights benefits it creates a society which can peacefully coexist with the whole of the world community. It appears fundamentally obvious that activities pursued by democracies are substantially better than the activities pursued by totalitarian regimes like Cuba, North Korea, Sudan, Iraq, Iran, Syria, and Libya. While it has long been suspected that stable democracies firmly committed to human rights do not make war on each other, nor do they abuse their own people, the empirical evidence now demonstrates this correlation. Debate on this point is over.

Thus, the central question now becomes how best to quickly impress solid human rights values in other national entities. Most certainly, human rights values become solid and irreversible only through the development of institutions designed to promote them. Institutionalization must be the criterion. While the desires for freedom will ultimately destroy a totalitarian system, freedom and human rights are not self perpetuating; they can only be sustained through the creation of concrete law-based institutions.

In order to foster democratic ideals and human rights in countries like Afghanistan, the United States must learn from the recent past in its failure to liberate the people of Iraq from the evil of Saddam Hussein at the close of the Gulf War. The United States must accept that it has an obligation to assist any country endeavoring to create governments grounded in basic human rights. Liberated nations in the War on Terror will eagerly embrace the principles of liberal democracy and self-determination, but will need immediate assistance to implement an institutional framework to accommodate their desires for the full range of human rights. Without meaningful assistance to translate the battle cry of human rights into an institutional framework, it is naive to assume that democratic values and human rights will germinate

Apart from the normal pressures associated with building democratic institutions, the escalating and often uncontrollable level of disorder and violence in many of the new democracies forcefully supports the idea that the United States must assist in the creation and maintenance of fledgling democratic governments. Aside from country specific issues, whether one concentrates on sectarian fragmentation or religious bias, the euphoric hope for instant world peace and greater human rights in the wake of the War on Terror is presumptuous—the globe is a dangerous place. Indeed, the danger of global terrorism is far more pronounced than ever before. Today, due to the growth of terrorist activities throughout the world, it is not only uncertain where the next attack will occur, but virtually impossible to take a defensive posture against every potential attack. The modern al-Que'ada-styled terrorist cannot be deterred by the threat of force—these murderers welcome death.

In the minds of much of the world, the vision of freedom is synonymous with the words—the United States of America. People yearn for governments that can guarantee the social, political, and economic freedoms of human rights. Does this mean, however, that the United States should take the lead in assisting these nations to translate desire into reality? Should the United Nations, another nation, or another group of nations, fulfill the mission?

In a pragmatic light, true collective security has always required a dominant leader. In the twentieth century, that has often meant the United States, particularly since World War II. In truth, the lesson of the Gulf War was the same as the Korean War, the United Nations or any other coalition does not have the capacity to guarantee the security of its members absent the direct participation of the United States. In the first major challenge of world terrorism it was the active influence of the United States that built the necessary coalition force to respond.

The contention that America stands as the role model for the world is only part of the truth. To a substantial degree, the tyranny of communism met its end precisely because America generally has always been the world's beacon for broad principles of human rights. These principles of human rights are now necessary to ensure the destruction of terrorism as well. From this perspective, the United States has a continuing responsibility to the community of nations to promote human rights. The United States cannot afford to be indifferent to the moral values that are the true source of its global influence. Judged by any positive standard, be it in the field of human rights, self-determination, economic opportunity, or privacy related to property and person, the United States stands out as a positive model. But America's most fundamental value does not reside in her military might or industrial complex. Those mighty pillars merely provide support for the United States' most enduring commodity—human rights flourishing under a systemic respect for the rule of law.

America, like great nations before her, has related all of these positive human rights values to a strong heritage of law institutionalized into its government. The founders of the nation established certain fundamental democratic institutions, and subsequent generations have generally exhibited the moral values and discipline required to maintain those institutions. American democracy continues to boast that men can rise to eminence in nearly any profession unaided by the advantages related to hereditary preferment. For over 200 years this boast of freedom and human rights has echoed throughout the world, penetrating even the strongest iron curtain of communism. As a consequence, together with American force of arms, several totalitarian regimes have been swept into the dust of history. More than any other nation, America has demonstrated that human rights and the by-products of human rights—economic success and social well being—are worth promoting and protecting.

Therefore, if democracies shun aggression, terrorism and hate, it is in the best interest of the United States to expend the necessary time, effort, and money to adequately assist those nations who have exhibited the will to embark on democracy's path. In this context, the United States must rapidly assess the ramifications of this important responsibility and offer assistance to the fledgling Afghan government before the window of opportunity closes and the chance for democracy is lost. The most significant danger in the War on Terror is that the global movement toward democratic reform, which started with the collapse of the Soviet Union will fail, signaling a return to totalitarianism, a more dangerous world, or even a Third World War.

Arguments that the Western European nations should take the lead in fostering the development of greater human rights and democracy have proven to be contentious. One need look no further than the conflict in the backyard of the European community itself, the former Yugoslavia, to conclude that either individually or collectively, Western Europe is not able to quickly solve even its own problems. Although Germany may be best suited to take on a leadership role in Europe, the historical suspicion of German militarism, justified or not, makes such an event is highly unlikely.

For similar reasons, the Far East will not allow Japan, a powerhouse of the region, to assert a more dominant leadership role. It remains for the United States to continue to extend its influence in the region, particularly in the face of the destabilizing effect of an aggressive and nuclear armed North Korea.

It is far too early to tell if the United Nations might one day fill the vacuum, though its record in peacekeeping actions since 1989 has often proved impressive. Still, hopes that the United Nations might evolve into a truly effective world collective security organization have not materialized. It seems unlikely that the United Nations can fulfill such a position on its own.

In the final analysis, there is as yet no viable substitute for United States dominance in the international arena. For the time being, it is apparent that history has chosen the United States as the nation most suited to assist in promoting human rights in the War on Terror for three reasons. First, the United States emerged from the Cold War as the foremost power in the world, a power that possesses the necessary capability to influence change. Second, many governments in Western Europe, East Asia, and the Middle East, whether allies of the United States or not, want the United States to continue to lead. Third, despite its own internal faults and shortcomings in the realm of human rights, it is well recognized that the United States has always been the foremost champion of values related to human rights and democratic ideals.

Interestingly, many of these impressions have not been made by the civilian arm of the United States, but by its military forces stationed throughout the world. The United States military has been—and continues to be—an excellent ambassador for positive change.

Finally, those who argue that the United States should not become involved in assisting the growth of human rights and democratic movements because there is no domestic benefit are incorrect. The United States chose not to become involved after World War I, and the resulting costs in terms of life lost and property destroyed were extremely high. Conversely, the United States did choose to become actively engaged after World War II and the resulting benefits were substantial, producing "the longest period of uninterrupted peace in Europe in 400 years, the highest level of economic prosperity and sustained economic growth in the history of the Western World, and the defeat of totalitarianism in Eastern Europe."[2] The United States wisely rolled up its sleeves and rooted out Nazi ideology, Italian fascism, and Japanese militarism. These evils were replaced with liberal democratic values which led to strongly rooted constitutional democracies at peace with their people and with the world community.

The spread of human rights and democracy around the world helps United States security, improves global stability, and increases economic prosperity. Thus, promoting governments who desire human rights and democracy benefits American national security directly—a more democratic world is a safer world. President George W. Bush has demonstrated an understanding of the paradigm of terrorism and war avoidance; his administration must stay the course and develop viable programs to fully promote the paradigm.

Gauged in terms of maintaining peace and stability—critical goals in the world community—it is time for the United States to exercise new thinking in terms of pursuing a foreign policy that promotes real programs to assist new democracies institutionalize human rights principles. Armed with the fact that human rights is the cornerstone of democracy and democracy is the foundation of building a better world, the United States must shift its role as the chief advocator of human rights to the chief promoter.

The United States has an opportunity and an obligation to assist in the historic potential for advancing human rights throughout the world community. Without question, the opening for constructive change is far wider than after the First or Second World Wars or the end of the Cold War. The events of September 11, 2001, have unleashed a tremendous moral clarity in America and the civilized world for the creation of governments that are truly based on protecting human rights and living with their neighbors in peace and prosperity.

In order to push the global movement towards expanding human rights, America must develop a strong and practical strategy that can truly assist the struggling and emerging governments to get out of the totalitarian shadows in which they stand by institutionalizing human rights values. If the doctrines of human rights can be inculcated, for example, in Afghanistan, the benefits will lead to a stabilized country capable of contributing as a full partner to a more peaceful, humane, and free world.

Endnotes

1. "How to Liberate Iraq," *Wall Street Journal,* Oct. 8, 2002, at A22.

2. Brigadier General James R. Harding and John A. Pitts, "The Challenge of Peace," *Military Review*, July 1991, at 2.

Appendices

Appendix A

Selected Provisions of the Charter of the United Nations

June 26, 1945, 59 Stat. 1031, T.S. 993, 3 Bevans 1153, entered into force Oct. 24, 1945.

PREAMBLE

WE THE PEOPLES OF THE UNITED NATIONS DETERMINED

- to save succeeding generations from the scourge of war, which twice in our lifetime has brought untold sorrow to mankind, and

- to reaffirm faith in fundamental human rights, in the dignity and worth of the human person, in the equal rights of men and women and of nations large and small, and

- to establish conditions under which justice and respect for the obligations arising from treaties and other sources of international law can be maintained, and

- to promote social progress and better standards of life in larger freedom,

AND FOR THESE ENDS

- to practice tolerance and live together in peace with one another as good neighbors, and

- to unite our strength to maintain international peace and security, and

- to ensure by the acceptance of principles and the institution of methods, that armed force shall not be used, save in the common interest, and

- to employ international machinery for the promotion of the economic and social advancement of all peoples,

HAVE RESOLVED TO COMBINE OUR EFFORTS TO ACCOMPLISH THESE AIMS

Accordingly, our respective Governments, through representatives assembled in the city of San Francisco, who have exhibited their full powers found to be in good and due form, have agreed to the present Charter of the United Nations and do hereby establish an international organization to be known as the United Nations.

CHAPTER I
PURPOSES AND PRINCIPLES

Article 1
The Purposes of the United Nations are:
1. To maintain international peace and security, and to that end: to take effective collective measures for the prevention and removal of threats to the peace, and for the suppression of acts of aggression or other breaches of the peace, and to bring about by peaceful means, and in conformity with the principles of justice and international law, adjustment or settlement of international disputes or situations which might lead to a breach of the peace;
2. To develop friendly relations among nations based on respect for the principle of equal rights and self-determination of peoples, and to take other appropriate measures to strengthen universal peace;
3. To achieve international cooperation in solving international problems of an economic, social, cultural, or humanitarian character, and in promoting and encouraging respect for human rights and for fundamental freedoms for all without distinction as to race, sex, language, or religion; and
4. To be a center for harmonizing the actions of nations in the attainment of these common ends.

Article 2

The Organization and its Members, in pursuit of the Purposes stated in Article 1, shall act in accordance with the following Principles.

1. The Organization is based on the principle of the sovereign equality of all its Members.
2. All Members, in order to ensure to all of them the rights and benefits resulting from membership, shall fulfill in good faith the obligations assumed by them in accordance with the present Charter.
3. All Members shall settle their international disputes by peaceful means in such a manner that international peace and security, and justice, are not endangered.
4. All Members shall refrain in their international relations from the threat or use of force against the territorial integrity or political independence of any state, or in any other manner inconsistent with the Purposes of the United Nations.
5. All Members shall give the United Nations every assistance in any action it takes in accordance with the present Charter, and shall refrain from giving assistance to any state against which the United Nations is taking preventive or enforcement action.
6. The Organization shall ensure that states which are not Members of the United Nations act in accordance with these Principles so far as may be necessary for the maintenance of international peace and security.
7. Nothing contained in the present Charter shall authorize the United Nations to intervene in matters which are essentially within the domestic jurisdiction of any state or shall require the Members to submit such matters to settlement under the present Charter; but this principle shall not prejudice the application of enforcement measures under Chapter VII.

CHAPTER II
MEMBERSHIP

Article 3

The original Members of the United Nations shall be the states which, having participated in the United Nations Conference on International Organization at San Francisco, or having previously signed the Declaration by United Nations of January 1, 1942, sign the present Charter and ratify it in accordance with Article 110.

Article 4
1. Membership in the United Nations is open to all other peace-loving states which accept the obligations contained in the present Charter and, in the judgment of the Organization, are able and willing to carry out these obligations.
2. The admission of any such state to membership in the United Nations will be effected by a decision of the General Assembly upon the recommendation of the Security Council.

Article 5
A member of the United Nations against which preventive or enforcement action has been taken by the Security Council may be suspended from the exercise of the rights and privileges of membership by the General Assembly upon the recommendation of the Security Council. The exercise of these rights and privileges may be restored by the Security Council.

Article 6
A Member of the United Nations which has persistently violated the Principles contained in the present Charter may be expelled from the Organization by the General Assembly upon the recommendation of the Security Council.

CHAPTER III
ORGANS

Article 7
1. There are established as the principal organs of the United Nations: a General Assembly, a Security Council, an Economic and Social Council, a Trusteeship Council, an International Court of Justice, and a Secretariat.
2. Such subsidiary organs as may be found necessary may be established in accordance with the present Charter.

Article 8
The United Nations shall place no restrictions on the eligibility of men and women to participate in any capacity and under conditions of equality in its principal and subsidiary organs.

Appendix A: Selected Provisions of the Charter . . .

CHAPTER IV
THE GENERAL ASSEMBLY

Composition

Article 9
1. The General Assembly shall consist of all the Members of the United Nations.
2. Each member shall have not more than five representatives in the General Assembly.

Functions and Powers

Article 10
The General Assembly may discuss any questions or any matters within the scope of the present Charter or relating to the powers and functions of any organs provided for in the present Charter, and, except as provided in Article 12, may make recommendations to the Members of the United Nations or to the Security Council or to both on any such questions or matters.

Article 11
1. The General Assembly may consider the general principles of cooperation in the maintenance of international peace and security, including the principles governing disarmament and the regulation of armaments, and may make recommendations with regard to such principles to the Members or to the Security Council or to both.
2. The General Assembly may discuss any questions relating to the maintenance of international peace and security brought before it by any Member of the United Nations, or by the Security Council, or by a state which is not a Member of the United Nations in accordance with Article 35, paragraph 2, and, except as provided in Article 12, may make recommendations with regard to any such questions to the state or states concerned or to the Security Council or to both. Any such question on which action is necessary shall be referred to the Security Council by the General Assembly either before or after discussion.
3. The General Assembly may call the attention of the Security Council to situations which are likely to endanger international peace and security.

4. The powers of the General Assembly set forth in this Article shall not limit the general scope of Article 10.

Article 12
1. While the Security Council is exercising in respect of any dispute or situation the functions assigned to it in the present Charter, the General Assembly shall not make any recommendation with regard to that dispute or situation unless the Security Council so requests.
2. The Secretary-General, with the consent of the Security Council, shall notify the General Assembly at each session of any matters relative to the maintenance of international peace and security which are being dealt with by the Security Council and shall similarly notify the General Assembly, or the Members of the United Nations if the General Assembly is not in session, immediately the Security Council ceases to deal with such matters.

Article 13
1. The General Assembly shall initiate studies and make recommendations for the purpose of:
a. promoting international cooperation in the political field and encouraging the progressive development of international law and its codification;
b. promoting international cooperation in the economic, social, cultural, educational, and health fields, and assisting in the realization of human rights and fundamental freedoms for all without distinction as to race, sex, language, or religion.
2. The further responsibilities, functions and powers of the General Assembly with respect to matters mentioned in paragraph 1(b) above are set forth in Chapters IX and X.

Article 14
Subject to the provisions of Article 12, the General Assembly may recommend measures for the peaceful adjustment of any situation, regardless of origin, which it deems likely to impair the general welfare or friendly relations among nations, including situations resulting from a violation of the provisions of the present Charter setting forth the Purposes and Principles of the United Nations.

Appendix A: Selected Provisions of the Charter . . .

Article 15
1. The General Assembly shall receive and consider annual and special reports from the Security Council; these reports shall include an account of the measures that the Security Council has decided upon or taken to maintain international peace and security.
2. The General Assembly shall receive and consider reports from the other organs of the United Nations.

Article 16
The General Assembly shall perform such functions with respect to the international trusteeship system as are assigned to it under Chapters XII and XIII, including the approval of the trusteeship agreements for areas not designated as strategic.

Article 17
1. The General Assembly shall consider and approve the budget of the Organization.
2. The expenses of the Organization shall be borne by the Members as apportioned by the General Assembly.
3. The General Assembly shall consider and approve any financial and budgetary arrangements with specialized agencies referred to in Article 57 and shall examine the administrative budgets of such specialized agencies with a view to making recommendations to the agencies concerned.

Voting

Article 18
1. Each member of the General Assembly shall have one vote.
2. Decisions of the General Assembly on important questions shall be made by a two-thirds majority of the members present and voting. These questions shall include: recommendations with respect to the maintenance of international peace and security, the election of the non-permanent members of the Security Council, the election of the members of the Economic and Social Council, the election of members of the Trusteeship Council in accordance with paragraph 1(c) of Article 86, the admission of new Members to the United Nations, the suspension of the rights and privileges of membership, the expulsion of Members, questions relating to the operation of the trusteeship system, and budgetary questions.

3. Decisions on other questions, Composition including the determination of additional categories of questions to be decided by a two-thirds majority, shall be made by a majority of the members present and voting.

Article 19
A Member of the United Nations which is in arrears in the payment of its financial contributions to the Organization shall have no vote in the General Assembly if the amount of its arrears equals or exceeds the amount of the contributions due from it for the preceding two full years. The General Assembly may, nevertheless, permit such a Member to vote if it is satisfied that the failure to pay is due to conditions beyond the control of the Member.

Procedure

Article 20
The General Assembly shall meet in regular annual sessions and in such special sessions as occasion may require. Special sessions shall be convoked by the Secretary-General at the request of the Security Council or of a majority of the Members of the United Nations.

Article 21
The General Assembly shall adopt its own rules of procedure. It shall elect its President for each session.

Article 22
The General Assembly may establish such subsidiary organs as it deems necessary for the performance of its functions.

CHAPTER V
THE SECURITY COUNCIL

Article 23
1. The Security Council shall consist of fifteen Members of the United Nations. The Republic of China, France, the Union of Soviet Socialist Republics, the United Kingdom of Great Britain and Northern Ireland, and the United States of America shall be permanent members of the Security Council. The General Assembly shall elect ten other Members of the United Nations to be non-permanent members of the Security

Council, due regard being specially paid, in the first instance to the contribution of Members of the United Nations to the maintenance of international peace and security and to the other purposes of the Organization, and also to equitable geographical distribution.

2. The non-permanent members of the Security Council shall be elected for a term of two years. In the first election of the non-permanent members after the increase of the membership of the Security Council from eleven to fifteen, two of the four additional members shall be chosen for a term of one year. A retiring member shall not be eligible for immediate re-election.

3. Each member of the Security Council shall have one representative.

Functions and Powers

Article 24
1. In order to ensure prompt and effective action by the United Nations, its Members confer on the Security Council primary responsibility for the maintenance of international peace and security, and agree that in carrying out its duties under this responsibility the Security Council acts on their behalf.
2. In discharging these duties the Security Council shall act in accordance with the Purposes and Principles of the United Nations. The specific powers granted to the Security Council for the discharge of these duties are laid down in Chapters VI, VII, VIII, and XII.
3. The Security Council shall submit annual and, when necessary, special reports to the General Assembly for its consideration.

Article 25
The Members of the United Nations agree to accept and carry out the decisions of the Security Council in accordance with the present Charter.

Article 26
In order to promote the establishment and maintenance of international peace and security with the least diversion for armaments of the world's human and economic resources, the Security Council shall be responsible for formulating, with the assistance of the Military Staff Committee referred to in Article 47, plans to be submitted to the Members of the United Nations for the establishment of a system for the regulation of armaments.

Voting

Article 27
1. Each member of the Security Council shall have one vote.
2. Decisions of the Security Council on procedural matters shall be made by an affirmative vote of nine members.
3. Decisions of the Security Council on all other matters shall be made by an affirmative vote of nine members including the concurring votes of the permanent members; provided that, in decisions under Chapter VI, and under paragraph 3 of Article 52, a party to a dispute shall abstain from voting.

Procedure

Article 28
1. The Security Council shall be so organized as to be able to function continuously. Each member of the Security Council shall for this purpose be represented at all times at the seat of the Organization.
2. The Security Council shall hold periodic meetings at which each of its members may, if it so desires, be represented by a member of the government or by some other specially designated representative.
3. The Security Council may hold meetings at such places other than the seat of the Organization as in its judgment will best facilitate its work.

Article 29
The Security Council may establish such subsidiary organs as it deems necessary for the performance of its functions.

Article 30
The Security Council shall adopt its own rules of procedure, including the method of selecting its President.

Article 31
Any Member of the United Nations which is not a member of the Security Council may participate, without vote, in the discussion of any question brought before the Security Council whenever the latter considers that the interests of that Member are specially affected.

Article 32

Any Member of the United Nations which is not a member of the Security Council or any state which is not a Member of the United Nations, if it is a party to a dispute under consideration by the Security Council, shall be invited to participate, without vote, in the discussion relating to the dispute. The Security Council shall lay down such conditions as it deems just for the participation of a state which is not a Member of the United Nations.

CHAPTER VI
PACIFIC SETTLEMENT OF DISPUTES

Article 33

1. The parties to any dispute, the continuance of which is likely to endanger the maintenance of international peace and security, shall, first of all, seek a solution by negotiation, enquiry, mediation, conciliation, arbitration, judicial settlement, resort to regional agencies or arrangements, or other peaceful means of their own choice.
2. The Security Council shall, when it deems necessary, call upon the parties to settle their dispute by such means.

Article 34

The Security Council may investigate any dispute, or any situation which might lead to international friction or give rise to a dispute, in order to determine whether the continuance of the dispute or situation is likely to endanger the maintenance of international peace and security.

Article 35

1. Any Member of the United Nations may bring any dispute, or any situation of the nature referred to in Article 34, to the attention of the Security Council or of the General Assembly.
2. A state which is not a Member of the United Nations may bring to the attention of the Security Council or of the General Assembly any dispute to which it is a party if it accepts in advance, for the purposes of the dispute, the obligations of pacific settlement provided in the present Charter.
3. The proceedings of the General Assembly in respect of matters brought to its attention under this Article will be subject to the provisions of Articles 11 and 12.

Article 36
1. The Security Council may, at any stage of a dispute of the nature referred to in Article 33 or of a situation of like nature, recommend appropriate procedures or methods of adjustment.
2. The Security Council should take into consideration any procedures for the settlement of the dispute which have already been adopted by the parties.
3. In making recommendations under this Article the Security Council should also take into consideration that legal disputes should as a general rule be referred by the parties to the International Court of Justice in accordance with the provisions of the Statute of the Court.

Article 37
1. Should the parties to a dispute of the nature referred to in Article 33 fail to settle it by the means indicated in that Article, they shall refer it to the Security Council.
2. If the Security Council deems that the continuance of the dispute is in fact likely to endanger the maintenance of international peace and security, it shall decide whether to take action under Article 36 or to recommend such terms of settlement as it may consider appropriate.

Article 38
Without prejudice to the provisions of Articles 33 to 37, the Security Council may, if all the parties to any dispute so request, make recommendations to the parties with a view to a pacific settlement of the dispute.

CHAPTER VII
ACTION WITH RESPECT TO THREATS TO THE PEACE, BREACHES OF THE PEACE, AND ACTS OF AGGRESSION

Article 39
The Security Council shall determine the existence of any threat to the peace, breach of the peace, or act of aggression and shall make recommendations, or decide what measures shall be taken in accordance with Articles 41 and 42, to maintain or restore international peace and security.

Article 40
In order to prevent an aggravation of the situation, the Security Council may, before making the recommendations or deciding upon the measures provided for in Article 39, call upon the parties concerned to comply with such provisional measures as it deems necessary or desirable. Such provisional measures shall be without prejudice to the rights, claims, or position of the parties concerned. The Security Council shall duly take account of failure to comply with such provisional measures.

Article 41
The Security Council may decide what measures not involving the use of armed force are to be employed to give effect to its decisions, and it may call upon the Members of the United Nations to apply such measures. These may include complete or partial interruption of economic relations and of rail, sea, air, postal, telegraphic, radio, and other means of communication, and the severance of diplomatic relations.

Article 42
Should the Security Council consider that measures provided for in Article 41 would be inadequate or have proved to be inadequate, it may take such action by air, sea, or land forces as may be necessary to maintain or restore international peace and security. Such action may include demonstrations, blockade, and other operations by air, sea, or land forces of Members of the United Nations.

Article 43
1. All Members of the United Nations, in order to contribute to the maintenance of international peace and security, undertake to make available to the Security Council, on its call and in accordance with a special agreement or agreements, armed forces, assistance, and facilities, including rights of passage, necessary for the purpose of maintaining international peace and security.
2. Such agreement or agreements shall govern the numbers and types of forces, their degree of readiness and general location, and the nature of the facilities and assistance to be provided.
3. The agreement or agreements shall be negotiated as soon as possible on the initiative of the Security Council. They shall be concluded between the Security Council and Members or between the Security Council and groups of Members and shall be subject to ratification by

the signatory states in accordance with their respective constitutional processes.

Article 44
When the Security Council has decided to use force it shall, before calling upon a Member not represented on it to provide armed forces in fulfillment of the obligations assumed under Article 43, invite that Member, if the Member so desires, to participate in the decisions of the Security Council concerning the employment of contingents of that Member's armed forces.

Article 45
In order to enable the United Nations to take urgent military measures Members shall hold immediately available national air-force contingents for combined international enforcement action. The strength and degree of readiness of these contingents and plans for their combined action shall be determined, within the limits laid down in the special agreement or agreements referred to in Article 43, by the Security Council with the assistance of the Military Staff Committee.

Article 46
Plans for the application of armed force shall be made by the Security Council with the assistance of the Military Staff Committee.

Article 47
1. There shall be established a Military Staff Committee to advise and assist the Security Council on all questions relating to the Security Council's military requirements for the maintenance of international peace and security, the employment and command of forces placed at its disposal, the regulation of armaments, and possible disarmament.
2. The Military Staff Committee shall consist of the Chiefs of Staff of the permanent members of the Security Council or their representatives. Any Member of the United Nations not permanently represented on the Committee shall be invited by the Committee to be associated with it when the efficient discharge of the Committee's responsibilities requires the participation of that Member in its work.
3. The Military Staff Committee shall be responsible under the Security Council for the strategic direction of any armed forces placed at the disposal of the Security Council. Questions relating to the command of such forces shall be worked out subsequently.

4. The Military Staff Committee, with the authorization of the Security Council and after consultation with appropriate regional agencies, may establish regional subcommittees.

Article 48
1. The action required to carry out the decisions of the Security Council for the maintenance of international peace and security shall be taken by all the Members of the United Nations or by some of them, as the Security Council may determine.
2. Such decisions shall be carried out by the Members of the United Nations directly and through their action in the appropriate international agencies of which they are members.

Article 49
The Members of the United Nations shall join in affording mutual assistance in carrying out the measures decided upon by the Security Council.

Article 50
If preventive or enforcement measures against any state are taken by the Security Council, any other state, whether a Member of the United Nations or not, which finds itself confronted with special economic problems arising from the carrying out of those measures shall have the right to consult the Security Council with regard to a solution of those problems.

Article 51
Nothing in the present Charter shall impair the inherent right of individual or collective self-defense if an armed attack occurs against a Member of the United Nations, until the Security Council has taken measures necessary to maintain international peace and security. Measures taken by Members in the exercise of this right of self-defense shall be immediately reported to the Security Council and shall not in any way affect the authority and responsibility of the Security Council under the present Charter to take at any time such action as it deems necessary in order to maintain or restore international peace and security.

CHAPTER VIII
REGIONAL ARRANGEMENTS

Article 52
1. Nothing in the present Charter precludes the existence of regional arrangements or agencies for dealing with such matters relating to the maintenance of international peace and security as are appropriate for regional action, provided that such arrangements or agencies and their activities are consistent with the Purposes and Principles of the United Nations.
2. The Members of the United Nations entering into such arrangements or constituting such agencies shall make every effort to achieve pacific settlement of local disputes through such regional arrangements or by such regional agencies before referring them to the Security Council.
3. The Security Council shall encourage the development of pacific settlement of local disputes through such regional arrangements or by such regional agencies either on the initiative of the states concerned or by reference from the Security Council.
4. This Article in no way impairs the application of Articles 34 and 35.

Article 53
1. The Security Council shall, where appropriate, utilize such regional arrangements or agencies for enforcement action under its authority. But no enforcement action shall be taken under regional arrangements or by regional agencies without the authorization of the Security Council, with the exception of measures against any enemy state, as defined in paragraph 2 of this Article, provided for pursuant to Article 107 or in regional arrangements directed against renewal of aggressive policy on the part of any such state, until such time as the Organization may, on request of the Governments concerned, be charged with the responsibility for preventing further aggression by such a state.
2. The term enemy state as used in paragraph 1 of this Article applies to any state which during the Second World War has been an enemy of any signatory of the present Charter.

Article 54
The Security Council shall at all times be kept fully informed of activities undertaken or in contemplation under regional arrangements or by regional agencies for the maintenance of international peace and security.

Appendix A: Selected Provisions of the Charter . . .

. . .

IN FAITH WHEREOF the representatives of the Governments of the United Nations have signed the present Charter.

DONE at the city of San Francisco the twenty-sixth day of June, one thousand nine hundred and forty-five.

Appendix B

United Nations Security Council Resolution 1368 (2001)

The Security Council,

Reaffirming the principles and purposes of the Charter of the United Nations,

Determined to combat by all means threats to international peace and security caused by terrorist acts,

Recognizing the inherent right of individual or collective self-defence in accordance with the Charter,

1. *Unequivocally condemns* in the strongest terms the horrifying terrorist attacks which took place on 11 September 2001 in New York, Washington (D.C.) and Pennsylvania and *regards* such acts, like any act of international terrorism, as a threat to international peace and security;

2. *Expresses* its deepest sympathy and condolences to the victims and their families and to the People and Government of the United States of America;

3. *Calls* on all States to work together urgently to bring to justice the perpetrators, organizers and sponsors of these terrorist attacks and *stresses* that those responsible for aiding, supporting or harbouring the perpetrators, organizers and sponsors of these acts will be held accountable;

4. *Calls also* on the international community to redouble their efforts to prevent and suppress terrorist acts including by increased cooperation and full implementation of the relevant international anti-terrorist con-

ventions and Security Council resolutions, in particular resolution 1269 of 19 October 1999;

5. *Expresses* its readiness to take all necessary steps to respond to the terrorist attacks of 11 September 2001, and to combat all forms of terrorism, in accordance with its responsibilities under the Charter of the United Nations;

6. *Decides* to remain seized of the matter.

Appendix C

Statement by the North Atlantic Council (September 12, 2001)

On September 12th, the North Atlantic Council met again in response to the appalling attacks perpetrated yesterday against the United States.

The Council agreed that if it is determined that this attack was directed from abroad against the United States, it shall be regarded as an action covered by *Article 5* of the Washington Treaty, which states that an armed attack against one or more of the Allies in Europe or North American shall be considered an attack against them all.

The commitment to collective self-defence embodied in the Washington Treaty was first entered into in circumstances very different from those that exist now, but it remains no less valid and no less essential today, in a world subject to the scourge of international terrorism. When the Heads of State and Government of NATO met in Washington in 1999, they paid tribute to the success of the Alliance in ensuring the freedom of its members during the Cold War and in making possible a Europe that was whole and free. But they also recognised the existence of a wide variety of risks to security, some of them quite unlike those that had called NATO into existence. More specifically, they condemned terrorism as a serious threat to peace and stability and reaffirmed their determination to combat it in accordance with their commitments to one another, their international commitments and national legislation.

Article 5 of the Washington Treaty stipulates that in the event of attacks falling within its purview, each Ally will assist the Party that has been attacked by taking such action as it deems necessary. Accordingly, the

United States' NATO Allies stand ready to provide the assistance that may be required as a consequence of these acts of barbarism.

Appendix D

Authorization for Use of Military Force (Public Law 107-40, 107th Congress)

Joint Resolution

To authorize the use of United States Armed Forces against those responsible for the recent attacks launched against the United States. NOTE: Sept. 18, 2001—[S.J. Res. 23]

Whereas, on September 11, 2001, acts of treacherous violence were committed against the United States and its citizens; and

Whereas, such acts render it both necessary and appropriate that the United States exercise its rights to self-defense and to protect United States citizens both at home and abroad; and

Whereas, in light of the threat to the national security and foreign policy of the United States posed by these grave acts of violence; and

Whereas, such acts continue to pose an unusual and extraordinary threat to the national security and foreign policy of the United States; and

Whereas, the President has authority under the Constitution to take action to deter and prevent acts of international terrorism against the United States: Now, therefore, be it

Resolved by the Senate and House of Representatives of the United States of America in Congress assembled, NOTE: Authorization for Use of Military Force. 50 USC 1541 note.

SECTION 1. SHORT TITLE.

This joint resolution may be cited as the "Authorization for Use of Military Force."

SEC. 2. AUTHORIZATION FOR USE OF UNITED STATES ARMED FORCES.

(a) In General.—That the President is authorized to use all necessary and appropriate force against those nations, organizations, or persons he determines planned, authorized, committed, or aided the terrorist attacks that occurred on September 11, 2001, or harbored such organizations or persons, in order to prevent any future acts of international terrorism against the United States by such nations, organizations or persons.

(b) War Powers Resolution Requirements.—
(1) Specific statutory authorization.—Consistent with section 8(a)(1) of the War Powers Resolution, the Congress declares that this section is intended to constitute specific statutory authorization within the meaning of section 5(b) of the War Powers Resolution.
[[Page 115 STAT. 225]]
(2) Applicability of other requirements.—Nothing in this resolution supercedes any requirement of the War Powers Resolution.

Approved September 18, 2001.

Appendix E

War Powers Resolution (Public Law 93-148, 93rd Congress, H. J. Res. 542, November 7, 1973)

Joint Resolution

Concerning the war powers of Congress and the President.

Resolved by the Senate and the House of Representatives of the United States of America in Congress assembled,

SHORT TITLE
SECTION 1.
This joint resolution may be cited as the "War Powers Resolution."

PURPOSE AND POLICY
SEC. 2.
(a) It is the purpose of this joint resolution to fulfill the intent of the framers of the Constitution of the United States and insure [sic] that the collective judgement of both the Congress and the President will apply to the introduction of United States Armed Forces into hostilities, or into situations where imminent involvement in hostilities is clearly indicated by the circumstances, and to the continued use of such forces in hostilities or in such situations.
(b) Under article I, section 8, of the Constitution, it is specifically provided that the Congress shall have the power to make all laws necessary and proper for carrying into execution, not only its own powers but also all other powers vested by the Constitution in the Government of the United States, or in any department or officer thereof.

(c) The constitutional powers of the President as Commander-in-Chief to introduce United States Armed Forces into hostilities, or into situations where imminent involvement in hostilities is clearly indicated by the circumstances, are exercised only pursuant to (1) a declaration of war, (2) specific statutory authorization, or (3) a national emergency created by attack upon the United States, its territories or possessions, or its armed forces.

CONSULTATION
SEC. 3.
The President in every possible instance shall consult with Congress before introducing United States Armed Forces into hostilities or into situation where imminent involvement in hostilities is clearly indicated by the circumstances, and after every such introduction shall consult regularly with the Congress until United States Armed Forces are no longer engaged in hostilities or have been removed from such situations.

REPORTING
SEC. 4.
(a) In the absence of a declaration of war, in any case in which United States Armed Forces are introduced—
(1) into hostilities or into situations where imminent involvement in hostilities is clearly indicated by the circumstances;
(2) into the territory, airspace or waters of a foreign nation, while equipped for combat, except for deployments which relate solely to supply, replacement, repair, or training of such forces; or
(3) in numbers which substantially enlarge United States Armed Forces equipped for combat already located in a foreign nation; the president shall submit within 48 hours to the Speaker of the House of Representatives and to the President pro tempore of the Senate a report, in writing, setting forth—
(A) the circumstances necessitating the introduction of United States Armed Forces;
(B) the constitutional and legislative authority under which such introduction took place; and
(C) the estimated scope and duration of the hostilities or involvement.
(b) The President shall provide such other information as the Congress may request in the fulfillment of its constitutional responsibilities with

respect to committing the Nation to war and to the use of United States Armed Forces abroad

(c) Whenever United States Armed Forces are introduced into hostilities or into any situation described in sub section (a) of this section, the President shall, so long as such armed forces continue to be engaged in such hostilities or situation, report to the Congress periodically on the status of such hostilities or situation as well as on the scope and duration of such hostilities or situation, but in no event shall he report to the Congress less often than once every six months.

CONGRESSIONAL ACTION
SEC. 5.
(a) Each report submitted pursuant to section 4(a)(1) shall be transmitted to the Speaker of the House of Representatives and to the President pro tempore of the Senate on the same calendar day. Each report so transmitted shall be referred to the Committee on Foreign Affairs of the House of Representatives and to the Committee on Foreign Relations of the Senate for appropriate action. If, when the report is transmitted, the Congress has adjourned sine die or has adjourned for any period in excess of three calendar days, the Speaker of the House of Representatives and the President pro tempore of the Senate, if they deem it advisable (or if petitioned by at least 30 percent of the membership of their respective Houses) shall jointly request the President to convene Congress in order that it may consider the report and take appropriate action pursuant to this section.

(b) Within sixty calendar days after a report is submitted or is required to be submitted pursuant to section 4(a)(1), whichever is earlier, the President shall terminate any use of Untied States Armed Forces with respect to which such report was submitted (or required to be submitted), unless the Congress

(1) has declared war or has enacted a specific authorization for such use of United States Armed Forces,
(2) has extended by law such sixty-day period, or
(3) is physically unable to meet as a result of an armed attack upon the United States. Such sixty-day period shall be extended for not more than an additional thirty days if the President determines and certifies to the Congress in writing that unavoidable military necessity respecting the safety of United States Armed Forces requires the continued use of such armed forces in the course of bringing about a prompt removal of such forces.

(c) Notwithstanding subsection (b), at any time that United States Armed Forces are engaged in hostilities outside the territory of the United States, its possessions and territories without a declaration of war or specific statutory authorization, such forces shall be removed by the President if the Congress so directs by concurrent resolution.

CONGRESSIONAL PRIORITY PROCEDURES FOR JOINT RESOLUTION OR BILL
SEC. 6.
(a) Any joint resolution or bill introduced pursuant to section 5(b) at least thirty calendar days before the expiration of the sixty-day period specified in such section shall be referred to the Committee on Foreign Affairs of the House of Representatives or the Committee on Foreign Relations of the Senate, as the case may be, and such committee shall report one such joint resolution or bill, together with its recommendations, not later than twenty-four calendar days before the expiration of the sixty-day period specified in such section, unless such House shall otherwise determine by the yeas and nays.
(b) Any joint resolution or bill so reported shall become the pending business of the House in question (in the case of the Senate the time for debate shall be equally divided between the proponents and the opponents), and shall be voted on within three calendar days thereafter, unless such House shall otherwise determine by yeas and nays.
(c) Such a joint resolution or bill passed by one House shall be referred to the committee of the other House named in subsection (a) and shall be reported out not later than fourteen calendar days before the expiration of the sixty-day period specified in section 5(b). The joint resolution or bill so reported shall become the pending business of the House in question and shall be voted on within three calendar days after it has been reported, unless such House shall otherwise determine by yeas and nays.
(d) In the case of any disagreement between the two Houses of Congress with respect to a joint resolution or bill passed by both Houses, conferees shall be promptly appointed and the committee of conference shall make and file a report with respect to such resolution or bill not later than four calendar days before the expiration of the sixty-day period specified in section 5(b). In the event the conferees are unable to agree within 48 hours, they shall report back to their respective Houses in disagreement. Notwithstanding any rule in either House concerning the printing of conference reports in the Record or concerning any de-

lay in the consideration of such reports, such report shall be acted on by both Houses not later than the expiration of such sixty-day period.

CONGRESSIONAL PRIORITY PROCEDURES FOR CONCURRENT RESOLUTION
SEC. 7.
(a) Any concurrent resolution introduced pursuant to section 5(b) at least thirty calendar days before the expiration of the sixty-day period specified in such section shall be referred to the Committee on Foreign Affairs of the House of Representatives or the Committee on Foreign Relations of the Senate, as the case may be, and one such concurrent resolution shall be reported out by such committee together with its recommendations within fifteen calendar days, unless such House shall otherwise determine by the yeas and nays.
(b) Any concurrent resolution so reported shall become the pending business of the House in question (in the case of the Senate the time for debate shall be equally divided between the proponents and the opponents), and shall be voted on within three calendar days thereafter, unless such House shall otherwise determine by yeas and nays.
(c) Such a concurrent resolution passed by one House shall be referred to the committee of the other House named in subsection (a) and shall be reported out by such committee together with its recommendations within fifteen calendar days and shall thereupon become the pending business of such House and shall be voted on within three calendar days after it has been reported, unless such House shall otherwise determine by yeas and nays.
(d) In the case of any disagreement between the two Houses of Congress with respect to a concurrent resolution passed by both Houses, conferees shall be promptly appointed and the committee of conference shall make and file a report with respect to such concurrent resolution within six calendar days after the legislation is referred to the committee of conference. Notwithstanding any rule in either House concerning the printing of conference reports in the Record or concerning any delay in the consideration of such reports, such report shall be acted on by both Houses not later than six calendar days after the conference report is filed. In the event the conferees are unable to agree within 48 hours, they shall report back to their respective Houses in disagreement.

INTERPRETATION OF JOINT RESOLUTION
SEC. 8.
(a) Authority to introduce United States Armed Forces into hostilities or into situations wherein involvement in hostilities is clearly indicated by the circumstances shall not be inferred—
(1) from any provision of law (whether or not in effect before the date of the enactment of this joint resolution), including any provision contained in any appropriation Act, unless such provision specifically authorizes the introduction of United States Armed Forces into hostilities or into such situations and stating that it is intended to constitute specific statutory authorization within the meaning of this joint resolution; or
(2) from any treaty heretofore or hereafter ratified unless such treaty is implemented by legislation specifically authorizing the introduction of United States Armed Forces into hostilities or into such situations and stating that it is intended to constitute specific statutory authorization within the meaning of this joint resolution.
(b) Nothing in this joint resolution shall be construed to require any further specific statutory authorization to permit members of United States Armed Forces to participate jointly with members of the armed forces of one or more foreign countries in the headquarters operations of high-level military commands which were established prior to the date of enactment of this joint resolution and pursuant to the United Nations Charter or any treaty ratified by the United States prior to such date.
(c) For purposes of this joint resolution, the term "introduction of United States Armed Forces" includes the assignment of member of such armed forces to command, coordinate, participate in the movement of, or accompany the regular or irregular military forces of any foreign country or government when such military forces are engaged, or there exists an imminent threat that such forces will become engaged, in hostilities.
(d) Nothing in this joint resolution—
(1) is intended to alter the constitutional authority of the Congress or of the President, or the provision of existing treaties; or
(2) shall be construed as granting any authority to the President with respect to the introduction of United States Armed Forces into hostilities or into situations wherein involvement in hostilities is clearly indicated by the circumstances which authority he would not have had in the absence of this joint resolution.

SEPARABILITY CLAUSE
SEC. 9.
If any provision of this joint resolution or the application thereof to any person or circumstance is held invalid, the remainder of the joint resolution and the application of such provision to any other person or circumstance shall not be affected thereby.

EFFECTIVE DATE
SEC. 10.
This joint resolution shall take effect on the date of its enactment.

Appendix F

President's Letter to Congress on American Response to Terrorism (October 9, 2001)

Office of the Press Secretary
October 9, 2001

President's Letter to Congress on American Response to Terrorism

Text of a Letter from the President to the Speaker of the House of Representatives and the President Pro Tempore of the Senate
October 9, 2001

Dear Mr. Speaker: (Dear Mr. President:)

At approximately 12:30 p.m. (EDT) on October 7, 2001, on my orders, U.S. Armed Forces began combat action in Afghanistan against Al Qaida terrorists and their Taliban supporters. This military action is a part of our campaign against terrorism and is designed to disrupt the use of Afghanistan as a terrorist base of operations.

We are responding to the brutal September 11 attacks on our territory, our citizens, and our way of life, and to the continuing threat of terrorist acts against the United States and our friends and allies. This follows the deployment of various combat-equipped and combat support forces to a number of locations in the Central and Pacific Command areas of operations, as I reported to the Congress on September 24, to prepare for the campaign to prevent and deter terrorism.

I have taken these actions pursuant to my constitutional authority to conduct U.S. foreign relations as Commander in Chief and Chief Executive. It is not possible to know at this time either the duration of combat operations or the scope and duration of the deployment of U.S. Armed Forces necessary to counter the terrorist threat to the United States. As I have stated previously, it is likely that the American campaign against terrorism will be lengthy. I will direct such additional measures as necessary in exercise of our right to self-defense and to protect U.S. citizens and interests.

I am providing this report as part of my efforts to keep the Congress informed, consistent with the War Powers Resolution and Public Law 107-40. Officials of my Administration and I have been communicating regularly with the leadership and other members of Congress, and we will continue to do so. I appreciate the continuing support of the Congress, including its enactment of Public Law 107-40, in these actions to protect the security of the United States of America and its citizens, civilian and military, here and abroad.

Sincerely,
GEORGE W. BUSH

Appendix G

The United States Constitution (Selected Provisions)

We the People of the United States, in Order to form a more perfect Union, establish Justice, insure domestic Tranquility, provide for the common defence, promote the general Welfare, and secure the Blessings of Liberty to ourselves and our Posterity, do ordain and establish this Constitution for the United States of America.

Article I

Section 1

All legislative Powers herein granted shall be vested in a Congress of the United States, which shall consist of a Senate and House of Representatives.

. . .

Section 8

Clause 1: The Congress shall have Power To lay and collect Taxes, Duties, Imposts and Excises, to pay the Debts and provide for the common Defence and general Welfare of the United States; but all Duties, Imposts and Excises shall be uniform throughout the United States;

Clause 2: To borrow Money on the credit of the United States;

Clause 3: To regulate Commerce with foreign Nations, and among the several States, and with the Indian Tribes;

Clause 4: To establish an uniform Rule of Naturalization, and uniform Laws on the subject of Bankruptcies throughout the United States;

Clause 5: To coin Money, regulate the Value thereof, and of foreign Coin, and fix the Standard of Weights and Measures;

Clause 6: To provide for the Punishment of counterfeiting the Securities and current Coin of the United States;

Clause 7: To establish Post Offices and post Roads;

Clause 8: To promote the Progress of Science and useful Arts, by securing for limited Times to Authors and Inventors the exclusive Right to their respective Writings and Discoveries;

Clause 9: To constitute Tribunals inferior to the supreme Court;

Clause 10: To define and punish Piracies and Felonies committed on the high Seas, and Offences against the Law of Nations;

Clause 11: To declare War, grant Letters of Marque and Reprisal, and make Rules concerning Captures on Land and Water;

Clause 12: To raise and support Armies, but no Appropriation of Money to that Use shall be for a longer Term than two Years;

Clause 13: To provide and maintain a Navy;

Clause 14: To make Rules for the Government and Regulation of the land and naval Forces;

Clause 15: To provide for calling forth the Militia to execute the Laws of the Union, suppress Insurrections and repel Invasions;

Clause 16: To provide for organizing, arming, and disciplining, the Militia, and for governing such Part of them as may be employed in the Service of the United States, reserving to the States respectively, the Appointment of the Officers, and the Authority of training the Militia according to the discipline prescribed by Congress;

Clause 17: To exercise exclusive Legislation in all Cases whatsoever, over such District (not exceeding ten Miles square) as may, by Cession of particular States, and the Acceptance of Congress, become the Seat of the Government of the United States, and to exercise like Authority over all Places purchased by the Consent of the Legislature of the State in which the Same shall be, for the Erection of Forts, Magazines, Arsenals, dock-Yards, and other needful Buildings;—And

Clause 18: To make all Laws which shall be necessary and proper for carrying into Execution the foregoing Powers, and all other Powers

Appendix G: The United States Constitution . . .

vested by this Constitution in the Government of the United States, or in any Department or Officer thereof.

. . .

Article II

Section 1

Clause 1: The executive Power shall be vested in a President of the United States of America. He shall hold his Office during the Term of four Years, and, together with the Vice President, chosen for the same Term, be elected, as follows

. . .

Section 2

Clause 1: The President shall be Commander in Chief of the Army and Navy of the United States, and of the Militia of the several States, when called into the actual Service of the United States; he may require the Opinion, in writing, of the principal Officer in each of the executive Departments, upon any Subject relating to the Duties of their respective Offices, and he shall have Power to grant Reprieves and Pardons for Offences against the United States, except in Cases of Impeachment.

Clause 2: He shall have Power, by and with the Advice and Consent of the Senate, to make Treaties, provided two thirds of the Senators present concur; and he shall nominate, and by and with the Advice and Consent of the Senate, shall appoint Ambassadors, other public Ministers and Consuls, Judges of the supreme Court, and all other Officers of the United States, whose Appointments are not herein otherwise provided for, and which shall be established by Law: but the Congress may by Law vest the Appointment of such inferior Officers, as they think proper, in the President alone, in the Courts of Law, or in the Heads of Departments.

. . .

GO. WASHINGTON—President and deputy from Virginia

[Signed also by the deputies of twelve States.]

Appendix H

Universal Declaration of Human Rights

PREAMBLE

Whereas recognition of the inherent dignity and of the equal and inalienable rights of all members of the human family is the foundation of freedom, justice and peace in the world,

Whereas disregard and contempt for human rights have resulted in barbarous acts which have outraged the conscience of mankind, and the advent of a world in which human beings shall enjoy freedom of speech and belief and freedom from fear and want has been proclaimed as the highest aspiration of the common people,

Whereas it is essential, if man is not to be compelled to have recourse, as a last resort, to rebellion against tyranny and oppression, that human rights should be protected by the rule of law,

Whereas it is essential to promote the development of friendly relations between nations,

Whereas the peoples of the United Nations have in the Charter reaffirmed their faith in fundamental human rights, in the dignity and worth of the human person and in the equal rights of men and women and have determined to promote social progress and better standards of life in larger freedom,

Whereas Member States have pledged themselves to achieve, in cooperation with the United Nations, the promotion of universal respect for and observance of human rights and fundamental freedoms,

Whereas a common understanding of these rights and freedoms is of the greatest importance for the full realization of this pledge,

Now, therefore,

The General Assembly,

Proclaims this Universal Declaration of Human Rights as a common standard of achievement for all peoples and all nations, to the end that every individual and every organ of society, keeping this Declaration constantly in mind, shall strive by teaching and education to promote respect for these rights and freedoms and by progressive measures, national and international, to secure their universal and effective recognition and observance, both among the peoples of Member States themselves and among the peoples of territories under their jurisdiction.

Article 1

All human beings are born free and equal in dignity and rights. They are endowed with reason and conscience and should act towards one another in a spirit of brotherhood.

Article 2

Everyone is entitled to all the rights and freedoms set forth in this Declaration, without distinction of any kind, such as race, colour, sex, language, religion, political or other opinion, national or social origin, property, birth or other status.

Furthermore, no distinction shall be made on the basis of the political, jurisdictional or international status of the country or territory to which a person belongs, whether it be independent, trust, non-self-governing or under any other limitation of sovereignty.

Article 3

Everyone has the right to life, liberty and security of person.

Article 4

No one shall be held in slavery or servitude; slavery and the slave trade shall be prohibited in all their forms.

Article 5

No one shall be subjected to torture or to cruel, inhuman or degrading treatment or punishment.

Article 6

Everyone has the right to recognition everywhere as a person before the law.

Article 7

All are equal before the law and are entitled without any discrimination to equal protection of the law. All are entitled to equal protection against any discrimination in violation of this Declaration and against any incitement to such discrimination.

Article 8

Everyone has the right to an effective remedy by the competent national tribunals for acts violating the fundamental rights granted him by the constitution or by law.

Article 9

No one shall be subjected to arbitrary arrest, detention or exile.

Article 10

Everyone is entitled in full equality to a fair and public hearing by an independent and impartial tribunal, in the determination of his rights and obligations and of any criminal charge against him.

Article 11

1. Everyone charged with a penal offence has the right to be presumed innocent until proved guilty according to law in a public trial at which he has had all the guarantees necessary for his defence.

2. No one shall be held guilty of any penal offence on account of any act or omission which did not constitute a penal offence, under national or international law, at the time when it was committed. Nor shall a heavier penalty be imposed than the one that was applicable at the time the penal offence was committed.

Article 12

No one shall be subjected to arbitrary interference with his privacy, family, home or correspondence, nor to attacks upon his honour and reputation. Everyone has the right to the protection of the law against such interference or attacks.

Article 13

1. Everyone has the right to freedom of movement and residence within the borders of each State.

2. Everyone has the right to leave any country, including his own, and to return to his country.

Article 14

1. Everyone has the right to seek and to enjoy in other countries asylum from persecution.

2. This right may not be invoked in the case of prosecutions genuinely arising from non-political crimes or from acts contrary to the purposes and principles of the United Nations.

Article 15

1. Everyone has the right to a nationality.

2. No one shall be arbitrarily deprived of his nationality nor denied the right to change his nationality.

Article 16

1. Men and women of full age, without any limitation due to race, nationality or religion, have the right to marry and to found a family. They are entitled to equal rights as to marriage, during marriage and at its dissolution.

2. Marriage shall be entered into only with the free and full consent of the intending spouses.

3. The family is the natural and fundamental group unit of society and is entitled to protection by society and the State.

Article 17

1. Everyone has the right to own property alone as well as in association with others.

2. No one shall be arbitrarily deprived of his property.

Article 18

Everyone has the right to freedom of thought, conscience and religion; this right includes freedom to change his religion or belief, and freedom, either alone or in community with others and in public or private, to manifest his religion or belief in teaching, practice, worship and observance.

Article 19

Everyone has the right to freedom of opinion and expression; this right includes freedom to hold opinions without interference and to seek, receive and impart information and ideas through any media and regardless of frontiers.

Article 20

1. Everyone has the right to freedom of peaceful assembly and association.

2. No one may be compelled to belong to an association.

Article 21

1. Everyone has the right to take part in the government of his country, directly or through freely chosen representatives.

2. Everyone has the right to equal access to public service in his country.

3. The will of the people shall be the basis of the authority of government; this will shall be expressed in periodic and genuine elections which shall be by universal and equal suffrage and shall be held by secret vote or by equivalent free voting procedures.

Article 22

Everyone, as a member of society, has the right to social security and is entitled to realization, through national effort and international co-operation and in accordance with the organization and resources of each State, of the economic, social and cultural rights indispensable for his dignity and the free development of his personality.

Article 23

1. Everyone has the right to work, to free choice of employment, to just and favourable conditions of work and to protection against unemployment.

2. Everyone, without any discrimination, has the right to equal pay for equal work.

3. Everyone who works has the right to just and favourable remuneration ensuring for himself and his family an existence worthy of human dignity, and supplemented, if necessary, by other means of social protection.

4. Everyone has the right to form and to join trade unions for the protection of his interests.

Article 24

Everyone has the right to rest and leisure, including reasonable limitation of working hours and periodic holidays with pay.

Article 25

1. Everyone has the right to a standard of living adequate for the health and well-being of himself and of his family, including food, clothing, housing and medical care and necessary social services, and the right to security in the event of unemployment, sickness, disability, widowhood, old age or other lack of livelihood in circumstances beyond his control.

2. Motherhood and childhood are entitled to special care and assistance. All children, whether born in or out of wedlock, shall enjoy the same social protection.

Article 26

1. Everyone has the right to education. Education shall be free, at least in the elementary and fundamental stages. Elementary education shall be compulsory. Technical and professional education shall be made generally available and higher education shall be equally accessible to all on the basis of merit.

2. Education shall be directed to the full development of the human personality and to the strengthening of respect for human rights and fundamental freedoms. It shall promote understanding, tolerance and friendship among all nations, racial or religious groups, and shall further the activities of the United Nations for the maintenance of peace.

3. Parents have a prior right to choose the kind of education that shall be given to their children.

Article 27

1. Everyone has the right freely to participate in the cultural life of the community, to enjoy the arts and to share in scientific advancement and its benefits.

2. Everyone has the right to the protection of the moral and material interests resulting from any scientific, literary or artistic production of which he is the author.

Article 28

Everyone is entitled to a social and international order in which the rights and freedoms set forth in this Declaration can be fully realized.

Article 29

1. Everyone has duties to the community in which alone the free and full development of his personality is possible.

2. In the exercise of his rights and freedoms, everyone shall be subject only to such limitations as are determined by law solely for the purpose of securing due recognition and respect for the rights and freedoms of others and of meeting the just requirements of morality, public order and the general welfare in a democratic society.

3. These rights and freedoms may in no case be exercised contrary to the purposes and principles of the United Nations.

Article 30

Nothing in this Declaration may be interpreted as implying for any State, group or person any right to engage in any activity or to perform any act aimed at the destruction of any of the rights and freedoms set forth herein.

Appendix I

International Covenant on Civil and Political Rights

Adopted and opened for signature, ratification and accession by General Assembly resolution 2200A (XXI) of 16 December 1966.

Entry into force 23 March 1976, in accordance with Article 49

Preamble

The States Parties to the present Covenant,

Considering that, in accordance with the principles proclaimed in the Charter of the United Nations, recognition of the inherent dignity and of the equal and inalienable rights of all members of the human family is the foundation of freedom, justice and peace in the world,

Recognizing that these rights derive from the inherent dignity of the human person,

Recognizing that, in accordance with the Universal Declaration of Human Rights, the ideal of free human beings enjoying civil and political freedom and freedom from fear and want can only be achieved if conditions are created whereby everyone may enjoy his civil and political rights, as well as his economic, social and cultural rights,

Considering the obligation of States under the Charter of the United Nations to promote universal respect for, and observance of, human rights and freedoms,

Realizing that the individual, having duties to other individuals and to the community to which he belongs, is under a responsibility to strive for the promotion and observance of the rights recognized in the present Covenant,

Agree upon the following articles:

Part I

Article 1
1. All peoples have the right of self-determination. By virtue of that right they freely determine their political status and freely pursue their economic, social and cultural development.
2. All peoples may, for their own ends, freely dispose of their natural wealth and resources without prejudice to any obligations arising out of international economic co-operation, based upon the principle of mutual benefit, and international law. In no case may a people be deprived of its own means of subsistence.
3. The States Parties to the present Covenant, including those having responsibility for the administration of Non-Self-Governing and Trust Territories, shall promote the realization of the right of self-determination, and shall respect that right, in conformity with the provisions of the Charter of the United Nations.

Part II

Article 2
1. Each State Party to the present Covenant undertakes to respect and to ensure to all individuals within its territory and subject to its jurisdiction the rights recognized in the present Covenant, without distinction of any kind, such as race, colour, sex, language, religion, political or other opinion, national or social origin, property, birth or other status.
2. Where not already provided for by existing legislative or other measures, each State Party to the present Covenant undertakes to take the necessary steps, in accordance with its constitutional processes and with the provisions of the present Covenant, to adopt such laws or other measures as may be necessary to give effect to the rights recognized in the present Covenant.
3. Each State Party to the present Covenant undertakes:
(a) To ensure that any person whose rights or freedoms as herein recognized are violated shall have an effective remedy, notwithstanding that

the violation has been committed by persons acting in an official capacity;
(b) To ensure that any person claiming such a remedy shall have his right thereto determined by competent judicial, administrative or legislative authorities, or by any other competent authority provided for by the legal system of the State, and to develop the possibilities of judicial remedy;
(c) To ensure that the competent authorities shall enforce such remedies when granted.

Article 3
The States Parties to the present Covenant undertake to ensure the equal right of men and women to the enjoyment of all civil and political rights set forth in the present Covenant.

Article 4
1. In time of public emergency which threatens the life of the nation and the existence of which is officially proclaimed, the States Parties to the present Covenant may take measures derogating from their obligations under the present Covenant to the extent strictly required by the exigencies of the situation, provided that such measures are not inconsistent with their other obligations under international law and do not involve discrimination solely on the ground of race, colour, sex, language, religion or social origin.
2. No derogation from articles 6, 7, 8 (paragraphs I and 2), 11, 15, 16 and 18 may be made under this provision.
3. Any State Party to the present Covenant availing itself of the right of derogation shall immediately inform the other States Parties to the present Covenant, through the intermediary of the Secretary-General of the United Nations, of the provisions from which it has derogated and of the reasons by which it was actuated. A further communication shall be made, through the same intermediary, on the date on which it terminates such derogation.

Article 5
1. Nothing in the present Covenant may be interpreted as implying for any State, group or person any right to engage in any activity or perform any act aimed at the destruction of any of the rights and freedoms recognized herein or at their limitation to a greater extent than is provided for in the present Covenant.

2. There shall be no restriction upon or derogation from any of the fundamental human rights recognized or existing in any State Party to the present Covenant pursuant to law, conventions, regulations or custom on the pretext that the present Covenant does not recognize such rights or that it recognizes them to a lesser extent.

Part III

Article 6
1. Every human being has the inherent right to life. This right shall be protected by law. No one shall be arbitrarily deprived of his life.
2. In countries which have not abolished the death penalty, sentence of death may be imposed only for the most serious crimes in accordance with the law in force at the time of the commission of the crime and not contrary to the provisions of the present Covenant and to the Convention on the Prevention and Punishment of the Crime of Genocide. This penalty can only be carried out pursuant to a final judgement rendered by a competent court.
3. When deprivation of life constitutes the crime of genocide, it is understood that nothing in this article shall authorize any State Party to the present Covenant to derogate in any way from any obligation assumed under the provisions of the Convention on the Prevention and Punishment of the Crime of Genocide.
4. Anyone sentenced to death shall have the right to seek pardon or commutation of the sentence. Amnesty, pardon or commutation of the sentence of death may be granted in all cases.
5. Sentence of death shall not be imposed for crimes committed by persons below eighteen years of age and shall not be carried out on pregnant women.
6. Nothing in this article shall be invoked to delay or to prevent the abolition of capital punishment by any State Party to the present Covenant.

Article 7
No one shall be subjected to torture or to cruel, inhuman or degrading treatment or punishment. In particular, no one shall be subjected without his free consent to medical or scientific experimentation.

Article 8
1. No one shall be held in slavery; slavery and the slave-trade in all their forms shall be prohibited.

2. No one shall be held in servitude.

3. (a) No one shall be required to perform forced or compulsory labour;

(b) Paragraph 3 (a) shall not be held to preclude, in countries where imprisonment with hard labour may be imposed as a punishment for a crime, the performance of hard labour in pursuance of a sentence to such punishment by a competent court;

(c) For the purpose of this paragraph the term "forced or compulsory labour" shall not include:

(i) Any work or service, not referred to in subparagraph (b), normally required of a person who is under detention in consequence of a lawful order of a court, or of a person during conditional release from such detention;

(ii) Any service of a military character and, in countries where conscientious objection is recognized, any national service required by law of conscientious objectors;

(iii) Any service exacted in cases of emergency or calamity threatening the life or well-being of the community;

(iv) Any work or service which forms part of normal civil obligations.

Article 9

1. Everyone has the right to liberty and security of person. No one shall be subjected to arbitrary arrest or detention. No one shall be deprived of his liberty except on such grounds and in accordance with such procedure as are established by law.

2. Anyone who is arrested shall be informed, at the time of arrest, of the reasons for his arrest and shall be promptly informed of any charges against him.

3. Anyone arrested or detained on a criminal charge shall be brought promptly before a judge or other officer authorized by law to exercise judicial power and shall be entitled to trial within a reasonable time or to release. It shall not be the general rule that persons awaiting trial shall be detained in custody, but release may be subject to guarantees to appear for trial, at any other stage of the judicial proceedings, and, should occasion arise, for execution of the judgement.

4. Anyone who is deprived of his liberty by arrest or detention shall be entitled to take proceedings before a court, in order that court may decide without delay on the lawfulness of his detention and order his release if the detention is not lawful.

5. Anyone who has been the victim of unlawful arrest or detention shall have an enforceable right to compensation.

Article 10
1. All persons deprived of their liberty shall be treated with humanity and with respect for the inherent dignity of the human person.
2. (a) Accused persons shall, save in exceptional circumstances, be segregated from convicted persons and shall be subject to separate treatment appropriate to their status as unconvicted persons;
(b) Accused juvenile persons shall be separated from adults and brought as speedily as possible for adjudication.
3. The penitentiary system shall comprise treatment of prisoners the essential aim of which shall be their reformation and social rehabilitation. Juvenile offenders shall be segregated from adults and be accorded treatment appropriate to their age and legal status.

Article 11
No one shall be imprisoned merely on the ground of inability to fulfil a contractual obligation.

Article 12
1. Everyone lawfully within the territory of a State shall, within that territory, have the right to liberty of movement and freedom to choose his residence.
2. Everyone shall be free to leave any country, including his own.
3. The above-mentioned rights shall not be subject to any restrictions except those which are provided by law, are necessary to protect national security, public order (ordre public), public health or morals or the rights and freedoms of others, and are consistent with the other rights recognized in the present Covenant.
4. No one shall be arbitrarily deprived of the right to enter his own country.

Article 13
An alien lawfully in the territory of a State Party to the present Covenant may be expelled therefrom only in pursuance of a decision reached in accordance with law and shall, except where compelling reasons of national security otherwise require, be allowed to submit the reasons against his expulsion and to have his case reviewed by, and be represented for the purpose before, the competent authority or a person or persons especially designated by the competent authority.

Article 14

1. All persons shall be equal before the courts and tribunals. In the determination of any criminal charge against him, or of his rights and obligations in a suit at law, everyone shall be entitled to a fair and public hearing by a competent, independent and impartial tribunal established by law. The press and the public may be excluded from all or part of a trial for reasons of morals, public order (ordre public) or national security in a democratic society, or when the interest of the private lives of the parties so requires, or to the extent strictly necessary in the opinion of the court in special circumstances where publicity would prejudice the interests of justice; but any judgement rendered in a criminal case or in a suit at law shall be made public except where the interest of juvenile persons otherwise requires or the proceedings concern matrimonial disputes or the guardianship of children.

2. Everyone charged with a criminal offence shall have the right to be presumed innocent until proved guilty according to law.

3. In the determination of any criminal charge against him, everyone shall be entitled to the following minimum guarantees, in full equality:

(a) To be informed promptly and in detail in a language which he understands of the nature and cause of the charge against him;

(b) To have adequate time and facilities for the preparation of his defence and to communicate with counsel of his own choosing;

(c) To be tried without undue delay;

(d) To be tried in his presence, and to defend himself in person or through legal assistance of his own choosing; to be informed, if he does not have legal assistance, of this right; and to have legal assistance assigned to him, in any case where the interests of justice so require, and without payment by him in any such case if he does not have sufficient means to pay for it;

(e) To examine, or have examined, the witnesses against him and to obtain the attendance and examination of witnesses on his behalf under the same conditions as witnesses against him;

(f) To have the free assistance of an interpreter if he cannot understand or speak the language used in court;

(g) Not to be compelled to testify against himself or to confess guilt.

4. In the case of juvenile persons, the procedure shall be such as will take account of their age and the desirability of promoting their rehabilitation.

5. Everyone convicted of a crime shall have the right to his conviction and sentence being reviewed by a higher tribunal according to law.

6. When a person has by a final decision been convicted of a criminal offence and when subsequently his conviction has been reversed or he has been pardoned on the ground that a new or newly discovered fact shows conclusively that there has been a miscarriage of justice, the person who has suffered punishment as a result of such conviction shall be compensated according to law, unless it is proved that the non-disclosure of the unknown fact in time is wholly or partly attributable to him.
7. No one shall be liable to be tried or punished again for an offence for which he has already been finally convicted or acquitted in accordance with the law and penal procedure of each country.

Article 15
1. No one shall be held guilty of any criminal offence on account of any act or omission which did not constitute a criminal offence, under national or international law, at the time when it was committed. Nor shall a heavier penalty be imposed than the one that was applicable at the time when the criminal offence was committed. If, subsequent to the commission of the offence, provision is made by law for the imposition of the lighter penalty, the offender shall benefit thereby.
2. Nothing in this article shall prejudice the trial and punishment of any person for any act or omission which, at the time when it was committed, was criminal according to the general principles of law recognized by the community of nations.

Article 16
Everyone shall have the right to recognition everywhere as a person before the law.

Article 17
1. No one shall be subjected to arbitrary or unlawful interference with his privacy, family, home or correspondence, nor to unlawful attacks on his honour and reputation.
2. Everyone has the right to the protection of the law against such interference or attacks.

Article 18
1. Everyone shall have the right to freedom of thought, conscience and religion. This right shall include freedom to have or to adopt a religion or belief of his choice, and freedom, either individually or in commu-

nity with others and in public or private, to manifest his religion or belief in worship, observance, practice and teaching.
2. No one shall be subject to coercion which would impair his freedom to have or to adopt a religion or belief of his choice.
3. Freedom to manifest one's religion or beliefs may be subject only to such limitations as are prescribed by law and are necessary to protect public safety, order, health, or morals or the fundamental rights and freedoms of others. 4. The States Parties to the present Covenant undertake to have respect for the liberty of parents and, when applicable, legal guardians to ensure the religious and moral education of their children in conformity with their own convictions.

Article 19
1. Everyone shall have the right to hold opinions without interference.
2. Everyone shall have the right to freedom of expression; this right shall include freedom to seek, receive and impart information and ideas of all kinds, regardless of frontiers, either orally, in writing or in print, in the form of art, or through any other media of his choice.
3. The exercise of the rights provided for in paragraph 2 of this article carries with it special duties and responsibilities. It may therefore be subject to certain restrictions, but these shall only be such as are provided by law and are necessary:
(a) For respect of the rights or reputations of others;
(b) For the protection of national security or of public order (ordre public), or of public health or morals.

Article 20
1. Any propaganda for war shall be prohibited by law.
2. Any advocacy of national, racial or religious hatred that constitutes incitement to discrimination, hostility or violence shall be prohibited by law.

Article 21
The right of peaceful assembly shall be recognized. No restrictions may be placed on the exercise of this right other than those imposed in conformity with the law and which are necessary in a democratic society in the interests of national security or public safety, public order (ordre public), the protection of public health or morals or the protection of the rights and freedoms of others.

Article 22
1. Everyone shall have the right to freedom of association with others, including the right to form and join trade unions for the protection of his interests.
2. No restrictions may be placed on the exercise of this right other than those which are prescribed by law and which are necessary in a democratic society in the interests of national security or public safety, public order (ordre public), the protection of public health or morals or the protection of the rights and freedoms of others. This article shall not prevent the imposition of lawful restrictions on members of the armed forces and of the police in their exercise of this right.
3. Nothing in this article shall authorize States Parties to the International Labour Organization Convention of 1948 concerning Freedom of Association and Protection of the Right to Organize to take legislative measures which would prejudice, or to apply the law in such a manner as to prejudice, the guarantees provided for in that Convention.

Article 23
1. The family is the natural and fundamental group unit of society and is entitled to protection by society and the State.
2. The right of men and women of marriageable age to marry and to found a family shall be recognized.
3. No marriage shall be entered into without the free and full consent of the intending spouses.
4. States Parties to the present Covenant shall take appropriate steps to ensure equality of rights and responsibilities of spouses as to marriage, during marriage and at its dissolution. In the case of dissolution, provision shall be made for the necessary protection of any children.

Article 24
1. Every child shall have, without any discrimination as to race, colour, sex, language, religion, national or social origin, property or birth, the right to such measures of protection as are required by his status as a minor, on the part of his family, society and the State.
2. Every child shall be registered immediately after birth and shall have a name.
3. Every child has the right to acquire a nationality.

Article 25
Every citizen shall have the right and the opportunity, without any of the distinctions mentioned in article 2 and without unreasonable restrictions:
(a) To take part in the conduct of public affairs, directly or through freely chosen representatives;
(b) To vote and to be elected at genuine periodic elections which shall be by universal and equal suffrage and shall be held by secret ballot, guaranteeing the free expression of the will of the electors;
(c) To have access, on general terms of equality, to public service in his country.

Article 26
All persons are equal before the law and are entitled without any discrimination to the equal protection of the law. In this respect, the law shall prohibit any discrimination and guarantee to all persons equal and effective protection against discrimination on any ground such as race, colour, sex, language, religion, political or other opinion, national or social origin, property, birth or other status.

Article 27
In those States in which ethnic, religious or linguistic minorities exist, persons belonging to such minorities shall not be denied the right, in community with the other members of their group, to enjoy their own culture, to profess and practice their own religion, or to use their own language.

Part IV

Article 28
1. There shall be established a Human Rights Committee (hereafter referred to in the present Covenant as the Committee). It shall consist of eighteen members and shall carry out the functions hereinafter provided.
2. The Committee shall be composed of nationals of the States Parties to the present Covenant who shall be persons of high moral character and recognized competence in the field of human rights, consideration being given to the usefulness of the participation of some persons having legal experience.

3. The members of the Committee shall be elected and shall serve in their personal capacity.

...

Part V

Article 46
Nothing in the present Covenant shall be interpreted as impairing the provisions of the Charter of the United Nations and of the constitutions of the specialized agencies which define the respective responsibilities of the various organs of the United Nations and of the specialized agencies in regard to the matters dealt with in the present Covenant.

Article 47
Nothing in the present Covenant shall be interpreted as impairing the inherent right of all peoples to enjoy and utilize fully and freely their natural wealth and resources.

Part VI

Article 48
1. The present Covenant is open for signature by any State Member of the United Nations or member of any of its specialized agencies, by any State Party to the Statute of the International Court of Justice, and by any other State which has been invited by the General Assembly of the United Nations to become a Party to the present Covenant.
2. The present Covenant is subject to ratification. Instruments of ratification shall be deposited with the Secretary-General of the United Nations.
3. The present Covenant shall be open to accession by any State referred to in paragraph 1 of this article.
4. Accession shall be effected by the deposit of an instrument of accession with the Secretary-General of the United Nations.
5. The Secretary-General of the United Nations shall inform all States which have signed this Covenant or acceded to it of the deposit of each instrument of ratification or accession.

Article 49
1. The present Covenant shall enter into force three months after the date of the deposit with the Secretary-General of the United Nations of the thirty-fifth instrument of ratification or instrument of accession.
2. For each State ratifying the present Covenant or acceding to it after the deposit of the thirty-fifth instrument of ratification or instrument of accession, the present Covenant shall enter into force three months after the date of the deposit of its own instrument of ratification or instrument of accession.

Article 50
The provisions of the present Covenant shall extend to all parts of federal States without any limitations or exceptions.

Article 51
1. Any State Party to the present Covenant may propose an amendment and file it with the Secretary-General of the United Nations. The Secretary-General of the United Nations shall thereupon communicate any proposed amendments to the States Parties to the present Covenant with a request that they notify him whether they favour a conference of States Parties for the purpose of considering and voting upon the proposals. In the event that at least one third of the States Parties favours such a conference, the Secretary-General shall convene the conference under the auspices of the United Nations. Any amendment adopted by a majority of the States Parties present and voting at the conference shall be submitted to the General Assembly of the United Nations for approval.
2. Amendments shall come into force when they have been approved by the General Assembly of the United Nations and accepted by a two-thirds majority of the States Parties to the present Covenant in accordance with their respective constitutional processes.
3. When amendments come into force, they shall be binding on those States Parties which have accepted them, other States Parties still being bound by the provisions of the present Covenant and any earlier amendment which they have accepted.

Article 52
Irrespective of the notifications made under article 48, paragraph 5, the Secretary-General of the United Nations shall inform all States referred to in paragraph I of the same article of the following particulars:
(a) Signatures, ratifications and accessions under article 48;

(b) The date of the entry into force of the present Covenant under article 49 and the date of the entry into force of any amendments under article 51.

Article 53
1. The present Covenant, of which the Chinese, English, French, Russian and Spanish texts are equally authentic, shall be deposited in the archives of the United Nations.
2. The Secretary-General of the United Nations shall transmit certified copies of the present Covenant to all States referred to in article 48.

Appendix J

Joint Resolution to Authorize the Use of United States Armed Forces Against Iraq

Whereas the Iraq Liberation Act (Public Law 105-338) expressed the sense of Congress that it should be the policy of the United States to support efforts to remove from power the current Iraqi regime and promote the emergence of a democratic government to replace that regime;

Whereas on September 12, 2002, President Bush committed the United States to 'work with the United Nations Security Council to meet our common challenge' posed by Iraq and to 'work for the necessary resolutions,' while also making clear that 'the Security Council resolutions will be enforced, and the just demands of peace and security will be met, or action will be unavoidable';

Whereas the United States is determined to prosecute the war on terrorism and Iraq's ongoing support for international terrorist groups combined with its development of weapons of mass destruction in direct violation of its obligations under the 1991 cease-fire and other United Nations Security Council resolutions make clear that it is in the national security interests of the United States and in furtherance of the war on terrorism that all relevant United Nations Security Council resolutions be enforced, including through the use of force if necessary;

Whereas Congress has taken steps to pursue vigorously the war on terrorism through the provision of authorities and funding requested by the President to take the necessary actions against international terrorists and terrorist organizations, including those nations, organizations or persons who planned, authorized, committed or aided the terrorist attacks that occurred on September 11, 2001, or harbored such persons or organizations;

Whereas the President and Congress are determined to continue to take all appropriate actions against international terrorists and terrorist organizations, including those nations, organizations or persons who planned, authorized, committed or aided the terrorist attacks that occurred on September 11, 2001, or harbored such persons or organizations;

Whereas the President has authority under the Constitution to take action in order to deter and prevent acts of international terrorism against the United States, as Congress recognized in the joint resolution on Authorization for Use of Military Force (Public Law 107-40); and

Whereas it is in the national security of the United States to restore international peace and security to the Persian Gulf region: Now, therefore, be it

Resolved by the Senate and House of Representatives of the United States of America in Congress assembled,

SECTION 1. SHORT TITLE.

This joint resolution may be cited as the 'Authorization for the Use of Military Force Against Iraq'.

SEC. 2. SUPPORT FOR UNITED STATES DIPLOMATIC EFFORTS.

The Congress of the United States supports the efforts by the President to - (1) strictly enforce through the United Nations Security Council all relevant Security Council resolutions applicable to Iraq and encourages him in those efforts; and (2) obtain prompt and decisive action by the Security Council to ensure that Iraq abandons its strategy of delay, evasion and noncompliance and promptly and strictly complies with all relevant Security Council resolutions.

SEC. 3. AUTHORIZATION FOR USE OF UNITED STATES ARMED FORCES.

(a) AUTHORIZATION- The President is authorized to use the Armed Forces of the United States as he determines to be necessary and appropriate in order to -

(1) defend the national security of the United States against the continuing threat posed by Iraq; and

(2) enforce all relevant United Nations Security Council resolutions regarding Iraq.

(b) PRESIDENTIAL DETERMINATION- In connection with the exercise of the authority granted in subsection (a) to use force the President shall, prior to such exercise or as soon thereafter as may be feasible, but no later than 48 hours after exercising such authority, make available to the Speaker of the House of Representatives and the President pro tempore of the Senate his determination that -

(1) reliance by the United States on further diplomatic or other peaceful means alone either (A) will not adequately protect the national security of the United States against the continuing threat posed by Iraq or (B) is not likely to lead to enforcement of all relevant United Nations Security Council resolutions regarding Iraq; and

(2) acting pursuant to this resolution is consistent with the United States and other countries continuing to take the necessary actions against international terrorists and terrorist organizations, including those nations, organizations or persons who planned, authorized, committed or aided the terrorists attacks that occurred on September 11, 2001.

(c) WAR POWERS RESOLUTION REQUIREMENTS-

(1) SPECIFIC STATUTORY AUTHORIZATION- Consistent with section 8(a)(1) of the War Powers Resolution, the Congress declares that this

section is intended to constitute specific statutory authorization within the meaning of section 5(b) of the War Powers Resolution.

(2) APPLICABILITY OF OTHER REQUIREMENTS- Nothing in this resolution supersedes any requirement of the War Powers Resolution.

SEC. 4. REPORTS TO CONGRESS. (a) The President shall, at least once every 60 days, submit to the Congress a report on matters relevant to this joint resolution, including actions taken pursuant to the exercise of authority granted in section 3 and the status of planning for efforts that are expected to be required after such actions are completed, including those actions described in section 7 of Public Law 105-338 (the Iraq Liberation Act of 1998).

(b) To the extent that the submission of any report described in subsection (a) coincides with the submission of any other report on matters relevant to this joint resolution otherwise required to be submitted to Congress pursuant to the reporting requirements of Public Law 93-148 (the War Powers Resolution), all such reports may be submitted as a single consolidated report to the Congress.

(c) To the extent that the information required by section 3 of Public Law 102-1 is included in the report required by this section, such report shall be considered as meeting the requirements of section 3 of Public Law 102-1.

About the Author

Jeffrey F. Addicott is an assistant professor of law at St. Mary's University School of Law, San Antonio, Texas, where he teaches a variety of subjects, including national security law. In 2000, after twenty years of active duty, he retired from the United States Army Judge Advocate General's Corps as a lieutenant colonel. During his tenure in the military, Professor Addicott served in a variety of senior legal positions throughout the world including Legal Advisor for United States Army First Special Forces Group; Deputy Chief, International Law Division, Pentagon; Senior Legal Advisor for United States Army Special Forces Command; and Deputy Staff Judge Advocate for United States Southern Command. Professor Addicott holds a doctor of juridical science (SJD) and a master of laws (LLM) from the University of Virginia of School of Law, a master of laws (LLM) from the Judge Advocate General's School, a juris doctor (JD) from the University of Alabama School of Law, and a bachelor of arts with honors in government (BA) from the University of Maryland.

Index

A

Act of war, 6, 17, 20–21, 29, 34, 51–52
Afghanistan, 5, 11, 19, 31–34, 37, 39, 53, 60, 62–65, 70, 78, 96–97, 102, 109, 115, 138–139, 158, 172, 179, 198, 202–205, 207, 209–210, 214
Afghan army, 33
Aggression, 2–3, 13, 23–24, 26–29, 36, 40, 45, 48–52, 56, 86, 98, 115, 137–143, 152, 178–183, 185–191, 194, 199–200, 202, 216
al-Qa'eda, 9, 11–12, 18–20, 32–34, 39, 41–45, 47, 51–53, 59–60, 62–63, 65, 68, 70, 78, 82, 84, 97, 102, 109, 111, 115–116, 138, 171, 191, 199–200
American Bar Association, 15, 68
American Civil War, 67, 74, 119
Appeasement, 25, 142–143, 177, 179, 181, 183, 200
Application of Yamashita, 67, 86
Anti–war movement, 106, 180, 184, 193
Anticipatory self-defense, 45–46, 51
Antiterrorism, 17–18, 60, 80, 166
Arms Export Control Act, 166
Articles of War, 67, 85

Assassination, 3, 13, 19, 59–60, 77–78, 85, 92, 207
Attorney General, 69, 71–72, 76, 88
Aum Shinrikyo, 9, 15
Axis, 25, 39, 53, 67, 143, 186, 194
Axis of evil, 39
Azzam, Abdallah, 18

B

Battle of the Bulge, 67
Belligerents, 62, 66–67, 82
Bill of Rights, 144, 147, 159
bin Laden, Osama (Usama), 5, 18–19, 42
bin Laden videotape, 19, 41
Bowra, Kenneth, 211
British, 7, 84, 143, 145, 186
British Crown, 145
Brooke Amendment, 169
Bush administration, 32, 49, 51, 62–63, 83, 116, 187–188
Bush, George H., 51, 177, 185, 187–189
Bush, George W., 17, 29, 33, 39, 50, 53, 115, 177, 179, 181, 185, 198, 218

C

Calley, Jr., William L., 103, 130

Caroline Doctrine, 45
Carnivore, 77
Catholic Church, 53, 192–193
Central Intelligence Agency (CIA), 5, 11
Cheney, Dick, 40, 53
Chamberlain, Neville, 25
China, 27, 141, 164
Churchill, Winston, 186
Civil and Political Covenant, 153–154, 160–161, 174–175
Civil liberties, 12, 59, 80, 159
Clinton administration, 43, 60
Clinton, William Jefferson, 14, 78
Cold War, 1, 51, 137, 143, 150, 157–158, 178, 183, 189, 199–200, 217–218
Collective security, 23, 173, 177–178, 185, 191, 215, 217
Communism, 172, 178, 201, 215–216
Counterproliferation, 45–46, 52, 56
Counterterrorism, 17–18, 61, 76, 81, 205
Counterproliferation self-help, 45–46, 52, 56
Confederate forces, 67
Covenant on Civil and Political Rights, 154, 160–161, 174–175
Crimes against humanity, 64, 83, 86
Cuba, 5, 31, 40, 62, 82, 87, 214

D

Declaration of Independence, 145
Defense Advanced Research Projects Agency (DARPA), 77
Defense against Weapons of Mass Destruction (NLD), 61, 81
Defense Security Assistance Agency, 165

Democracy, 12, 52–53, 96, 101, 137–139, 143–148, 155, 168, 197–200, 203–205, 209, 213–214, 216, 218
Democratic values, 52, 137, 139, 142, 144–145, 148, 166, 178, 190–191, 198, 201, 208, 213–214, 218
Department of Defense, 18, 73–74, 87, 89, 165
Department of Justice, 18, 70, 74, 88
Deuteronomy, 118, 133
Desert Storm, 134, 184, 209
Diplomatic privilege, 7
Due process, 59–60, 62, 64, 71, 83, 88, 163

E

Economic and Social Council (ESOSOC), 159
Economic Support Fund, 166
Ecclesiastes, 95
Electronic eavesdropping, 76
English common law, 73
Executive Branch, 31, 61, 167, 169
Ex Parte Milligan, 66–67, 85
Ex Parte Quirin, 67–68, 85

F

Federal Aviation Administration, 79
Federal Bureau of Investigation (FBI), 16, 18, 33, 70, 77, 88, 93
Federal Rules of Civil Procedure, 88
Field Manual 27-10 (FM 27–10), 62
First strike, 56
Fifth Amendment, 71
Fourteenth Amendment, 59
Foreign Assistance Act, 165, 202, 211

Index 291

Foreign Military Financial Program (FMFP), 166
Force multipliers, 197–198, 201
Ford, Gerald, 77
Framers, 23, 31, 145–148, 178
Frank, Anne, 139–140
Franklin, Benjamin, 145
Franks, Tommy, 137

G

Geneva Conventions, 24–25, 48, 53, 62–63, 82–83, 99–100, 107, 117, 126, 130–131, 152, 171, 174
General Assembly, 2, 28, 153, 157, 159–160, 188, 195
Genocide, 43, 54, 65, 83, 142, 153–154
German saboteurs, 67, 85
Green Berets (see also Special Forces), 37, 89, 198, 205–208, 211
Gulf War, 31, 33, 52, 96, 121, 131, 133, 177–180, 182–185, 187–188, 190–191, 193–194, 199, 214–215
Guantanamo Bay, 62

H

Hadayat, Hesham Mohamed, 11
Hamas, 9, 41
Hebrews, 118, 133
Hegel, Georg, 95
Highjacking, 61
Hickenlooper Amendment, 169
Hitler, Adolph, 186
Homefront support, 120–121
Homeland security, 73, 79, 81, 199
Hostages, 61, 171
Howard, Dick, 147, 173

Human rights, 2, 12, 40, 42–43, 47–48, 52, 100, 102, 120, 137–142, 146–164, 166, 168–175, 178, 187–189, 197–198, 200–201, 203–205, 208–211, 213–218
  First generation, 154, 157, 162, 170–171
  Gross violations, 97, 139, 154, 169–171, 210
  Second generation, 154–156, 178, 200
  Third generation, 155
Humanitarian intervention, 47, 56
Human Rights Commission, 159–160
Human Rights Committee, 158, 160–161
Hussein, Saddam, 47–48, 51, 96, 102, 133, 177, 179, 182–184, 190–191, 202, 213–214

I

Illegal aliens, 70–72, 76
Immigration, 3, 59–60, 70–72, 75–76, 88, 90–91
Indo-China War, 101, 106, 127
Inter-American Commission on Human Rights, 163
International Committee of the Red Cross (ICRC), 83, 162
International law, 2, 6–8, 12, 15, 20, 28–29, 35, 40, 45, 50, 53, 55–56, 62, 64–65, 78, 82–83, 91, 96, 98–99, 125–126, 133, 135, 148–151, 153–157, 174, 178, 180, 192–193
International Law Commission, 2, 15
International Military Education and Training (IMET), 166, 168, 211
International Tribunal, 64, 67, 86

Iran, 5, 11, 31, 34, 39, 53, 116, 138, 172, 214
Iraq, 5, 11, 33–34, 39–40, 43, 47–48, 50–51, 53, 56–57, 75, 115–116, 138, 141, 172, 182–184, 187, 189–190, 194–195, 198, 202, 209, 214, 219
Islam, 19, 41, 54, 141
Israel, 1, 10, 13, 42, 45, 47, 56, 75, 172

J

Jackson, Robert, 80
Jeremiah, 181, 192
Jihad, 41
Jus ad bellum, 98, 152
Jus in bello, 97–98, 119, 152

K

Karzai, Hamid, 39
Kennedy Amendment, 168–170
Kennedy, John F., 205, 209
Kellogg-Briand Pact, 24, 26, 35
Khobar Towers, 63
Kirkpatrick, Jeanne J., 20, 34
King, Coretta Scott, 193
KISS, 49
Korean War, 31, 52, 178, 194, 215
Kuwait, 33–34, 48, 51, 56, 180, 182–185, 187, 189–190, 194–196

L

Lackawanna, 17
Lake, Anthony, 43, 55, 138
Law of Land Warfare (FM 27–10), 63
Law of Nations, 66, 148
Law of War, 12, 14, 21, 35, 53, 57, 62–64, 67–68, 82, 85, 92, 95–102, 107–108, 111–113, 116–122, 124–125, 130–131, 133–135, 162, 209
Gross breaches, 97
Simple breaches, 100
League of Nations, 23–24, 35, 181, 186
Lee, Robert E., 101, 123–125
Locke, John, 144
London Naval Charter, 24
Lone-wolf terrorism, 10
Lowery, Joseph, 184, 193
Libya, 5, 16, 31, 40, 92, 138, 172, 214

M

MacArthur, Douglas, 101, 197
Maktab al-Khidamat, 18
Madsen v. Kinsella, 66, 85
McVeigh, Timothy, 11, 15
Meadlo, Paul, 111
Medina, Ernest, 103, 113
Medina Standard, 113
Middle East, 33, 54, 89, 116, 143, 168, 171–172, 178, 190, 200, 209, 213, 217
Military Assistance Command Vietnam (MACV), 107, 131
Military commissions, 66–69, 82, 85, 87
Military tribunals, 59–60, 62, 65–68, 85–86
Milligan, Lambdin, 66–67, 85
Mobile Training Teams, 167
Moore, John Norton, 13, 127, 141, 173
Moslem, 18
Munich Agreement, 25
Murder, 5–8, 10–11, 39, 41, 43–45, 47, 50–51, 54, 64, 67, 77–78, 84–

86, 92, 102, 106, 113–114, 128, 130, 140, 142, 154, 171, 200
My Lai, 95–97, 101–102, 104–108, 110–112, 114–115, 117, 120–121, 123, 125–132

N

National Defense Authorization Act, 4, 53
National Security Council, 60, 165
National Security Strategy of the United States, 46, 56
Nazis, 42
New Age, 186, 189–191
New paradigm, 54, 137, 142, 156, 198
New World Order, 57, 86, 177, 185–191, 194–196
Nixon, Richard, 31, 105
Noncombatants, 78, 96, 99–100, 103–104, 106–107, 109, 119, 130
Non-governmental organizations (NGO), 137, 161–162, 164, 171
North Atlantic Treaty Organization (NATO), 17, 20–21, 29, 32, 36
North Korea, 5, 39, 52–53, 194, 214, 217
North Vietnam, 101–102, 108, 116, 127, 141
Northern Alliance, 32
Northern Command, 73–74
North Korea, 5, 39, 52–53, 194, 214, 217
Nuremberg Trials, 67, 86

O

Office of Homeland Security, 79, 81
Oklahoma City bombing, 11, 15, 81, 85
Operations other than war, 199

Organization of American States (OAS), 163, 175
Osiraq, 47, 56

P

Paine, Thomas, 155
Palestinian Authority, 9–10
Pan Am Flight 800, 6
Passive personal principle, 65
Patrick, William C., 10
Patrick, III, William C., 10
Patriot Act, 3, 13–14, 62, 71–72, 82
Peace-building, 158
Peacekeeping operations, 166, 211
Peers Report, 105–111, 117, 123, 127–132
Pentagon, 11, 17, 20, 60, 73, 77, 89, 91, 133
Pope John Paul II, 183, 193
Posse Comitatus Act, 73–74, 89–90
Power of the purse, 167
Preemptive self–defense, 45–46
Preventative self–defense, 45, 51
Prisoners of war, 62–63, 82–83, 96–97, 99–100, 119, 126, 174

Q

Quadrennial Defense Review (QDR), 73

R

Radical regime syndrome, 141
RAND Study, 143
Reconstruction, 73–74
Reagan, Ronald, 77
Reign of Terror, 1, 12–13, 152
Renatus, Flavius Vegetius, 177
Reciprocity, 8, 119, 121
Ridenhour, Rod, 105

Rogue states, 26, 40, 42, 45–47, 50, 52, 115
Rousseau, Jean–Jacques, 144
Rule of Law, 1, 6, 8–9, 17, 21–24, 26–27, 39, 42, 44, 47–53, 77–78, 80, 96–97, 107, 120, 135, 140–142, 166, 177–182, 185, 187–189, 191–192, 203, 205, 216
Rummel, R.J., 54, 142
Rumsfeld, Donald, 37, 74

S

Scott, James, 193, 209
Search and destroy, 111, 132
Secretary general, 160, 182
Secretary of defense, 15, 46, 68–70, 74
Secretary of dtate, 3, 45, 170, 187
Security assistance, 164–170, 202–203, 208, 211
Security Assistance Organization, 165
Security Council, 13, 21, 26–28, 50–52, 56, 60, 164–165, 182, 187, 194–195
Self–defense, 2, 8–9, 21–22, 24, 26–29, 32, 36, 40, 45–47, 51, 53, 55–56, 78, 98, 182, 206
Sennacherib, 179
Sherman, William T., 14, 119
Simpkin, Richard, 205, 211
Sixth Amendment, 67
Slavery, 54, 149, 154
Sleeper terrorist cells, 11
Son My, 103–104, 111, 127–129
Somalia, 31, 209
South Vietnam, 102–103, 106, 108–109, 115–116
Special Forces, 32, 37, 89, 122, 134, 168, 197–198, 205–211

Special Operations Forces, 32–33, 121, 198, 206
Stalinism, 42, 179
State defense force, 75, 90
State Department, 5, 11, 40, 167, 170–172
Suicide bomber, 1, 13
Symington-Glenn Amendment, 169

T

Taliban, 11, 19, 32–34, 37, 39, 44, 50–51, 54, 62–63, 65, 70, 78, 82, 97, 102, 115–116, 138, 141, 203
Task Force Barker, 103, 107, 110, 129, 132
Technical Assistance Field Teams, 167
Technical Assistance Teams, 167
Terror, 1, 6, 10–15, 17–21, 33–34, 39–40, 42–49, 51–53, 55, 59, 68, 70, 72, 77–81, 88–89, 95–98, 100, 102, 114–117, 121–122, 126, 138, 143, 152, 156, 158, 171–172, 177–178, 182, 185–186, 191–192, 197–202, 206–207, 211, 213–217
  Individual, 1, 6, 10–11, 13, 21–22, 27–28, 34, 36, 55, 63, 71–72, 79, 91, 106–108, 112, 114, 123, 131, 140, 142, 144–147, 149–152, 154–158, 161–163, 165, 167, 182, 204, 208
  State-sponsored, 1, 5–8, 11, 16, 44–45
  State-supported, 1, 5–6, 11, 19, 44–45
  Sub-State, 1, 5–6, 9–11, 33, 42
Terrorism, 1–7, 9–11, 13–17, 19–22, 29–30, 33–34, 37, 39–44, 47–48, 51–56, 59–61, 65, 68, 71–74,

76, 79–81, 84–85, 88–89, 137–143, 146, 156, 172–173, 179, 198–201, 207–208, 213, 215–216, 218

Terrorist, 1–15, 17–22, 29–30, 32–33, 39–47, 52, 54, 59–65, 70–72, 74–75, 77, 80–81, 88, 92, 138, 166, 172, 199, 201, 215

Terrorist statute, 65

Thieme, Jr., Robert B., 173

Thompson, Jr., Hugh C., 104

Torture, 19, 100, 102, 109, 117–118, 154, 162, 170–171

Total depravity of man, 140

Totalitarian(ism), 5–6, 40, 42, 46, 48, 52, 120, 138–139, 141–143, 148, 150–151, 155, 157, 190, 197–199, 203, 205, 213–214, 216, 218

Tytle, Alexander Frasier, 146

U

Unified Command, 52, 165, 194, 205

Uniform Code of Military Justice, 64, 85

United Nations (U.N.), 2, 13, 15, 20–21, 25–29, 33–37, 40, 42–45, 47–48, 50–52, 55–57, 78, 82–83, 98, 126, 133, 137, 142, 149, 152–153, 155–164, 172–175, 177–178, 180–182, 184–185, 187–189, 191, 194–195, 202, 215, 217

U.N. General Assembly, 28, 157, 195

U.N. High Commissioner for Human Rights, 158, 161

U.N. Human Rights Committee, 158, 160–161

U.N. Security Council, 27, 51, 56

U.N. Security Council Resolution 678, 33–34, 37, 51, 194

U.N. Security Council Resolution 1368, 21–22, 29

U.N. Sub–Commission on Human Rights, 2

U.N. Charter Article 1, 26, 28, 30, 40, 43, 142, 152, 156, 163

U.N. Charter Article 2, 27–29, 180, 182

U.N. Charter Article 5, 29, 36, 163

U.N. Charter Article 23, 27

U.N. Charter Article 24, 27

U.N. Charter Article 27, 7, 27

U.N. Charter Article 51, 27–28, 45, 50, 55, 78, 98, 181–183

Universal Declaration of Human Rights, 149, 153, 159, 162, 170, 174

United States Constitution, 30, 36, 59, 66, 147

United States Special Operations Command, 205

Universal Declaration of Human Rights, 149, 153, 159, 162, 170, 174

Universal principle of jurisdiction, 65

Unlawful belligerents, 62

U.S. v Yunis, 64

V

Vienna Convention on Diplomatic Relations, 7, 15

Vietnam War, 31, 96, 101, 106, 108, 110, 117, 120, 127

Viet Cong, 96, 101–103, 109, 128

Virtual state, 12, 138

von Clausewitz, Karl, 120, 134

W

Washington, George, 80
War between the States, see American Civil War
War crimes, 14, 62–65, 67–68, 83, 86–87, 96, 100, 102, 112–114, 121–123, 190
War on Terror, 10–12, 17–18, 21, 39–40, 43–49, 51–52, 59, 72, 77–80, 95–98, 100, 114–117, 121–122, 126, 138, 143, 156, 158, 171–172, 177–178, 182, 185, 191–192, 197–202, 206–207, 213–217
Weapons of mass destruction, 1, 4–7, 9–12, 39–40, 42–44, 46–47, 52, 56, 59, 61, 75, 80–81, 179
Weapons of mass murder, 5, 7, 10, 39, 43–45, 47, 50–51, 142, 200
Webster, Daniel, 45, 146
Weinberger, Casper, 7, 15
West, Rebecca, 143
Westphalia, 22
Wilson, Woodrow, 23, 173, 179
Wiretapping, 76
Wolfolwitz, Paul, 46
World Conference on Human Rights, 148
World Trade Center, 9, 19–20, 60, 80
World War I, 23, 25, 118, 217
World War II, 25, 53, 65, 67, 76, 86, 113, 118, 131, 143, 151, 177, 186, 192, 215, 217

Y

Yamashita Standard, 67, 86, 113–114
Yousef, Ramzi Ahmad, 9

Yunis, Fawaz, 64, 83

Z

Zadvydas v. Davis, 72, 88
Zionism, 188